Letters from the Edge

12 Women of the World Write Home

Illustrations inside this book:
Zimbabwe – Clive Offley
China – Peter Wingham (35), Clive Offley (39)
Bolivia – Alan Hughes
India – Miriam McCurdy (75, 82), Sarah John (88)
Pakistan – Miriam McCurdy
Nigeria – Miriam McCurdy
Russia and Chechnya – Miriam McCurdy (145), Sarah John (153)
Colombia – Sarah John
Mongolia – Sarah John
Lebanon – Sarah John
Mauritius – Sarah John
Egypt – Sarah John

About the **New Internationalist**

The **New Internationalist** is an independent not-for-profit publishing co-operative. Our mission is to report on issues of global justice. We publish informative current affairs and popular reference titles, complemented by world food, photography and gift books as well as calendars, diaries, maps and posters – all with a global justice world view.

If you like this book, you'll also enjoy the **New Internationalist** magazine. Each month has a main theme, such as *Ethical Travel* or *Nuclear Weapons,* as well as a Special Feature such as *Guilt* or *How to Get Out of Iraq.* In addition there are music, film and book reviews, country profiles, interviews and worldwide news.

To find out more about the **New Internationalist**, visit our website at **www.newint.org**

Letters from the Edge

12 Women of the World Write Home

New Internationalist

Letters from the Edge
First published in 2008 by
New Internationalist™ Publications Ltd
55 Rectory Road
Oxford OX4 1BW, UK
www.newint.org
New Internationalist is a registered trade mark.

Front cover image:
Illustrations by Sarah John; Photograph by Dieter Telemans/Panos

Back cover illustrations: Sarah John

Edited by Chris Brazier
Designed by Simon Loffler

 Printed on recycled paper by T J International Limited, Cornwall, UK who hold environmental accreditation ISO 14001.

British Library Cataloguing-in-Publication Data.
A catalogue for this book is available from the British Library.

Library of Congress Cataloguing-in-Publication Data.
A catalogue for this book is available from the Library of Congress.

ISBN 978-1-904456-97-1

FOREWORD

These letters – from 12 women in different locations around the world, written over a period of two decades – have a timeless quality to them. They weave together a patchwork picture of our world that is very different from the standard portrait painted in news media dominated by disasters, atrocities or political pronouncements. This is not conventional travel writing, where a visitor skims across the surface of a new location, picking out the exotic morsels that loom into view. Whether they are written from the remotest part of the Mongolian steppe in midwinter, from Beirut as it stoically faces up to the latest car bomb, or from an island in the Indian Ocean, they tell the human stories of ordinary people – as fresh, insightful and, often, as moving today as they were when they were written.

When the *New Internationalist* magazine began its popular *Letter from...* series in 1986, there was certainly no thought that it would still be appearing more than two decades later. We had simply responded to an intriguing proposal by a young woman then working as a teacher in rural Zimbabwe. Yvonne Burgess wrote beautifully about the Shona culture around her but also very thoughtfully about the relationship between rich and poor worlds – and her own compromised part in that relationship. By the time Yvonne returned to Scotland it was evident to us that there would be a gaping hole where her column had been – and so the Letters became a series, and Carol Davis took up the story of how she grappled with Chinese culture a decade or so after the death of Mao.

This was very much the original conception – a woman from the rich world living and working in (rather than just traveling through) the Global South, acting as a thoughtful, observant representative of our mainly Western readership but also as an active bridge between cultures.

No sooner had that model been established than it was refined and diversified. The next correspondent, Susanna Rance, had married and had children with an Aymara man in Bolivia and thus wrote about the indigenous culture with the extra insight and engagement that situation afforded. And the correspondent after that, Mari Marcel Thekaekara, was born and bred in India – though there was an intriguing twist in that she too was in a way an outsider, often writing about the perspective of the indigenous people or *adivasi* with whom she lived and worked, whose own outlook on life was as different from her own background in Kolkata (Calcutta) as it was from that of her readers.

That the correspondents were always women was not planned at the outset but it soon came to seem important. One of the reasons why these Letters are still a pleasure and an education to read today is that the women writing them are trying to get us under the skin of a country and a culture, portraying the lives and thoughts of ordinary people. And while men may dominate the world of politics and wars that makes up the daily news, it is women who are the lead actors in the dramas of everyday life yet their stories are never normally told. This was something our fifth correspondent, Maria del Nevo, excelled at, homing in with both passion and insight on the plight of the women she saw around her in Pakistan.

Over the years since, the Letters have ranged across the continents and cultures – from urban Nigeria to rural Mongolia, from civil-war-torn Lebanon to civil-war-torn Colombia, from Russia's capital to its troubled colony Chechnya, from the Indian Ocean island of Mauritius to their current location in Cairo.

Reading these Letters together, there are many common themes. There is a fascination with how people are named in other cultures, for example: from the Mongolian 'Son of the Cosmos' to the Nigerian 'God is worth worshipping', from the Zimbabwean 'Thank you' to the Chinese 'Colorful Clouds at Dusk'. There is also a recurrent awareness of the seriousness with which 'magic' or the paranormal is treated in other cultures – as when Susanna Rance resorts to some unconventional healing when her daughter falls ill, or when Louisa Waugh encounters a female shaman. Yet paradoxically, for all that they focus on the differences between peoples, on the cultural distinctiveness of their particular locale, the Letters as a whole convey an overwhelming sense of how alike human beings are the world over – with similar hopes and dreams, similar concerns for family and community, and for making ends meet.

This book is dedicated to former *New Internationalist* co-operative member Maria del Nevo, the only one of its contributors who was not able to play an active part in approving its contents (to understand why, see Maria's biographical section on page 91).

CONTENTS

Letters from Mawere (Zimbabwe) by Yvonne Burgess 1986-1987

Letters from the Yellow River (China) by Carol Davis 1988-1989

Letters from La Paz (Bolivia) by Susanna Rance 1989-1990

CONTENTS

Letters from Tamil Nadu (India) by Mari Marcel Thekaekara 1991-1992

Letters from Lahore (Pakistan) by Maria del Nevo 1992-1993

Letters from Lagos (Nigeria) by Elizabeth Obadina 1993-1995

CONTENTS

Letters from Russia and Chechnya by Olivia Ward 1995-1997

Letters from Atlantis (Colombia) by Jenny James 1997-1998

Letters from Tsengel (Mongolia) by Louisa Waugh 1998-1999

CONTENTS

Letters from Beirut (Lebanon) by Reem Haddad 1999-2006

Letters from Bambous (Mauritius) by Lindsey Collen 2006-2007

Letters from Cairo (Egypt) by Maria Golia 2007-2008

Letters from Mawere (Zimbabwe) 1986-1987

Yvonne Burgess

Living in Africa in the 1980s was a pivotal experience for Yvonne. On her return to Scotland in 1989, she moved to Fife, north of Edinburgh, and spent ten years writing (her book *The Myth of Progress* was published in 1996), playing in a ceilidh band, working with music and writing groups, and growing vegetables. Since 2001 she has been directing community choirs in Edinburgh – work that came to her originally through teaching friends the songs she learned in the Zimbabwean village of Mawere.

Thanks to a beautiful stroke of synchronicity, Yvonne has recently got back in touch (by mobile phone) with her friends in Mawere. Some Edinburgh friends who play *mbira* (the traditional Zimbabwean sacred instrument) recently attended an AIDS awareness festival of song and dance at the very school where she taught. The leader of the Grassroots drama and music troupe that organized the festival comes from Mawere and remembers her from his goat-herding days.

'For all the economic and physical suffering that Zimbabweans are having to bear,' says Yvonne, ' – and this did not begin in the 1990s, but in the 1890s or even earlier, with the Zulu migrations north to escape the upheavals of European settlement and war further south – there is more continuity, courage and lust for life in Zimbabwe than we in the West find easy to credit.'

Changes in Zimbabwe

The Zimbabwe Yvonne Burgess described in the 1980s was a very different entity in political terms from the Zimbabwe of today, even though Robert Mugabe has led the country throughout the period.

In the mid-1980s Mugabe was still relatively fresh from his triumph as victorious guerrilla leader and first Prime Minister (subsequently President) of the newly independent nation that emerged from the ashes of white-supremacist Rhodesia in 1980. In 1986 4,500 farmers (almost all of them white) still owned 50 per cent of the land, including all its most productive rain-fed areas, while 4,000,000 Africans squeezed onto communally owned lands lacking in rainfall, infrastructure and communications. This legacy of white supremacy remained undisturbed in the 1980s – part of the independence deal struck with Britain. Nevertheless, Mugabe's policies aimed at empowering small black farmers met with significant international approval and the maize harvest quadrupled within a few years as they were given more control over their own destiny. Early repressive tendencies – including the murder of many members of the opposition in Matabeleland – tended to be glossed over by international observers who saw Mugabe as a generally progressive influence in southern Africa.

The 1990s, however, saw Mugabe becoming increasingly autocratic and he began talking about the possibility of a one-party state. The economy began to stagnate, in part because of IMF-imposed structural adjustment programs, and frustration rose among veterans of Mugabe's guerrilla forces who had expected a quicker dividend from independence. Land reform measures allowing white land to be expropriated and redistributed by the State had been introduced in 1990 but this still proceeded at a modest pace until 1996, when war veterans took over six farms by force. The Government responded by expropriating 841 farms by the end of the year but many of these went to Mugabe's cronies instead of being redistributed as smallholdings. The pattern was set for the ensuing decade, as Mugabe descended into dictatorship, rigging elections so as to see off the threat of the Movement for Democratic Change, clamping down on independent media and seizing more farmland. The economy went into a nosedive as inflation spiraled to a world-leading 150,000 per cent, food production plummeted and international isolation and sanctions bit deep. In March 2008 the opposition victory in the presidential election was so sweeping that it initially seemed the 84-year-old Mugabe, with the eyes of the world fully opon him, would have no option but to concede defeat. Instead he clung desperately to power, not releasing the electoral results and resorting to tried and tested tactics of intimidation. A run-off between Mugabe and the clear winner of the first round, Morgan Tsvangirai, was due to take place but no date had been set by the time this book went to press.

The rural life that Yvonne describes will have changed markedly. But the rhythms of everyday life she notices still apply in most rural parts of Africa – and her meditations on the gap between rich world and poor are sadly still entirely relevant to the Zimbabwe of today.

Golden eggs

Yvonne explains why she has chosen to teach in a system that is so far removed from students' lives.

Our students walk up to two-and-a-half hours to get to school by 7.20am (by the sun!), and they are supposed to stay till 4.00pm Monday to Friday, though there is no food at school for them, and no lessons in the afternoons. When fruits, maize and sweet potatoes are out of season, those with a few cents will buy a tiny packet of cellophane-wrapped biscuits or half a loaf of white bread, or a bottle of Pepsi or Fanta; most eat nothing till they get home.

At school we study, obviously, syllabuses inherited from Britain and Rhodesia, which still, in spite of changes in style and content, stress the advantages, or rather necessities, of 'modern' living: fluency in English being number one. Geography is about manufacturing and mining as well as 'land use' according to good old settler priorities – in other words, the best land is most 'efficiently' used in large-scale commercial farming. The new science course concentrates more on biology but still cannot avoid mysteries like electricity and atom-splitting. Even recent English textbooks are full of comprehension passages about boarding schools and city life, for that is mainly what Zimbabwean writers in English have experienced.

Yet at home, our students live in a totally different world, relying on traditional skills of agriculture, building, fishing, trapping and crafts. (At school, agriculture is a 'boys' subject', matching needlework for girls, done half-heartedly for all the rhetoric about 'Education and Production'.) Their families can barely subsist on their exhausted fields, with few hands to till because all the children are at school and yet somehow they must find 60 Zimbabwean dollars per child each term (for me, this is the worst part) hoping one day it will produce a golden egg to repay their sacrifices; convinced that without this crippling investment, things can only get worse.

Why do they believe this? Why accept that progress can only come on the terms of 'modern', city-led life, on European terms?

To grasp this we need to talk about the cultural and spiritual dislocation that accompanies all these material contrasts in standards of living.

Every night under the stars, or in the moonlight, we hear the drums talking across the plain, telling us that somewhere beer has been brewed in honor of the ancestors, and a family has gathered to drink, sing and dance together, to solve a pressing problem of illness or misfortune by observing an ancient ritual.

But at assembly every morning, when hymns and choruses are sung and the Headteacher delivers sermons and harangues about fees and discipline, no mention is ever made of any traditional belief or custom. They are ignored in public as an archaic embarrassment, by 'educated' modern leaders whose attitudes often strike us as a caricature of their missionary and colonial predecessors – even though most of them probably consult traditional healers, and observe many rituals in their families at home in the communal areas.

Yet who are we, British expatriates, to sneer? We are the successors of earlier European interferers we now criticize ideologically. Alongside the Headteacher and leagues of officials, we are co-beneficiaries of the international economic system grid that is still unchallenged, and condemns our local friends to exhausted land, increasing hardship and cultural alienation.

So why am I here? And more – why do I want to stay? I am here because I know the system is the same wherever I live, and I want to understand better what is happening in our world by facing these contradictions where they confront me most clearly, living with them and writing about them. On this level, being here is not a comfortable experience. But comfort comes on the human level, in new relationships, hours shared eating, singing, working, or exchanging skills.

Next year I hope to be still working in the community, not as a school teacher but with school leavers and others involved in local co-operative ventures. However, I cannot say I am here only or mainly for others' sakes – 'community development' and my own 'development' have come to mean almost the same thing.

Calling cards

A constant stream of visitors competes with Yvonne's need to write and reflect.

One thing about sitting down and trying to write in a rural situation is that, unless it is after nine at night, you are liable to be interrupted.

Yesterday, while I was writing to my sister, there were four different knocks at the door. Just as I began, a young friend came to ask me to buy a school shirt for him next time I go to town: he gave me 12 Zimbabwean dollars – the price of the shirt – from his monthly wage of Z$20. He works in his uncle's butcher's shop, seven days a week, 14 hours a day – wage non-negotiable, since it was a 'family favor' to give him the job. We agreed that he would come with me and that we would make a day of it next week. Although the town is only one dollar's – or one hour's – bus ride away, it will be only his third visit ever. We drank some tea and ate bread and tomatoes and then he left to walk home down the one-and-a half-hour-long path around the mountain.

As soon as I settled down again with my pen, Mercy called by to remind me that she wants to visit her relatives on Monday – I had agreed to pay her bus fare. In return she later agreed to help the family of a friend of mine to carry a huge load of grass for rethatching their kitchen. The grass had been stored in the branches of a tree and had to be taken – on foot, an hour's walk up and down a steep hill – to a spot where the ox-cart could come to collect it.

While she was still with me, Mr Sibanda, the teacher who lives in the next house to mine, knocked on my door. Beer bottle in hand, he invited me over to admire his new four-piece suite. I had been surprised the previous day by the unfamiliar sound of a delivery van driving over the grass past my house, and was glad of an opportunity – my first – to see inside his house.

The new furniture took up most of the central room: two very smart, square mini-sofas and two matching armchairs – Z$1,500 with ten months to pay. Next, he told me, comes the kitchen unit. The trouble is, the room is full already.

I sat comfortably on the firm foam rubber, feeling the rough, tweedy texture of the upholstery and discussing the need for washable covers (which, he said, his wife will deal with when she polishes the cement floor) and I realized how accustomed I have become to seeing these jarring juxtapositions – between Mercy's lack of bus fare and the teacher's sitting room, bulging with new furniture – of basic needs and flaunted surplus. At first I felt nauseated all the time. But I have had to learn to live with such crude contrasts. And I am beginning to appreciate that these conspicuous symbols of inequality are, in fact, only simpler (or perhaps more innocent) signs of the inequalities that underlie our whole economic and social system.

The fourth interruption, soon after I got back to my letter, was Blessing, the headteacher's maid, who is studying for her exams. She was returning a novel she had borrowed and asking for a replacement. I gave her a copy of *Equiano's Travels*, a 200-year-old narrative written by a West African man captured into slavery as a child, who educated himself while still a slave, and finally bought his freedom, to spend his later life campaigning against slavery.

The thing about these interruptions is that their demands are so concrete and direct. I can't ignore them: they push my writing aside and make me ask myself what is so important about what I am doing. Indeed, can anything be more important than these day-to-day encounters with other people sharing a struggle to survive, progress and make sense of our lives?

Pendulum swings

Moving house – and leaving the school.

I moved house on Sunday afternoon. My new home is only borrowed until I can build my own, but it is a beautiful collection of four small houses about 25 minutes' walk from the school. It nestles (as tourist brochures say) under the lower end of Vakwambo Mountain and looks north between hills to the lake and more mountains beyond. At sunset the loveliness makes your heart melt. (*Maneru!* – the evening greeting from a girl driving her goats home from the mountain as I write; rain-clouds grey above the trees; golden evening sunshine on the goats' backs as they run).

On Saturday I had my last cold shower in the neighboring teacher's house. And on Tuesday evening I washed at the river by the light of a four-day-old moon, picking my way across smooth granite rippling with water and moonlight in search of a suitable place for bathing and hairwashing, enjoying the secret signals of the fireflies under the trees and the raucous hilarity of the frogs. As I stripped off to wash, the frogs' laughter seemed cruder than ever, even threatening, while the sight of the moonlight on the moving water and the reflections of the stars in the still pools were still new enough to astonish me.

I was helped to move by my Zimbabwean friend Joseph and his brother and sister. We borrowed an elderly Peugeot estate car to carry my belongings most of the way over the steep (but not too steep) rock and swampy (not too swampy) field. Others, we were told, have driven all the way here, round the vegetable gardens by the stream and along the edge of the maize fields – but their cars probably had first and reverse gears that worked.

From the parked car we moved the stuff by wheelbarrow, head and hands: boxloads of books, papers, posters and kitchen paraphernalia in embarrassing quantities: clothes, tables, chairs, mats and mattresses, shelves and cement bricks. One load, littered in the grass beside the car, looked almost obscene and I resolved (again) to get rid of as much of it as possible.

And yet I like these things around me: they are my home, and they express my personality. A lot of what I think and say to others, for example, comes out of books; and I still seek confirmation, encouragement and further clarification in others' printed opinions. I like my clothes too – second-hand, home-made, shop-bought – though I do, gradually, give most of them away.

I have left my job at the school. My reasons are inconceivable to many local people. This morning my neighbor commented, politely probing: 'The children are difficult?' 'The children are fine,' I assured her. 'I'm not moving because of the children.' Further than that I was unable to explain, though I went on speaking. I often have this feeling of missing the mark completely when I am trying to use Shona, the language of a traditional rural culture with relatively constant human values and practice to express problems generated by the incessant self-revisions of our culture of galloping 'progress'.

Who, after all, are more contemptuously critical of the attitudes of the old white missionaries than young radical Europeans? Who are more uncomfortable in the mission-school system than teachers like me who belong to a later generation of the same onward-thrusting culture? And so who can blame rural people anywhere for being confused by or indifferent to the pendulum swings of our theories and values?

So my thoughts run on, refueled by the new experiences of living under thatch, drawing water from the well, washing at the river. Increasingly I feel conscious of living between two worldwide cultures; the culture of money and power and that of the poor and powerless.

I think the most challenging thing for me here will be living with my doors open in a sense that they have never been before.

A fine art
Discovering the importance of beer to the local community.

Today, Saturday, is full moon so I have had plenty of time to sit in the moonlight and think about the successes and failures that surround me. My African neighbors have successfully adapted some parts of the colonists' culture – like Christianity – to their own ends. My thoughts were prompted by the non-stop song, dance and preaching emanating from a meeting of local Methodists. The Methodists walked here from miles around. Yesterday three of my friends were busy cooking for their visitors. Last night as we sat round the fire in my neighbors' kitchen (I had gone over to borrow the cat for a night's mousing) we heard the African 'Oompah' of the *kudu* horn leading the local contingent up to church. Later still, the sound of a chorus of voices traveled down to us easily on the still air.

When I took the cat back this morning (no mice were caught), two of the women who had been cooking (they are known here as Vatete, the father's sister, and Amai, the mother) were brewing traditional seven-day beer. 'So we can get drunk,' said the aunt, laughing, frankly and without guilt.

Later this morning, Baba Fungisai, the father of one of my friends, passed by on his way up to church and invited me to follow. This family, by the way, is known by the name of the eldest daughter, although she is younger than her brother. She has more education than he, knocking a few generalizations for six! Father and daughter are well-known preaching and chorus-leading members of the local Methodist community. But I have never seen the mother or aunt there, and rarely the sons.

Churchgoers are not supposed to drink beer, play, dance or sing traditional music. These forms of recreation are associated with traditional beliefs and practices and so are condemned as pagan. Even beads are suspect, and not worn by Christians. Yet it does not make much difference whether somebody gets drunk to a drumbeat around a fire or gets carried away in the schoolyard by the Holy Spirit, to the rhythm of women's and children's feet pounding to the horn. Perhaps the Christians' voices will be hoarser on Monday from singing, the drinkers' headaches worse.

Beer-brewing provides a model of traditional – and successful – African business. As well as providing an age-old way of getting high in company, beer-brewing is both a serious ceremony and the most popular form of rural income generation. There are often special family reasons for particular brewings. Perhaps someone is ill, or has lost their job, or there is something to be thankful for. On the other hand, maybe examination fees need to be paid, or there are plans to buy an asbestos roof for the house being built, or someone has to be sent to see relatives.

Raising money is a fine art here. I often buy milk from my neighbors who also sell tangerines by the basket to local girls, who sell them at the township to bus passengers and others. In fact another neighbor came over yesterday to borrow a container for peanut butter she was grinding to sell in Gweru when she goes there to visit her family.

Given all this entrepreneurial activity, it is disappointing to see how most rural development promoters have not acknowledged the skills which local people use to make money. Their blindness is all the more evident because they spend so much of their time talking about appropriate technology and grassroots initiatives. But their ideas of appropriateness are closely tied in to Western ideas: they believe everything should be done on a huge scale, planned by those who will not do the work and are divorced from African village life. Families brew beer, and indeed district councils build huge beer-halls to raise funds for road construction, but as far as I know there has been no promotion of beer-brewing co-operatives!

Instead rural Zimbabwe is dotted with unwieldy and uneconomic co-operative projects relying on expensive inputs, transport and large, reliable markets. For example, people have been persuaded that raising commercial chickens for meat is a sure-fire co-operative profit-maker. In fact the 'experts' now realize that there is no adequate local market for broilers – which must be sold fast, as they eat expensive mash. An astute friend of mind has made money on broilers; but to divide her profit between 10 or 15 co-op members would make the three-month effort to raise 50 chicks absurd. The broiler market cannot sustain chick production in larger numbers.

In this environment the development planners often overlook the ways in which rural people have managed to blend their knowledge of local needs with Western-style concern for routine efficiency. Recently I visited a farmer in another area who was looking after chicks. He had built a round brooder of brick and thatch for the nights, and a wire-and-brick thatched run for daytime. The birds were kept in this run until big enough to be safe outside. At night predators were kept at bay by smoke being channeled round the brooder wall from an outside fireplace. The chicks raised in this way are sold for a little less than his commercial broilers – but the method of rearing them is much more economical. They can breed freely, so stocks don't need to be replenished from the outside, and they eat millet mixed with maize which is grown locally.

On its own, small-scale production will not eradicate poverty or hunger, but rural development programs must begin to take more account of people's existing skills and resources if they are to help prevent these evils. Small projects and co-operatives will be successful if they find local forms of expression, as has happened so exuberantly with Christianity.

Upon this rock

Choosing a site for a new house – away from the local church and the road.

I have spent two months visiting family and friends in Britain and the US. Returning to my new home reminds me of my reasons for choosing this site. Comparing my situation with the ones I have just come from, I think: how much nicer to pick out a lovely and convenient spot to build and then design your new home, instead of poring over a newspaper worrying about mortgages and interest rates.

Besides the view, I considered practical points like: how far away is the spring? How far to the road? (Could I push the bike there easily enough, or carry home a full gas bottle?) How exposed is the place to wind and lightning (a big killer in Zimbabwe)? Is the earth deep enough to dig a toilet pit? Do I have good neighbors? Will there be enough privacy? How close could the vegetable garden be?

Local people consider – before all else but the view – how visible their fields will be from the home in case of baboon raids, or straying goats and cattle. Then they think about how easily they can get water; and good grazing ground. For them the road and toilet would be less pressing needs.

In fact the kraalhead, a local leader, had suggested to me a site right beside the road where the local Methodist community was planning to build a church. Quite sheltered, overlooking the lake and close by the stream, it is a lovely spot. But living by the road has its drawbacks. Easy visibility to casual visitors makes break-ins more likely; it is exposed to noise from buses and trucks laboring up the steep hill; and there are constant greetings to exchange with passers-by on their way to and from school, clinic, grinding mill, shops and beer hall. Were the church to be built, up to four times a week there would be long, riotous evenings of preaching and singing – accompanied by rhythmic blasts of the *kudu* horn, the beat of aerosol can shakers and many feet. Finally, a home across the road would be likely to become a favorite spot for beer parties, which can last two or three days at a time!

So it seemed a better idea, on the whole, to find somewhere further from the road. The place I have chosen is flat and rocky, high above the valley. It looks northwest to the lake, and is sheltered by a ring of trees from lightning and the prevailing south wind. (The Shona word for south means 'rot the beans', since this wind often brings late, damaging rains, as it did this year).

When I showed her the place, my friendly neighbor Amai Tarisai

('Tarisai's mother') pointed to the knee-high remains of several round houses and told me her husband had grown up on this spot. The houses had been built in the traditional way, using a ring of poles plastered with mud. Nowadays people usually build with locally molded and fired bricks, which last much longer, especially when plastered with a mixture of mud and cement. Houses of stone are rarely built these days, though often in this area you come across a terracing wall or cattle kraal of milky-grey granite blocks shaped by fire, water and hammer. These rocks are small monuments to the magnificent Great Zimbabwe, which was the spiritual and political center of an ancient Shona trading empire.

No stone house for me: my bricks were molded and fired last July. I asked the local elders and officials for permission to build. Now, only the task of finishing the building remains.

The woman in green
Building the house raises a whole new set of issues.

The building of my house is teaching me new lessons. The housebuilder is the kraalhead's son Talenda ('Thank you') assisted by three young men, two of whom are brothers and live nearby. The thatcher lives 15 minutes' walk away. Besides indicating the wealth of useful skills locally available, this closeness has a significance I didn't appreciate at first – so I made a mistake over the water-carriers.

One morning last week a forceful woman in green from outside the village arrived at my door and suggested that she, her daughter and mother-in-law would carry my water, The next morning we sat in the round kitchen hut – the three women, the builder, his assistants and me – to thrash out rates.

At first no-one would come forward. The woman in green wanted me to set a daily amount. I said they should give me a fair suggestion. Worried that I had no idea how much water we'd need or how long carrying it might take, I asked Talenda to help me calculate what the builders would need and hurriedly consulted my labor budget. Then I cheerfully agreed to pay five Zimbabwean dollars a drum.

The following morning, the first day of building, I was seven kilometers away cycling down the mountainside to visit a co-operative bakery when the wife of that area's kraalhead hailed me. 'It pained my heart to hear of that five dollars,' she said gravely. 'You see this building here? That river over there? Two dollars per drum was the amount they earned.'

'It doesn't matter,' I answered, annoyed.

I got back on my bike, thinking that if I can afford to let these women have a bit over the odds, what does it have to do with everyone else? 'We don't want that "it doesn't matter"', she said.

It hit me almost immediately, with a sinking feeling, that my first reaction was wrong. Wage rates are not a private affair. I had acted hastily, without a full grasp of the situation. Why hadn't Talenda stopped me? Ashamed, I pedaled on to work.

That evening Talenda called in to tell me how the building had progressed. Two drums had been filled in by ten o'clock and the foundation was in place. Everything was fine.

'What,' I ventured, 'about the inflated water rates?'

His face clouded. 'Ah! That old woman – we did not know: she is dangerous. If she is there, she can make it so that I put my hand on this brick and it will never come off! We should pay them tomorrow for the work done and tell them we are waiting for some more materials to be delivered. Then we find people here who want to do the work for the usual rate. Ah! Five dollars a drum is too much.'

Relieved and amused as we both were, I felt that the charge of witchcraft was a graphic way of expressing two resentments. First, that I had taken on 'strangers' when neighbors were keen to be employed; second, that I was paying these strangers almost as much for a couple of hours' work as the men were getting for a full day!

Again, I am reminded that everything here is connected. A supposedly 'supernatural' explanation may be a substitute or metaphor for another very practical one. It is not hard to see why, quite apart from the prejudice and sentiment, people prefer to employ neighbors and relatives living close by than mabrakure ('you've come from far' – an insult in Shona). Getting from place to place is a slow business which can easily be interrupted by prior commitments closer to home.

I felt these considerations myself when I chose both the builder and the thatcher against more distant contenders. Besides fostering good relations with neighbors, if the builders live nearby I know where they are. We can see each other, therefore we can trust each other. It is much harder to be reliable at a distance, when your first commitments are those you live among.

These established and well-founded traditions of mutual support among neighbors and family often give rise to outraged cries about nepotism and tribalism in official circles. Of course these customs don't transfer well to government ministries and transnational companies. But it's important to remember that it is good to help those closest to you. It strengthens the ties of blood and neighborhood that work for the good of the community.

The so-called 'objective' Western models of impartiality and certified merit are a necessary part of our highly stratified societies. Maybe we should look again at traditional communities and ask ourselves if Western ways of life really represent a clear improvement on them.

Dancing under the full moon
Cultures collide at an engagement party.

Last night I went to a party in a club in the Modza District, a rural growth point about 80 kilometers away. I hitched there and as the sun went down was very lucky to be picked up by other guests heading for the same party. On the last 15 kilometers of dirt road we saw no other traffic.

The full moon had risen level with Orion (who hunts upside down in the Southern sky) by the time we had washed and changed at the nearby mission and driven to the club. As we walked in round the empty swimming pool to greet our hosts, an expatriate teacher and a Zimbabwean celebrating their engagement, I noticed how people were sitting in different groups. 'Ordinary' local women and girls, many with babies tied on their backs in towels, sat around the edge of the sandpit, watching. Expatriates congregated around the floodlit barbecue. Better-dressed black women sat chatting, babyless, in metal garden chairs in the shadow of a huge tree. And the local men, who were easily the biggest group, wandered freely in and out of the bar, mingled with the other groups, or sat drinking on the grass.

After greeting people, I joined a few at the edge of the pool who were playing *mbira*, traditional songs which call for playing of the mbira, or thumb piano, and *hosho*, or gourd rattle. It is rare to hear mbira in this area, where the drums reign supreme, although the home-made guitars of cooking oil cans or pots, wood and fishing twine, do seem to imitate its sound.

For a long while I was the only white in the group. Loud South African and American disco and funk continually drowned the soft rippling music, leaving only the sharp shaking of the hosho against the pounding stereo beat. A young man in jeans and tee-shirt danced 'robot' half-heartedly in front of the speaker, while by the poolside another, dressed in shirt and tie, shuddered and stomped with movements that recalled a chicken, a man plowing, a woman grinding grain – dance movements you can see performed with the same energy by a child of 3 or an elder of 70-plus.

Later on I was told that these are not the right steps for mbira music, but belong to the local tradition of drumming. But watching the two men dance, at the one time and in the one place to the music of two (or maybe three or four) different cultures, I was shown again the vast range of human experience that Zimbabweans have to span in their daily lives – from cowherd's whip to digital watch, wood fire to stereo.

A woman wanted to put her sleeping child to bed, so we walked along sandy paths in the moonlight to her candle-lit home, not yet electrified although the water was connected this week. On the way back, when a thorn went through my rubber sandals, she laughed apologetically about 'these houses in the bush'.

Approaching the club again, I noticed an unusually tall, windowless building painted yellow. 'For playing squash,' she explained and even as I tasted the irony of squash courts 'in the bush' she went on. 'But it is being used to store the drought-relief food, so the people are not happy, they cannot play squash.'

Back at the club, the gate-crashers were being politely asked to leave (and arguing their case with zest, for parties are expected to be public affairs). The man who owned the stereo, now very drunk, was picking fights in the bar over a missing record. The mbira group were still singing and playing their gentle hypnotic music. More and more men got up to dance by the pool side, as attention of blacks and whites gradually focused on this 'African culture'.

Suddenly a burly administrator in a dark three-piece suit hurled himself full length on the ground in front of me, howling, his body contracting in spasms – in imitation of possession by an ancestral spirit, the man sitting next to me explained reassuringly.

Earlier in the evening this same besuited local dignitary had addressed us at some length in English, while the groom's male relatives had heckled him across the pool for not using the 'little people's language'.

In Zimbabwe feelings about modern versus traditional are both strong and mixed – enthusiasm and resentment live together in the same breast. Perhaps this is why people like me feel extreme and contradictory responses to this place. Here you can feel loved and accepted at one moment, isolated and shut out at the next. Perhaps life here would be calmer if more people could say, like the fatherly middle-aged mbira player, nodding appreciatively to the disco beat, 'We have known this music also, but we do not need all that to enjoy our culture'.

Evening conversation

A visit to a black township opens up a world of difference.

If you come by bus into Chikumwe, a provincial township, you will be dropped, whether you like it or not, at the 'rank' outside the town. You then pay 30 cents for an emergency taxi ride, 15 cents for another bus, or you can walk for half an hour along sandy paths through scrub and by the side of sewage plants, to get to the so-called 'back entrance'.

Segregation persists in the town. Though there are no Asians or 'Coloreds' and only four whites in Chikumwe, different cultures meet here, and in the daytime they seem to clash. Reggae or Zimbabwe music pounds from the stereos; mothers call their children with names like Lawrence, Stanwell or Zvidzai; the ice-cream vendors' bells rattle insistently; crows squawk on the lookout for lizards; articulated lorries roar.

The houses in this new part of Chikumwe are tidy, four-room units of breeze block and asbestos, nicely designed except that they have no verandas and have been built in eye-wearying straight lines with about 15 feet between each house. This week I'm staying with Anne and John, two English friends who have chosen to live in Chikumwe while they work here for two years. Apart from doing without suburban luxuries – swimming pool, three bathrooms and a huge tree-shaded garden – living in the township has its trials for the Western expatriate.

A visitor from Canada recently looked up *Murungu!* – the greeting she'd heard shouted by children as she passed – and was a bit shaken to find it meant 'White!' (I have occasionally retorted *Mutema!* – which means 'black' – after checking there was an adult around to exchange proper greetings with and who might have a word with the children).

Now I can hear the wee boy next door playing his new game, which I call 'heavy traffic'. He runs behind a long piece of wire with two improvised wheels on the end (yesterday it was a bald tire), and as he runs keeps up a powerful droning whine that is hard to think through.

If you try asking children at play here, 'Is that a lorry?' or 'Are you mixing dough?' you will be told plainly: 'No, it's wire, shoe-polish, tins or mud'. Childhood in Zimbabwe is an experience that has not been molded by adults' romanticization of children and their worlds. Mud is mud, and not supplanted by – as a Western child would be likely to find – a specially developed product such as 'play dough' which is sold to adults for children.

Buying power, and the adoption of Western goods (which have greater status than local products) is very much in evidence. The most prestigious item I can see from the window, apart from the odd TV aerial, is a massive solar unit on the roof of the next house!

Income-generating and subsistence skills also flourish. As I write, a boy of 10 or so is walking past with a bunch of brooms made of grass, calling his wares. Every half hour or so I will hear a cry like: 'Ma-a-a-mango mamango panaapa!' ('Mangoes here!') as a woman or a boy passes with a basket. Peanut butter, hot maize cobs, tomatoes and milk come to the door. The milk comes with ice cream courtesy of one of Lyons Maid's tricycle men, who have great fun (and some disasters) going downhill, but pay heavily going up.

Yesterday afternoon, as I was baking by the open door, a neighbor's aunt beckoned me over. She and her niece were embroidering and chatting, sitting on the kitchen floor on pieces of 'African' printed cloth (known here as zambias). The Shona word for chatting, *kutandara*, also means spending time together, and has no sexist overtones of women wasting time or female gossiping.

We talked for a while about sewing and crocheting, and I showed them the two new mouse-holes in my favorite crocheted bodice, which my great-aunt bought in Palestine when she was a nurse there during World War Two.

The aunt would fix it for me if I could find the twine. 'You'll always find me here,' she said. 'I have to keep an eye on my niece in case she sees any men she prefers to her husband while he's at work.' Everyone laughed, but as a relative of the husband, the speaker's meaning was plain.

At sunset all these differences will be reconciled in a peaceful, peachy glow. Rows of rooftops, telegraph poles and wires will stand poetic against the embers; the low hills rolling away westwards will be golden; groups of youths will stroll along the streets not looking for trouble but having a good time. And women will raise their voices to their neighbors in evening conversation.

Speaking truth to fear

The pitfalls and pleasures of local ways of working.

This morning I put the kettle on the gas before going down to the Blair toilet* at the bottom of the maize field. The grass was high and golden in the morning sun. After breakfast of tea without milk and rolls with cheese and marmalade, I wrote myself reminders of what to discuss today at the 'Keep Trying' bakery, collected useful handouts and a picnic lunch, fetched the bike from its tiny sleeping house, pumped up the back tire and I was off.

It is a ten-minute ride to the road, first on a narrow path along the side of a field of parched maize and groundnuts, then down across the stream, up the smooth rounded granite and along the top, passing by my neighbor's home, down round her fields under the trees and up to the tarred road.

Laid for white tourists, this road hugs the flat land by the lakeside, going nowhere in particular, while the road south through the communal area which I soon turn onto is much busier, yet is untarred and in many places steep and treacherous. Passing the township, both brakes jammed on, I slither and judder down the newly regraveled surface, hoping for something to pass and pick me up, but also marveling at the open splendor of the valley scenery which surprises me afresh every time I look.

Nothing passes during the 13 kilometers to Dimatima. I slow down for some cows and greet many people but I don't usually have to stop now, even for elders. I've gradually learned how to carry on casual yet animated extended greetings, including weather and work comments and the odd joke, even respectful clapping (hand to shoulder) while pedaling past.

When I get to the township, three women have already prepared the bread dough in a bucket. I see they have made new breadpans of the right size out of empty cooking-oil cans from the US AID supplementary feeding program – these were brought out recently by a local agency who helped the women to build a new oven. They should make a bit more profit than they used to with the old, oversized pans they made from bigger oil cans.

The new oven is popular. The women are glad not to have to labor in their sweltering, smoke-filled little pole-and-dagga

* No relation to the former British prime minister (!) but a pit toilet with a vent-pipe and fly-screen originally designed by the Blair Institute near Harare, now widely known as the VIP (ventilated improved pit).

houses. Previously they had to remove embers from the long fire-pit to lay on corrugated metal sheets, then embed the breadpans in the cinders and replace the hot sheets over the hole.

The new mud-and-brick oven is designed around two used oil drums – a piece of 'appropriate technology' developed and introduced, in part, by an expatriate ex-colleague. It's nice to see it in action.

To my amused horror, I find myself urging the women to try baking buns (more sugar, more profit!) and working out the amounts for a trial run. With Government-subsidized bread prices, it is very hard to make a rural bakery worthwhile for 15 members by making bread alone, even mixing local maize meal with the flour. Though it depends, of course, on what you mean by 'worthwhile'. Certainly this bakery is not yet a going financial concern, but who can measure the value of the women's enthusiasm, optimism, pride and enjoyment of their co-operative effort? It was their own idea, started without help before I began my work as an adviser and I want to try and help them make it a success.

In between the business talk, people are coming and going with news of death or illness, words of praise and encouragement and proposals for mutual support between local co-operatives. Among the women, the talk is of *kubereka* (childbearing). A woman starting her 12th pregnancy says her mother scolded her when she heard: 'You will die!' She says her mother had six and then stopped.

Writing this down, I realize she is afraid, but this morning she shared her fear so publicly and laughed so heartily that this didn't strike me till now.

This morning, as often happens, the women urged me to marry here and have a family. They even jokingly offered me a brother or son – I used to think this was a straightforward, if surprising and rather frivolous show of openness to newcomers. But maybe it is rather a response to the real threat which we single expatriate women, with all our means and mobility, present to family structures here. Instead of being repressed, the frightening possibility is voiced, dramatized and laughed about and so acknowledged as part of life.

Everything from bereavement and marriage to the price of yeast is taken as it comes at these rural meetings. This contrasts with the 'proper' business practice of prioritizing, following an agenda, and excluding the personal (which often reappears with us in various professional disguises!). This way of working is often frustrating for me, of course, and it makes for economic inefficiency. But if efficiency ultimately aims at improving the quality of our life, there is surely another, more important, kind of efficiency here, in the holistic practice of these women and men.

Bulawayo to Birmingham

Musing on the state of Zimbabwe's women.

There's no doubt: rural Zimbabwean women are impressive. Full-voiced and muscular, they laugh loudly in welcome and slap hands to slam the point home. When they sing, dance, argue or rejoice, you know all about it. Beside them, the European 'development' worker can feel pale, weedy and underdeveloped.

Yet, the Western visitor asks, don't these women suffer blatant oppression by their menfolk that women in the West just wouldn't stand for? For Zimbabwe's women and their daughters do all the domestic work, including fetching firewood and water, and most of the cultivation.

When a rural woman marries, she must move to her husband's home. If they divorce, she must give up their children to him once they reach seven or eight years old. On top of this, women curtsy, eyes lowered, when greeting a man; kneel on the ground to give him his food or a mug of water and sit silent and to one side at public meetings while men dominate the discussion.

It is enough to make a Western feminist's soul self-ignite.

And yet... and yet, I notice that my rural women friends have strengths that I don't have – both inwardly and in the eyes of their society. In spite of all this patriarchal control they are undiminished. You can tell from the way they run their homes, refer to their husbands, greet and spend time with one another. They are not psychologically dependent on their men, who come and go as employment and the beer-hall dictate.

It may be that they have not spent years, as I have, glancing in magazines and shop windows for images to emulate, competing in class and career – measuring oneself by male-imposed standards. Happy side-effects, you may say, of their rural poverty.

But surely there is more to it than this. These women are farmers, mothers, providers and healers. Every day they are in the real world making a living for themselves and their families. As beer brewers,

midwives and mediums they carry on celebrating, conserving and interpreting life for their communities as they have done for centuries. They have a lot to be confident about.

To find out what has happened to Western women's traditions and confidence, I think we need to go back to the long and bloody period of witch-burning that ushered in the modern era in Europe and North America. The torture and murder of six to nine million wise women must have left a deep mark of terror and eradicated untold knowledge among Western women.

Inevitably women in Zimbabwe who earn salaries adopt many familiar middle-class norms of appearance and behavior. Women teachers come to school in elegant acrylic dresses. Their shoes are expensive and ornamental rather than practical. Urbanization leads to less enticing forms of dependence on men for unemployed women. Wives and daughters moving to the township find themselves without an extended family, without fields to cultivate or their own income. In the townships wife-beating seems to be much more common; male infidelity is almost a norm.

Probably the most dramatic effect of the townward drift on women is the increase in prostitution – or in being 'kept' by a man – and the public response. Every day you overhear a conversation, or read some outraged letter to the newspaper about the 'seductive wiles' of temptresses who 'lure' men into liaisons. Such misogynistic, hypocritical moralism flourishes in the panicky atmosphere of shabby bar-rooms from Bulawayo to Birmingham. Police have even made mass arrests of single women in the evening. Yet wife-beating is not a major issue.

Understanding the forces of modern patriarchy seems to be taking a very long time.

Letters from the Yellow River (China), 1988-1989

Carol Davis

Carol was born in North Wales in 1959. When she was six, she and her family moved to Botswana, where her parents taught at Swaneng Hill School on an initial two-year contract, though they finally stayed for eight years. On her return she was educated in Cheshire and at Liverpool University, where she completed a PhD in medieval literature in 1984.

Carol then taught English in China at a provincial university, returning for a second year in 1988, when her letters for the *New Internationalist* began. She studied written and spoken Chinese during that time, and used university vacations to travel widely in the country, visiting the northeastern city of Harbin to see the ice sculptures in February, and visiting Tibet too.

She is now a freelance journalist based in Liverpool, England, and writes for national newspapers and magazines mainly on health issues. She has two children, aged 12 and 14. She has since traveled widely in Cuba and Peru, but would love to return to China one day to see first hand how things have changed.

China

At the end of the 1980s, when Carol Davis was writing her letters from the city of Jinan in Shandong Province, China was still in the relatively early stages of opening up to the outside world. The power struggle following Mao Zedong's death in 1976 had been won by Deng Xiaoping, who had set the template for modern China in embracing the free market while retaining an iron grip on political power. The first Special Economic Zones were opened in 1978 and were followed by 14 more in the 1980s but across the board in the cities and the countryside 'capitalist' ventures were increasingly encouraged, while the social security system was broadly phased out.

Carol wrote her letters under the pseudonym 'Sue Robson' and was always careful to conceal her specific location, conscious of the need for discretion in a repressive state. The pressure for more democratic space was at the time coming increasingly from students like those she was teaching, and just as her letter series ended this pressure exploded into mass demonstrations. Sparked initially by the death of reformist symbol Hu Yaobang in April 1989, these waves of protest culminated in June in the occupation of Beijing's Tiananmen Square by students and workers claiming greater democratic rights – only for the regime to send in tanks to crush the uprising and initiate a massive clampdown on dissent.

China's story since then has followed a broadly similar pattern. The Communist Party has retained absolute power and still pays lip service to Maoist ideology while actually pursuing wealth, market share and profit with the single-minded vigor of born-again capitalists. Economic growth has been consistently extraordinary – averaging 9 per cent annually but often topping 10 per cent, fueled by a domestic boom in building and commercial development as well as by mushrooming exports. China now exerts a major influence on the global economy – the soaring prices of commodities, from copper to oil, are largely explained by China's hunger for them. Carol's letters convey a sense of the old frugal habits beginning to give way to consumerism – as well as of considerable faith in technological progress.

Yet for all the glistening skyscrapers and enthusiasm for consumption, China remains a culture apart – strong, independent and self-confident. Many of Carol's letters focused on the differences she encountered day-to-day in the way Chinese people approached life and looked at the world, from eating habits to naming their children – and these cultural markers have been little affected so far by the bushfires of economic growth.

Sea slugs and monkey brains

A welcoming banquet fit for a queen.

China has changed since I was here two years ago. In Beijing shops are stocked with increasing quantities of expensive electrical goods. Working mothers ignore more traditional staples to buy the newly arrived white sliced bread. Even at a quick glance there are signs that social divisions are growing. Well-dressed older men now pay the higher fare to travel through Beijing by minibus, avoiding the slow, jammed and steamy buses on which the youngest and strongest men fight their way to a few rickety seats. That leaves mothers, children and older people behind in the mad scramble for the doors when the bus arrives, to stand packed together, jolted and elbowed, for the long slow journeys.

But when we left the capital with its taxis playing Strauss over Beijing Radio and traveled on the diesel train through the countryside, we found that in the rural areas change comes more slowly. Big black pigs still snuffle around as women scrub their clothes in muddy pools; chickens pick around mud-bricked homes whose elaborate tiled roofs are adorned with stone beasts. The golden sweetcorn still hangs out in the sun to dry.

As the train pulled into our urban destination, seen dimly through the coal-fire smog, our future academic colleagues lined up to greet their strange and jet-lagged guests. We were escorted to our accommodation. It was a Soviet-built apartment with a walk-in wardrobe and red velvet curtains partitioning rooms. We found it embarrassingly palatial. And in a city feeding largely on rice and noodles in a thin soup of stock and vegetables, we learned our hosts were planning a splendid welcoming banquet.

Abundance, even superfluity, is the key to Chinese hospitality. Our university hosts led us into a room bedecked with tinsel and flashing fairy lights, and seated us around a circular table covered with elaborate cold starters. As young waitresses brought in a series of unfamiliar hot dishes, our hosts used their own chopsticks to fill our bowls again and again. Between 18 or so delicious courses, as our hosts turned the revolving center of the table to urge more of this dish or that, compliments were tossed back and forth. Greetings became elaborate as the leader indicated the four glasses in front of each of us. 'This red wine is to wish you a warm welcome. This *mao tai* (strong spirit) is to your continuing success with us. The third – light beer – is for your good health.' Someone pointed to the fourth glass – Chinese cola – and asked what that was for. He looked nonplussed for a moment, then improvised fast. 'And this, to your safe return home.'

At times there were shocks. 'Have some of this,' our host urged, ladling out generous portions. 'It's delicious. It's monkey brain.' There was a gasp, as we stared at the cream-colored glutinous substance floating in a thin gruel. 'It's a kind of mushroom. We call it monkey brain because it looks that way.' Quite the opposite happened with the 'sea cucumber': slimy, chewy, sweaty black; and fed to us in quantities – then redefined as 'sea slug'.

As one course followed another we began to wonder whether the meal would ever end. A whole fish in a rich sweet-and-sour sauce came as a relief to those of us who knew that fish tends to come near a banquet's close. By the time the waitresses had brought an extra course of fruit in deference to Western tastes, the banquet had done its work. We had been plied with hospitality so great that no-one could go away hungry. Indeed when our hosts tried to press still more on a woman's plate and she blurted, 'I can't – I'd be sick,' they looked quite delighted.

Rise and shine

The dawn chorus – and a lot more besides – starts up with the sun's first rays in the Yellow River valley.

I woke up well before six to take a look at early morning China – and found the little world outside my door was awake well before me. People scurried about in the pale dawn light down the narrow lane edged by the cucumber plants that everyone grows over domestic walls. While a few old ladies held wide-eyed babies in their arms, others rooted in huge communal dustbins to salvage cardboard and waste paper. People carrying thermos bottles of hot water from home to home stepped in time with military music already blasting from loudspeakers.

From every small courtyard came delicious breakfast smells. High above, mothers cooked on the open balconies of modern apartment buildings. Chairs and old bricks were piled around their stoves and pots of crimson geraniums and cacti stood on the ledges. When a balcony collapsed recently onto the one below, China Daily moralized: 'People who overload their balconies contribute to such accidents.' But in a country where space is at a premium, few are likely to listen.

Yet beyond the homes already coming to life, the broad roads are almost silent. Chinese roads are quiet anyway; apart from the occasional roar of a truck, the only sounds are of tinkling bicycle bells and the swish of a hundred cycle tires. This morning crowds of joggers mingle with the bikes. The runners and cyclists swerve around pedestrians who cheerfully ignore enormous billboards directing, 'Pedestrians should keep to the sidewalk'. Junctions are a mess of cyclists, runners and strollers, with rattletrap Liberation trucks veering through the lot. For at this hour the traffic lights are still switched off for the night.

When I reached the deep green canal in the center of the town and looked through the drooping willows to the red-and-gold pavilions, I found people on the opposite bank working intently on their breathing and their health. Facing the rising sun, which glowed red over the roofs topped with strange stone beasts, were crowds performing graceful tai chi movements. Dozens of hands reached up into the misty air, then spiraled sideways in graceful circles. A pair of white-bearded men stopped their exercises to chat, but swiveled wrists in supple circles while they talked. More old gentlemen simply sat watching and listening peacefully to the songs of pet birds they carried in cages.

Back on the road, I cycled through the dust raised by weary farmworkers who had risen early to pull carts laden with sweet potatoes into town. Wheels rattled on the tarmac as women passed by with trolleys filled with white eggs. A red-faced peasant hauled a vast cart full of baskets topped with his wife and big-eyed daughter. Women wearing the bright green-and-orange headscarves of countryfolk pulled oil-drums mounted on wheels and filled with the foul-smelling products of city latrines – en route to be used as fertilizer in the fields.

But faster than I could watch it all, China was waking up. Soon the streets were filled with schoolchildren, each with a knotted red scarf around her neck – a revolutionary symbol used as a badge of the Young Pioneers. On every corner street vendors were selling breakfast: deep-fried bread; sesame-topped rolls baked in oil drums beside the street; dough smeared with salt, herbs and garlic, folded and tossed in oil.

I rode back up the hill in a smog of morning coal fires and the traffic's diesel fumes, waited at traffic lights newly switched on, and saw that all the schoolchildren, the tai chi practitioners and the songbirds had disappeared.

Minding your own business

Invasion of privacy is an alien concept in China, as Carol finds out when she goes for a rear-end injection.

'You know my name in Chinese means "God",' said a new acquaintance provocatively, 'and so I know everything. I know many things about you. I know you're 28, have no children, graduated in 1984... and many other things too.'

I was amazed. I'd met this woman, who worked in the provincial education administration department, only two days before. 'How do you know?' At first she teased me, saying she had supernatural powers, but finally admitted happily: 'When we met on Monday, I told you I wanted to be your friend. So I looked out your application form in the office to find out more about you.'

In the West, documents such as application forms would come under the heading 'confidential'; and if we have seen a colleague's form we pretend we haven't. We might take a sneaky look to see whom a friend was writing to, but would not pick up the letter to read as Chinese visitors do. In the Post Office anyone already pasting stamps onto their letter will pick up yours to examine as well.

'Desk drawers are private territory in the West,' an English manual painstakingly explains, 'and it is impolite to read over someone's shoulder.'

Here, such Western obsession with confidentiality is replaced by an intrusive concern about other people's affairs. Gossip spreads like wildfire. Personal space is in short supply. At university, seven students packed into bunk beds lining a bedroom no bigger than a Western box room have to study, sleep, chat and live on top of each other. And if one has a cough, schoolmates and teachers will try to help. A kindly and paternalistic Dean will even escort teachers to the clinic and, as with me, stand watching until asked to leave during an injection in a place I'd rather not show the head of my department.

Such public concern about matters we would see as private extends to total strangers too. 'Aren't you cold?' the old lady asks as I park my bike and, paying a few cents, take the wooden tag that serves as a receipt. In temperatures that would constitute a hot summer's day elsewhere, but here is like spring or autumn, I shake my head. The old lady stares at me and bends to grip my bare ankle. 'You must wear more clothes,' she says firmly.

People cope with the crowds partly by ignoring them. Cyclists veer across the road without checking to see if someone else is behind them, as they invariably are. Passers-by walk straight in front of cameras – for if you waited for every photographer to take her picture, you would wait forever. And except in the posed photographs beloved by the Chinese, you're never alone. Perhaps that is part of the attraction of those ubiquitous photos of one person alone with a famous monument.

So while in the West we preserve a defended body-space, apologizing if we touch or are touched by someone else, in overcrowded China bodies invariably collide. While we say, 'Excuse me...', here people simply brush – or haul – you out of the way.

Yet even from a foreigner's viewpoint, it would be a mistake to think there is no individual space in this country. True there is no privacy in the toilets, for example – those smelly unpartitioned rooms lined with holes in the floor – but women on the lavatory preserve an aloof distance from each other.

And while on a packed train people start up conversations, offer cigarettes or sunflower seeds and play cards, they also withdraw if they want to. Among the noisy 'hard seat' carriages, sprawling with humanity as they are, a few retreat into meditative silence. In the midst of the anonymity of public life, they retire to perfect privacy inside their own heads.

Vibrate the Universe !

What's in a name? we ask in English. In China, names reflect changes in the political climate.

If you want to understand China's history, my students keep telling me, all you have to do is look around you – and listen. From the oldest grandmothers (their feet still tiny from binding in feudal China) to today's bright toddlers, almost every person in China bears a name evocative of the fears and longings of society at the time they were born.

So the names of my friends' grandfathers show the dreams of China's people in the years before Liberation: Get Rich, these old men are called, Have Luck, or Gain High Office. Babies born to intellectual families were sometimes given bookish names – adopted straight from literature, or having as an element 'book', 'ink' or 'poem'.

Some older names show an underlying sadness and hardship. Dog's Reject was a name supposed to turn devils away from a precious son — because after all, if not even a dog treasured the child, what devil would want him? A much-longed-for son might be given an ugly name — such as Er Tu, or Baldhead – simply to protect him. In those years of high infant mortality, parents often chose names which indicated that a child would be easy to bring up. And in families of nine or ten, parents gave younger children the hopeful name Jie – The End.

Those of my friends born around 1949 – the time of Liberation – are called Victory and New Country or Long March, Celebrate the Country, Peace and simple Liberation.

But among my students, now in their early twenties, names recall the outbreak of the Cultural Revolution. Red Guard, Defend the People, Protect Mao Zedong and May You Triumph Forever are the personal names of both men and women. Other students once had such names but have quietly changed them since. And when they choose they adopt names like Study Quickly, Fly Far and Wide and – my favorite – Colorful Clouds at Dusk.

The Chinese laugh at the idea that we in the West can have forgotten the meanings of our names: in China, everyone accepts that names have power. This is part of a culture in which the people – colloquially, the 'old hundred names' – assume language relates directly to the real world. It is in any case easier to believe this in a country where the written language is based on ideograms: words are pictures, and everyone can read a name's real meaning in the elements of a Chinese character. But Chinese also shows more linguistic inventiveness than English, creating new names while we use words from other languages. Thus the Chinese made up 'bear cat' and 'pocket rat', while we simply borrowed 'panda' and 'kangaroo'.

But Chinese names also show how disproportionately precious boy children still are in China. Boys are sometimes given girls' names: because fewer girls die, superstition has it that female names can protect from danger. Families of girls sometimes have such names as Pan Di, Zhap Di and Lai Di – Expect Brother, Call for Brother and Come Here Brother. Names are so powerful, the Chinese believe, that they can call boy children to the world.

Attitudes to women change slowly, one friend told me angrily. In her grandparents' time, women were often simply called by their husband's surname, then their father's, then shi — meaning 'married woman'. Her own grandmother was called Quiet, felt then to be a female virtue; her mother Pretty Pearl. Her sisters had names linked to quietness, kindness and shyness – and she was called after a flower. So when her elder sister had a baby girl and my friend was asked to name her niece, she thought hard. And in a generation where parents give their precious only children pretty but meaningless names such as Bao Bao or Ling Ling, she chose Zhen Hua – or Vibrate the Universe!

Sleeping in cars

Small ants and robots are part of a national fantasy in China.

'In 10 or 20 years' time,' reflected a 20-year-old when asked to think about China's future, 'our diet will be much better. Small ants and many other new foods will be on the table.'

Wonderfully inventive as I think the Chinese are in making artificial foods and in the ingenious use of existing ones, China's ideas of progress do not always match my Western ones. But what strikes me in conversations is not only the way people in this country see the future, but their firm belief that it will be progress. Ask anyone here how China is likely to change, and the answer will be optimistic.

'Our life will be richer and more comfortable, and food will be more delicious,' commented another young man. 'We will build our homes in the quiet countryside, and travel in our own cars. In the big modern cities there will be no traffic jams and no pollution.' While we see technology as bringing inevitable problems, Chinese young people imagine instead a romance of technology able to transcend all difficulties.

In a developing country where everyone aspires to own color televisions and huge fridges propped prominently in the corner of a living room, technology holds a charm long lost to someone hardened by the technological chaos of Western cities. 'In the future,' a young woman added dreamily, 'we teachers won't have to go to the classroom: we can just speak into a TV camera, and students can sit at home and watch us on their own TV screens. The students can ask the TV to borrow reference books, and check their homework. Machines will do all the hard work, and I'll be able to buy things in my own home by an auto-line to the shops.'

Here in the Yellow River valley, where there is little machinery to ease the burden of everyday tasks and huge loads of farm produce, logs and scrap-iron are hauled in carts pulled by men, a world where all the work is not hand-done is a rose-tinted dream. A favorite Chinese fantasy is a future world where robots take over the chores.

Perhaps one cultural difference is that the industrial world has experienced the technological miracle already, and found it wanting; perhaps to jaded Western youth, it is difficult to imagine a future of glorious change. Our teenagers, I believe, do not imagine that in a couple of decades life will be wonderful: quite the reverse. But unlike the West, people in China are forcibly involved in planning for a bright future. When the 13th Party Congress met in Beijing last October to plan the country's progress, leaders' speeches were circulated nationwide for workers and students to discuss in the weekly political study sessions over the next few months.

'We will have achieved the Four Modernizations by the end of the century,' the young woman explained confidently. 'We'll catch up with the developed countries. No-one will look down on our country, and everyone in the world will want to come here to see a very developed China.'

Working towards a glorious future is official policy: and so foreigners often dismiss the English language newspaper, *China Daily*, as propaganda. 'Balance of trade likely to be favorable', 'Power industry reaches milestone', 'State revenue on target' and 'Golden age of growth in Fujian Province' are the big headlines in the stack of recent papers beside my desk. For bad news, you have to turn to the back page – the foreign news. Western newspapers relish incest, murder cases, traffic accidents and other gloom. And so as someone accustomed to Western media, *China Daily* teeters between propaganda and simple economic optimism.

So life in China will be wonderful in 10 or 20 years' time – or almost. 'In the future,' one smart young man speculated, 'everyone will have a bright, shiny and very big car.' He hesitated. 'The roads will have to be wider, as China has so many people.' He thought again. 'We'll widen the roads and pull down all the old houses, and let people sleep in their cars.'

Jumping the queue

Any social connection can be a ticket to ride in China. And one favor begets another...

The first time I traveled alone in China, I was worried that I wouldn't be able to buy a train ticket. I had practised the appropriate sentences in careful Chinese and bought a phrase book, but in this country where it is commonly said 'the people are too many', trains are packed and tickets hard to buy.

I was in Harbin station near the Russian border on a dark January afternoon and outside the temperature was falling towards zero. There were three ticketsellers' windows, and above two I read my destination, 'Qiqihaer'. As I joined the first long queue, railway workers were busy scrubbing out the characters and when I reached the head of the line I was waved aside to the next window. I queued again under another 'Qiqihaer' sign. Soon workers erased this too, and I was abruptly told to join the third queue. I did so but the ticket seller sent me back to the first and the whole process began again.

My nearest friend was 1,500 kilometers away and I was desperate. I left the crowds and found a gold-braided railway official hovering near the entrance. 'Comrade,' I said in my baby Chinese, 'how do you buy a ticket? Here none, there none, there none.' He asked where I wanted to go, and when; he took my money, opened the door to the ticketsellers' office, and went round the back to buy my ticket from the clerk at the first window.

In China, people use figurative back doors all the time because there is simply too little of everything to go round. For a ticket to Beijing, the Chinese either queue several hours, or find a 'friend-of-a-friend' who works at the station to phone down the line and reserve a seat or sleeper. The Chinese 'back door' is the way to find decent housing, get your children into university, buy a superior brand of bicycle or even procure a delicious fish. One girl I knew never so much as bought a long-distance bus ticket. 'My father is Professor so-and-so,' she used to say, and get on free.

Guan xi or 'having connections' is frequently used to help friends or relatives. It mainly works as a regimented system of exchange. Ask someone to buy you a ticket, and they'll expect you to translate something, write a letter or sell hard currency. Everyone uses their *guan xi*. The university uses it to encourage factories to donate much-needed machinery. My own over-friendly students will suddenly ask for a preview of their marks or a guaranteed exam pass. When lotus root, oranges and lettuces are harvested, teachers can buy them cut-price and in return the university drafts bright graduates as farm laborers. The barter of commodities includes a trade in people.

Yet almost everyone condemns this institutionalized queue-jumping. The papers complain daily that to get permission for building sites, to run a business, even to change jobs you must give elaborate presents to bureaucrats; hospital patients pay a fortune getting treatment. Officials whose bribes run into hundreds of thousands of yuan are imprisoned. A few notorious wheelers and dealers in a nearby town are about to be investigated by regional government inspectors, but in the usual style these jokers will probably wine and dine the investigators and send them away happy. The children of professors and other important people have big apartments, comfortable jobs and scarce consumer goods. Ordinary people complain about this. It is corruption they say, and should be stopped.

In the West the equivalent of *guan xi* mainly operates at either end of the social scale, with the old boys' network at one end and 'the lads' at the other. But in China the system is spread throughout society. While I see *guan xi* as the inevitable result of a lumbering planned economy in which everyone is supposed to wait their turn and no-one wants to, the Chinese often describe it as an unfortunate habit left over from feudal times. '*Guan xi* and the back-door system will die in time,' a friend told me. 'As we get richer and facilities improve, people will be able to buy things more easily and *guan xi* will go. As for seeking out the friend-of-a-friend to phone another friend to ask for a ticket – well, we simply won't have time.'

Children of the moon

One night every year the full moon drives China's young people mad with excitement.

Rockets were shooting into the darkness long before the moon rose. The machine-gun rattle of firecrackers summoned us into the warm night, and we walked through the pink-paper debris of spent fireworks as little boys lit more, awaiting the results with fingers in ears and eyes screwed up. Then the moon came up.

It was gorgeous: huge, silver, a perfect circle rising above the city. And suddenly the streets were packed as China giggled its way into the year's second great holiday – the 'Moon' festival which celebrates Chinas's *qing nian*: 'fresh of years' or young people.

The moon rose above the campus, between the outstretched fingers of Mao's giant statue at whose feet students formed a circle. The teenagers crowded around a vacant patch of concrete where a tape-recorder blasted, waiting for someone to start dancing. But, bashful under the fairy lights and brilliant moon, no-one would.

More and more young people flocked around us as we sauntered through the dark night, until we had gathered a great horde. Joking, giggling, chatting, we swarmed towards the mountain on the city's edge.

The moon lit the polished stone steps as we began to ascend. Climbing a mountain is never a solitary experience in China but a mad rush upwards in an excited crowd. And this mob, all under 25, was more excitable than most. Whole gangs kept breaking away to start high-pitched card games, buy beer and apples from stalls lit by wax tapers, and – once – to join a party, merry-making under the pines. There, to the strumming of a fast guitar and a squeaking mouth organ, an excited couple danced under the moon's half-light.

From tunes warbled on flute and accordion to disco beats on passing ghetto-blasters, music was all around us as we climbed. Sometimes teenagers simply wandered along singing folk songs to the starry sky.

And deep within an ancient Buddhist temple, shuttered against the night, monks beat on an insistent, melancholy drum. Against the monastery's bolted gates, couples hovered in the shadows: although most institutions here forbid their students to have boy- or girlfriends, many youngsters break that rule today.

But most were single-sex groups, holding hands in camaraderie as they stumbled up the steps under the light of the great moon. Only a few dark shapes wandered solitary and sad. Some students told me that the mid-Autumn Festival brought them poignant reminders of home. The Moon Festival is traditionally a time for families to get together, but students often find they simply do not have the money – or the time – to stand all night in the 'hard seat' carriages amongst throngs of people going home to celebrate.

'I wish I was at home with my family,' said one girl mournfully. 'My father is preparing beer and mooncakes in the courtyard. He will invite our neighbors to join the family watching the moon. And then they will play games and tell jokes, and whoever wins will be rewarded with an apple.'

Inside the pagoda at the very top of the mountain, we opened beer and ate our mooncakes: flat and round, filled with dried fruit, impossibly red cherries and lurid green angelica. Outside on the mountain's silvered peak, teenagers sat in circles telling jokes and singing. In a country where most people have no radio, TV or cassette recorder, young people often take it in turns to sing lilting Chinese folksongs and the garbled words of Western pop. Some groups roared with laughter as boys began a 'crosstalk', producing greater and greater boasts to meet the others' straight-faced lies.

And still young people poured in their hundreds up the slopes to watch the moon, now shining high above the city. They shrieked and giggled, teetering up moonlit stone steps rubbed so smooth by centuries of feet that they were treacherous to trendy heels. The rockets had long ceased to whizz from the grey city spread below us, but throughout the night, firecrackers exploded suddenly, spasmodically from the suburbs.

Trashing the past

Old skills are junked as China moves towards a throwaway society.

The vegetable market closes at dusk. People hurry home with bits of meat loosely wrapped in squares of brown paper, leaving the ground littered with straw rope and abandoned baskets. There is very little waste paper and no plastic, for foodstuffs are not pre-packaged here but sold from a farmer's barrow or the back of a bike. A flimsy paper-bag costs as much as a Chinese pound of beansprouts. But the hand-woven wicker baskets used to carry oranges, lotus root, carrots and green celery from the countryside are dismantled in the market place, usually to be flung into the river.

These beautifully crafted panniers would sell for high prices in the West, but hours of labor and generations of skill are treated casually here. Everywhere in China sophisticated hand-made tools are used, and the Chinese assume that because anyone can make such things they have less value than, say, a plastic bag.

So a friend was embarrassed when I wanted to examine every object his family had made: the weathered pitchforks crafted from branching joints of trees; strong rope twisted from straw; bundles of sesame-seed stalks used as firewood after the seeds had been eaten; hand-woven winnowing baskets, and heavy clay pots for keeping water cool in hot summers. There was even a deep cellar under the chicken run that served as the family's freezer.

Chinese family economies are generally more adaptable and ingenious than those of Western households. A woman who farms land all year can make straw rope, pots and pitchforks in slack periods; she can cook noodles for the local factory; she grows her own cotton to stitch into winter padded jackets; and – unlike most of her Western counterparts – can strip down and mend her bike.

The same ingenuity applies to farming methods. The Chinese are expert at land use: they feed a quarter of the world's population on seven per cent of its arable land in a country littered with vast deserts and mountain tracts. A single piece of land may have rice growing in water, fish farmed amongst the rice, and ducks swimming on top eating the parasites that prey on rice. According to ancient ideas, the balance of yin and yang forces comprise an organic whole. Hence Chinese farmers maintain a balance between different species – and generally without the use of heavy machinery or artificial fertilizers.

While understanding technology in the West is usually a specialist's job, in China everyone is expected to understand the principles behind homespun machinery. The vendor at our market weighs the vegetables carefully in hand-held scales. He tells you the price per Chinese pound, and then merely points to the scales to show the weight. Sometimes he calculates the price on an abacus and then indicates the total. But if as a Westerner you cannot read the abacus, or the scales, it is bad luck, because the assumption is that everyone shares the skills that enable them to do this.

Another really good piece of basic, practical machinery whose workings are accessible to everyone, is the bicycle standing outside my front door. Like all Chinese bikes, it is an all-purpose workhorse: so strong it will probably go on and on, until like most other bikes on the road its seat leather is worn right through and every part has been patched by street-corner bike repairers. It bears little resemblance to bikes popular in the West, a fact ruefully noted by the Shanghai Bicycle Factory recently. They are now sacrificing the durability of their traditional line to manufacture a good-looking, light version aimed at an export market where people trade in bicycles regularly.

There are many other examples of the same thing. It looks as if this non-specialized homespun world, which requires so many skills from so many people, is about to change towards glossy factory-made consumerism. Indeed, the Government recently criticized those resourceful street-corner repair shops, where a spare part can be created with the most basic of equipment rather than ordered from a factory. It is finally uneconomical to go on and on repairing the sturdy Liberation trucks, they argued: far better to stimulate the economy by buying a glossy new vehicle, and throwing away the old.

Reaching for the sky
Sexual equality in a changing China.

'It's Women's Day today,' the local restaurant proprietor leaned over me. 'Did you know?' I did. Colleagues were busy organizing women's inter-department tug-of-war teams and distributing free cinema and dance tickets. These were for women only – though each woman got a second one for her partner.

It was a surprise, however, when the restaurateur produced a complimentary bottle of beer. 'Happy Women's Day!' he said. Then he stuck his head into the cooking alcove to bring out one delicious dish after another – all for free.

'But what about your wife?' I asked, pointing to the curtained alcove. 'If it's Women's Day why don't you do the cooking?'

He grinned. 'Oh, I can't. Relax. Eat slowly. Happy Women's Day.'

China is a country where almost everyone is acutely aware of the issue of women's equality, but locked into what are described as 'feudal habits'. Male students will tell you how far Chinese women have come since the pre-Liberation days of entrapment in the home. Yet those same male students appreciate a bit of female help when it comes to washing the sheets and still view bright girls who speak out in class as distinctly 'unfeminine'. Silence was a female virtue before Liberation – and still is. In today's 'lonely hearts' columns women describe themselves as 'dainty and silent' as they advertise for rich and powerful husbands.

While the new China has vastly improved women's position by training them to become teachers, doctors, bus drivers and bicycle menders, it remains harder for Chinese women to find jobs than men. When they do, they often have to accept a lower salary. There are other inequalities. Women workers will often leave work an hour before the regular lunch break – to go home and cook. Chinese meals may take half an hour to eat, but they usually take two hours to prepare. Now, if a man were to leave work early to prepare an elaborate lunch he would be ridiculed.

Some women I know are enraged by common proverbs such as: 'Men can do anything better'. Others tamely accept the lesser role complete with the frilly, impractical dress style typical of the new city woman. But for every woman teetering on high heels there is one clad in sexually undifferentiated work clothes, spattered with oil, mud or paint. Women may be thought of as weak but they are also required to be strong.

Culturally and politically, women still have a low profile in Chinese society. Women's calligraphy, art or even literature is relatively rare. When a painting is by a woman, the sign often points this out carefully – underlining the sense that this is an unusual occurrence. There are few women leaders, few women politicians and questions about feminist groups are met with incomprehension. Protest here is institutionalized – the Party does it for you.

But, compared with most countries in the world – my own included – the position of Chinese women is in many ways pretty good. Kindergarten facilities are excellent. Maternity leave is often generous, up to 18 months in many cases. Compared with China's feudal past, the change is remarkable. The country's new economic policies, however, may be threatening the benefits its women have gained.

Under the brigade system a woman could work part of the time in the fields and look after young children and the couple's elderly parents for the rest of the day. But as China adopts the 'responsibility system' with payment for work actually done, men are moving off the land to set up their own businesses in the cities. Many women are left behind to work the family's small plot of land, keeping home, caring for children and elderly parents, mending tools and in some cases boosting the family income by doing an evening job as well.

Today more women are following their husbands to the cities – often illegally. Without urban residence permits they find low-paid jobs in privately run restaurants or in the new family-managed sweatshops. Or they do piecework at home. Hundreds work as nannies and housemaids, for little more than their keep. Women, as Chairman Mao said, hold up half the sky – or perhaps, as Chinese society changes again, rather more than half.

Little emperors revisited

Why the Chinese spoilt brat is a myth.

When we go to lunch in the little street round the corner, the proprietors' three-year-old son rushes to meet us. We are made to wait while he shows his new toys; a scarlet tricycle, a pull-along duck, a space-age gun playing the tunes of eight different police sirens when you pull the trigger.

The other customers in the restaurant ignore him. If he starts playing with the keys attached to the back of their belts, they push him away. Chinese parents and teachers complain that today's children are being spoilt. Usually 'only' children, they are plied with expensive toys by an adoring circle of parents, grandparents, aunts and uncles. 'Little emperors', they are called. 'If he wanted the stars in the sky,' one parent told me, 'you would try to get them for him.'

But to my Western eyes, children here are remarkably unspoiled. It is just that the rules are different. Here, in China, people talk with horror of children playing games we happily permit in the West: teasing and even hitting an older relative, for example, to see them pretend pain and fear. In my view this restaurant's three-year-old is a model of good behavior: his tantrums are rare and only once did he complain about a lack of attention by peeing on the floor right between my feet and his mother's.

But China's children are expected to behave like little adults. This requirement may have been part of our own history too. Philip Aries' book *Centuries of Childhood* argues that in Europe's early history, children's lives were similar to those of adults. That was before a new 17th-century protectiveness evolved special ways to treat kids. In China today you only very occasionally hear someone using a baby voice or baby language when speaking to a child. And a British teacher I knew used to point out to me the oddness of Chinese children's drawing styles compared with those of Western children. While Western infants are quite happy to draw in ways that are characteristically 'childish', Chinese children rule careful lines and get quite frustrated in their attempts to produce pictures that do not look childish.

Chinese parents do, of course, shower love and attention on their children but it is always made quite clear that child's-play has to remain well within the limits of normal social behavior. The same control applies to adults in their treatment of children. You hardly ever see a parent hit a child. That would constitute too great a loss of face. But when I inquired about this I was told: 'they belt the kid later, in private'. Indeed there have been several cases in the press recently of 10- or 11-year-olds being so severely beaten for under-achievement at school that they died. A lot is expected of children here – and few allowances are made.

Another thing you rarely see is people crying – be they children or adults. Tears are saved for very serious troubles. So the adult response to a child's tears is more likely to be a brushing aside than an extension of sympathy. On an acupuncture ward I watched a doctor insert long copper needles into the scalp of a one-year-old and saw the baby howl when every ten minutes the needles were twisted to stimulate the body energy. The parents laughed, showed toys and jogged the baby up and down while wiping his tears. Older children bore the pain in stoic silence.

And while Western influences may be partly responsible for some more flexible attitudes towards education, rote learning and recitation are still primary in Chinese schools. A teacher may demonstrate how to write a particular ideogram on the board. But to write the word themselves Chinese children – those spoilt and individualistic 'little emperors'? – will practise writing individual strokes for hours on end until they can get this horizontal or that vertical line exactly right. It is difficult to imagine the average Western schoolchild being so uncomplainingly diligent.

Letters from La Paz (Bolivia), 1989-1990

Susanna Rance

Susanna continues to live in La Paz, further down the hill from the street market neighborhood which was her home when she wrote the 'Letters'. She still has a wonderful view of Mount Illimani from her 17th-floor apartment near the UMSA state university where she works as lecturer and researcher.

For some years Susanna combined consultancy work with doctoral studies at Trinity College Dublin, receiving her PhD in Sociology in 2003. Since 2006 she has worked with the postgraduate center for development studies, CIDES-UMSA, teaching research methodology and gender theories. Susanna has published on the Bolivian family planning debate, participatory advocacy, humane treatment and medical education, research ethics, sexual citizenship, medical discourse, and women's changing abortion practices. She is currently commencing a study on abortion and transnational migration, and is a member of CLACAI, the Latin American Consortium Against Unsafe Abortion.

Susanna's children, who appeared in the 'Letters', are now at universities in England: Nina doing Dance at DMU Leicester, and Amaru reading Politics, Philosophy and Economics at St Anne's College, Oxford. All three remain strongly attached to La Paz, and are firmly committed to Bolivia's current process of political and social transformation.

Changes in Bolivia

Rooted as they are in the Aymara culture of the family and community into which Susanna Rance had married, the letters included here prefigure the political revolution that has recently taken place in Bolivia, bringing indigenous peoples to the forefront.

Like many Latin American countries, Bolivia was blighted by military rule in the 1970s – when the populist nationalist Hernan Siles Zuazo won the presidency in 1982 it was after 18 years of military regimes. His announcement that Bolivia would not repay its debt caused consternation in international banking circles and the IMF and World Bank soon scuppered this, blocking trade and eventually prompting a fiscal crisis and hyperinflation. From 1985 through the years when Susanna was writing, neoliberal policies dominated successive governments, in line with the Thatcher-Reagan ideology dominating the West – mines were closed, subsidies withdrawn and state enterprises privatized.

In the late 1980s indigenous organizations began to form – the majority of Bolivians see themselves as indigenous but they have historically been marginalized. In 1990 there was a 750-kilometer mass march to the capital, La Paz, pleading for Land and Dignity. In 1993 the indigenous movements won the right for children to be educated in the Aymara, Quechua and Guaraní languages.

On the economic front, privatization continued, despite public opposition. In 2000 Bolivian resistance to privatization was celebrated worldwide when the people of Cochabamba successfully rebelled against a World Bank-imposed privatization of the local public water system. In 2003 there was further mass protest against the export of natural gas to the US via Chile; attempts to crush the revolt left scores dead but only increased the resistance. Eventually President Sanchez de Lozada was forced into exile by what became known as the 'October Revolution'.

The growing influence of indigenous movements and the resistance to globalized exploitation culminated in the landslide presidential victory of Evo Morales, the coca growers' union leader who became the country's first indigenous leader. On taking office in January 2006, Morales announced the nationalization of hydrocarbons. His Government followed up with progressive social measures funded by oil and gas revenues – a small annual grant for each child in education, free healthcare for children and a universal old-age pension.

Bolivia has always had a strong radical tradition – and that is reflected in Susanna's letters. But the insights the letters give us into the culture of one of the country's main indigenous groups are even more penetrating – and are politically prescient in a way that few would have anticipated at the time.

A style of death

Susanna's Aymara mother-in-law has died, and those who knew her mark her death in the Andean way.

Looking up from the computer, my boss shook his head: 'It must be strange for you – joining in those death rites so different from your own culture.'

He was right. My mother-in-law's death had brought convulsion to the whole family and not just because she was our much-loved Mami, the hub of the household, a true matriarch. Her passing set in motion a sequence of events which left me dizzy, as others around me prescribed how grief was to be expressed and exorcized.

At first I felt outside it all, as though my personal sorrow had little to do with the rituals I had been drawn into. But by the end of the week I too felt their cathartic effects and realized that the Aymara customs of dressing, wailing, embracing, eating, drinking, washing and burning had cleansed a part of my pain and brought a new bond with the family.

La Mamá died peacefully at dawn. Her frail body seemed a shadow of the vigorous woman who had given birth to nine children and lost six of them; who had spun and woven her hands raw to support the family; who had worked tirelessly on the land and run ahead of me down the tiny mountain paths, her hearty laugh and guttural Aymara phrases ringing in the air.

An early morning visit from my sister-in-law Julia brought home the most urgent concerns provoked by death: money, clothing and food. On hearing the news, our neighbor was aghast. 'Then why are you going round like this?' she reproached us, plucking the sleeve of Julia's blue cardigan. We fled to the market and combed the stalls for black garments to cover us from head to toe.

As we ran through the streets in the rain, Julia stopped, sobbing, to tell relatives, friends, unknown market traders, of her mother's death. The news started to fly, climbing up through the shanty towns, delivered by bus drivers to distant provinces so that long-lost relations managed to reach the city in time for the funeral the next day.

That night, the biggest room in the house was prepared for the wake. The guests sat talking quietly, sipping hot tea with grape liquor and chewing coca leaves. In contrast to their calm, El Papá would suddenly shout out in grief: 'I'm not going to die! I'll live for a hundred years!' was his protest against the violence of death.

Julia sobbed uncontrollably, rocking back and forth, dropping hot tears onto the glass window of the coffin. Her pain was not just allowed but approved, her wails cushioned on the shoulders of fellow mourners.

Before the funeral, Mami's coffin was gently placed in the courtyard, in the place where she liked to sit. Then we proceeded to the town cemetery. Death is loyal to social status; the better-off can afford to buy eternal rest at eye level, the poor rent temporary coffin spaces accessible only by ladder.

After the burial, we stood at the cemetery gate while 80 people stopped to embrace each of us in turn. Drained and exhausted, I was dismayed to hear that an uncle had invited the funeral party to drink beer in a nearby hall.

On trying to escape, I was firmly grabbed by the arm. 'You mustn't go! It's unlucky!' Three hours and several crates of beer later, alcohol had mellowed our spirits. Julia was laughing and El Papá was proudly showing crumpled photos of his war years. Libations were poured to the earth mother –Pachamama – and as the beer splashed to the ground, someone would say: 'Las penas!' Our woes poured away along with the offering.

Returning home that night I was shocked to see Mami's bed, mattress and belongings piled up in the yard. The next day her closest relatives would take her clothes to the river to be washed. Then most of them would be burned. La Mamá was really gone.

'Does the spirit live after you die?' asked my five-year-old daughter. All around us Mami's spirit permeated the walls she had built, the yards where she had sat in the sun, the family she had raised and nourished with her frail strong body.

Spiritual food

The many ways in which coca is used by ordinary Bolivians today.

An early morning phone call. It's Albertina. 'I'm going crazy waiting to see if I'm going to get this job or not! Do you know anyone who can read coca?' My friend is in luck. A *yatiri* – or soothsayer – has just come in from a rural province. Before setting off again by truck at dawn the next day, she will, for a price, read the future, offer warnings and advice.

She throws the coca leaves into the air. They float for a while before arranging themselves on the striped woven cloth. Albertina's face falls. The leaves have landed mainly dark side up, a sign of ill fortune. And two leaves have become entwined, their stalks facing downwards, showing that there is an obstacle in Albertina's way. 'This is what the coca knows,' concludes the soothsayer. 'You need to have a lot of faith.'

For over 2,000 years, the coca leaf has been part of the Andean life and ritual. Bolivians hold it proudly as a symbol of their cultural identity and their rich tradition of natural medicine. In recent years, Bolivia has become notorious as a supplier of the raw material for the international drugs industry. But the cocaine trade is barely two decades old – a mere upstart compared to the ancestral dignity of Mama Coca.

Visitors to La Paz are offered an infusion of coca leaves to ward off altitude sickness: *mate de coca* is on restaurant menus along with camomile or aniseed tea. On the market streets indigenous women weigh out the leaves by the pound on tin scales. Their best customers are the poor, who chew the leaf to dull hunger, cold and fatigue.

'How would you feel if you didn't have coca?' I asked Dionisio, a Quechua farmer from a valley community. 'We wouldn't feel like working,' he answered, plucking a few dark-green leaves from a small woven bag. 'It gives us strength, it quenches our thirst. We don't get so hungry. No coca, no work.'

For headaches, a couple of leaves are stuck to the temples, for the toothache to the jaw. A remedy for muscular pain? A poultice of coca leaves, well chewed to release their juices. Coca is the faithful companion of those in need, growing alongside them in their poverty of shallow, stony soil, on impossible slopes where nothing else will flourish.

But how did coca enter Andean culture in the first place? The legend goes like this. At the time of the Conquest when the Incas were being defeated by the Spanish invaders, a group of indigenous rebels took refuge in the house of an old and revered soothsayer, called Khana Chuyma. He was on the verge of death, but on seeing the suffering of his race personified in the unexpected guests, he asked the Sun God, Inti, for a lasting gift to the people. This gift should be neither gold nor riches, so that the ambitious white man could not snatch it away.

Inti granted the wish, and the soothsayer told his visitors: 'My children, go up to the nearest mountain top. There you will find some small plants with oval leaves. Look after them and cultivate them with care. They will give you food and comfort.

'But,' he warned, 'if the white man wants to do the same, and dares to use these leaves like you, they will have the opposite effect on him. Their juice, which will bring you strength and life, will become a repugnant, degenerating vice for your masters. While for you, the Indian race, coca will be a spiritual food, to them it will bring idiocy and madness.'

When Lake Titicaca overflowed its banks two years ago, destroying crops, drowning animals and submerging whole villages, some said

Pachamama, the earth mother, was angry at the abuse of the Sun God's gift. Nine-tenths of Bolivia's coca production now goes to supply the international drugs trade. Banana and coffee plants are ripped from the ground to make room for the lucrative coca bush. Young landless people leave highland communities to try their luck on the tropical Chapare coca plantations and street kids smoke and sell toxic cocaine-base cigarettes in the parks at night.

Meanwhile, back home, their parents and grandparents continue the ancient tradition of exchanging potatoes for coca – essential ingredient in life, death, ritual and necessity.

Bread for the living, bread for the dead

As the feisty women of Potosí prepare for All Saints Day, the sniff of revolution is never far away.

The smell of fresh-baked bread leads us down a cobbled alleyway, through a stone courtyard and into the suffocating warmth of the room by the oven wall. Eulogia, Fanny and Magdalena take a break from their work to tell us about the San Cristóbal bakery.

In this old quarter of the mining town of Potosí, bread is more than a daily staple. The bakery is part of a project run by local women, many of them daughters, wives and mothers of unemployed miners. They alternate shifts working in the bakery, health center, crèche and vegetable garden, making time for meetings to discuss community problems and pressure local authorities to improve conditions in their neighborhood.

'We never get much trade at the end of October,' says Fanny. 'Everyone's saving to come here and do their own baking for All Saints. That week, there were people in here day and night. Each family uses 10, 20, 50 pounds of flour, whatever they can afford, to make bread for their dead, and for the friends and relatives who come to visit their tombs.'

The 'tombs' prepared for 1 November, the Day of the Dead, are improvised shrines taking up half a family's living space, elaborately draped with clothes and sheets – black for the adult deceased, white for children. Symbols of Catholic and native religions jostle together on tables laden with crucifixes, candles, flower petals, coca leaves, faded photos, plates of food, tiny glasses of liquor and piles of bread in all shapes and sizes.

Gaudily painted plaster masks of horses, llamas, clowns, babies, farmers and miners stare up from plump figures of twisted dough which will be dry and hard by the time they are eaten. All Saints is about feeding the spirits, who announce their return home with a cold gust of wind which blows through the room at midday, making candles flicker and bringing the living a breath closer to their lost relatives.

Going from house to house to visit the tombs is an obligation as much as a social occasion. 'People criticize you if you don't go', says Eulogia, 'and the spirits may punish you.' Families wisely start their visits with those furthest from home, so as to end up near base by dawn as they stagger back, leaving a trail of lost hats, shoes and toddlers, the smallest babies slung haphazardly in shawls on their mothers' backs.

All Saints begins in sorrow as the dead are grieved for at home. Its mood of ceremony starts to mellow in flower-laden graveyards where earthenware jars of liquor have been smuggled in days before to outwit guards checking visitors for alcohol at the gate. But on the third day, the mourners climb to a sacred hilltop where they bid farewell to the spirits in the ritual Cacharpaya. The offerings of food are burned, and drinking, dancing and forfeit games give way to euphoria as the deceased are allowed to depart until the following year.

San Cristóbal had more than its share of dead last year. Freddy Oyala, 32, an active member of the community health center, was killed by a teargas grenade in a march protesting against state health and education cuts. Potosí turned into a battlefield, with a hundred wounded, as students, housewives and workers burst into the streets, enraged by the brutality of local police in trying to repress the protest.

'Whole families joined in the demonstration,' remembers Magdalena. 'Some went in to persuade their relatives to come home, but ended up staying for a fight until their clothes were torn into shreds. You could not help pitching in. You just get in there, without thinking of the consequences. We burned down the police headquarters and marched the cops out on the street in their underpants. We kept their helmets as trophies. They haven't dared to show their faces in any demonstrations since.'

The mood in the bakery gets more animated as each woman adds her anecdotes of barricades, Molotovs and people running along the rooftops. 'If you stay quiet and ask for nothing, you get nowhere,' says Eulogia. 'When you get tough, at least something starts moving, even if you have to shout a bit.'

After a moment of sudden silence, we take stock of the conversation. 'Funny, isn't it,' I say, 'how we started talking about bread...'

'And ended up with the revolution!' exclaims Fanny, throwing her woolen shawl around her shoulders.

Over the border

How do you support eight children as a single mother in Bolivia? Desperation breeds some ingenious solutions.

'Want to buy a pig?' asked a voice, as I carried Amaru downstairs to breakfast. Frankly, at 7.30am on a workday I had other things on my mind. Anyway our yard was scarcely big enough to hang out the nappies/diapers, let alone house a grunting beast.

'A pig? Are you crazy?' Then I saw Doña Andrea grinning up as she squatted in her wide skirts beside the bundle of farm produce she had brought to the city to sell. Her face radiated hope and goodwill.

'It's all right! They're not born yet!' Well, that was something. 'My sow is going to have piglets in a couple of weeks. I'm short of cash and I wondered... I mean, I'd raise it for you. It would be an investment.'

I got the picture. The idea still didn't fill me with enthusiasm, but I had to admire Doña Andrea's resourcefulness in finding yet another strategy to feed and clothe her eight children.

Bolivia is on the bottom rung as far as Latin American poverty levels go. The minimum monthly wage is worth $35. Only one worker in five has access to the social security system. Unemployment benefit is non-existent. So how do people survive?

The answer lies in the intricate web of activities performed by every family member old enough to bring in a bit of income. Two-thirds of the workforce are in the informal economy, outside the protection and control of labor laws. They rely on their ingenuity to improvise a living, running family workshops, shining shoes, doing errands or selling on the street.

Women, hampered by lack of capital and training, and with their youngest kids in tow, make up the majority of informal-sector workers. Jacinta was supporting three children, with her husband out of work.

She started off in the local markets selling detergent, soap and toothpaste smuggled from Peru. Having a good head for business, she soon graduated to bringing in contraband cameras and ghetto-blasters. With a bit of capital in hand, the next step was to become a money-changer.

Then a neighbor suggested a risky but profitable deal: investing all her capital in a cargo of cocaine. The neighbor got busted and ended up in jail. Jacinta lost everything. Shaken after her narrow escape, she started off at square one again with her market stall.

The middle classes also resort to activities on the fringes of illegality to make ends meet. My neighbor Leonora's job as a domestic-science teacher brought in barely enough money for bread and bus fares. But she kept on her evening teaching post because it gave her two daughters access to social-security healthcare.

In the daytime she sold fashion clothes to colleagues and friends. Then prices started to rocket. Few people could afford even contraband garments from neighboring Brazil. A new business started flourishing in La Paz: second-hand US clothing shipped south to Chile and brought back overland.

Once a fortnight Leonora would leave a supply teacher to manage her class and join the band of hardy clothes-traffickers who controlled the train, bus and truck routes over the mountains to Chile. Bargaining with wholesalers; hauling heavy loads around; shivering under tarpaulin at dawn; battling with corrupt customs officials: she would return from the four-day trip pale and exhausted.

Her two-bedroom house was piled to the roof with bales of used clothing. Leonora struggled to sell the merchandise and raise the capital for her next journey. But the idea was catching on and competition was fierce in the markets and on the contraband train. Her eldest daughter was starting university and the youngest would soon be leaving school.

Last week Leonora broke the news. 'I'm leaving. I'm going to the US to try my luck. I'll do anything. I'm not afraid of a bit of hard work so long as I can raise some cash. What's left for me here? I can't keep going like this. I've got to give the girls a future.'

By the end of the month Leonora will be on her way to Miami with two friends, one an engineer and the other a secretary. Their papers have been 'fixed' by a travel agency running an undercover emigration racket.

Bolivia is a country of six-and-a-half million inhabitants. A million more have gone abroad to live. For many, the trip north is just another step on the ladder of survival strategies: the only way up is across the border.

Trashing lives

At night on the city rubbish tip in La Paz, strange things start to happen...

Little Amaru looked down at the street and kicked a can with his red gumboots. 'We're near home aren't we,' he concluded.

'Yes, love, how do you know?' his dad replied.

'Because there's rubbish. That's life isn't it, Papi?'

The rubbish tip has been part of the scene since we moved to our market street seven years ago. By day it is invisible: only a layer of dust remains on the stretch of sidewalk where vendors sit selling fruit, vegetables and spicy food. Passers-by pause here to admire the spectacular view over shanty-town rooftops, across the crater-like basin of the city to the Andean ranges on the other side. Above them towers the snow-capped Mount Illimani, symbol and guardian of La Paz.

As night falls, the scene changes. The encroaching dark is a signal for people to emerge from nearby houses with boxes and bins to dump their trash. At first a discreet pile, the mound grows steadily until it covers the sidewalk almost knee-deep for 20 yards.

Then the scavengers move in. Flames flicker as they set light to the rubbish – not to reduce it to ashes but to see what is worth collecting. Poking around with sticks, they hold up promising finds to examine them, while eerie shadows move between the fires on the black tip.

Among the regulars at our dump are a pack of stray dogs, rooting around for bones and scraps. They compete with neighbors gleaning left-overs for their rabbits, sheep and pigs. Another group combs the refuse for tins, bottles and plastic containers to be sold on junk stalls.

Then come the children for whom the nightly forage produces not only improvised toys but anything which can conceivably be sold to raise a bit of cash. Some are street kids who rely on their ingenuity to keep alive. They take their night's work seriously and do the rounds of local houses, carting bundles of trash to the tip for a few pennies, and getting first pick of each load.

David, aged nine, empties our bin in the yard to pick out the salvageable items before he crams the rest into a sack to take to the dump. 'I can sell these in the Sunday market,' he says, carefully setting aside a bundle of *Time* magazines. A bottomless dustbin, a plastic oil container and a private selection of empty bottles have already been added to his private junk heap, waiting to be collected one day when he has time.

To some the rubbish tip is an eyesore. To others it means a chance to recycle whatever may still have a shred of use. Nothing is wasted and only the dregs are left, charred and thoroughly sifted, by the time the municipal refuse truck comes through at dawn the next day.

In La Paz, social status is marked by altitude, with the well-to-do preferring the balmier climate at the bottom of the city basin. Down there, trash is discreetly disposed of by aproned maids who run out with bins when the municipal truck comes by. The best-class rubbish is found at the gates of high-walled mansions, their privacy protected by barking Alsatians and uniformed guards.

Up at the top of the city, the refuse trucks are nowhere in sight. Dumps form haphazardly, filling crevices in the eroded landscape, littering wasteland and clogging streams. Kids play on the tips amidst swarms of flies. One organization of shanty-town women, concerned about the risk to their children's health, did a survey to find out where dumps were located and what they consisted of. The results were disconcerting: many tips were only meters from schools and markets. And one of their main components was human excrement, since few houses have toilets in the poorer zones.

The women set up a project to make cheap, home-built latrines with local materials. While that took shape, they organized a massive dump-clearing campaign, with voluntary teams working in each zone. Pregnant women and grandmothers kept the children entertained with puppet shows at a safe distance from the tips, while others worked together to pile up, burn and bury the rubbish.

The Town Hall, afraid of bad publicity, sent a convoy of refuse trucks around the shanty towns the day before the campaign. But the task of clearing hundreds of tips was too much for them to take on at the last minute.

'We're living on top of a load of trash,' said community leader Nélida, shovel in hand, a handkerchief tied bandit-style over her face against the dirt, smoke and dust. 'We're getting contaminated and our kids are getting sick. We have to deal with the problem ourselves, until the authorities remember we exist.'

Tickets to salvation

The religions rocking and rolling hope to Bolivia's poor.

People of all ages queued outside the huge, striped tent. Gradually the bustle and the music drew us in out of the cold night air. Hoisting the children onto our shoulders so they could peer over the sea of heads, we found ourselves witnessing a 'revival show' with energetic marketing techniques which seemed strangely out of place in the backstreets of a La Paz shanty town.

Tidy, blue-jeaned youths roused the public to clap and sing along to hymns set to fast rock rhythms. The close, steamy atmosphere became charged with enthusiasm as collection bags grew heavy with money; cassettes, stickers and 'cost-price' bibles sold like hot cakes by every tent pole.

After two hours, we felt stunned by the bombardment of music and emotion which drew several of those present into a state of trance. Swaying, trembling and weeping, many were already possessed by the time the star of the show – a Pentecostal preacher – leapt onto the stage to grab a microphone, impressively agile despite his tight suit. 'Let the Spirit touch you!' he roared, pointing aggressively at one spectator, then another, swearing that those who believed would be freed from their afflictions.

The blind, lame and sick fell into line and shuffled onto the stage to be saved and cured. 'Illness comes from sin and ignorance,' shouted the preacher. 'Out! Out! Out!' he yelled at the devils inhabiting his timorous guests, who were then ordered to move their wasted limbs and see with their sightless eyes. 'Let's hear it for Jesus!' he screamed finally, sweating under the floodlights. The show was a roaring success. People left in high spirits, helping the blind and lame out into the muddy field and down the unlit shanty-town alleyways.

Pushing our way out, we ran into Doña Elba from our corner shop, her sturdy two-year-old slung across her back, three older kids in tow. 'Good, wasn't it?' she beamed. 'I joined to get my husband converted, to make him stop drinking. They say it really works.' She trudged off back to the shop, her shawl flapping in the wind, the children trailing behind to pick up leaflets strewn on the ground.

Like most people in La Paz, Doña Elba regularly practises native Aymara rites. She pours libations of alcohol onto the ground for the Earth Mother, the Pachamama; reads coca leaves to see what fate has in store for her; and burns offerings of herbs, incense, sweets and animal fat to be consumed by the spirits in times of special need. But, faithful to tradition, she also got married and had her children baptized in a

Catholic church.

Salvation, for many Bolivians, is not an exclusive affair: allies in the struggle for survival can be sought in various spiritual quarters, without betraying one's basic beliefs. Bolivia has been a Catholic nation since colonial times. But most of the population also worship native deities, and over 400 churches and esoteric groups compete with the official creed for souls. The 'Vice-Ministry of Worship' admits the existence of 180 sects which have eluded official registration and control. Some of the more unconvincing are the Adorers of the Navel (of Nepalese origin), the itinerant Zombies for Bob, Seeing is Believing, and Ovnibol or unidentified flying object worshippers, who hang out in the historic mining town of Potosí.

'These groups go against the country's moral norms,' complains Vice-Minister Pedro Martinez, who organized the religious census. 'They conspire against family values, children's obedience to their parents and good morals.' His department tracks down acolytes of these clandestine groups, and takes steps to deal with them – like closing down vegetarian restaurants reputed to be façades for obscure activities carried out by the previously deported Hare Krishnas.

Other Catholics have a more self-critical attitude to the salvation boom and to the rapid growth of Pentecostal churches. 'Where are we failing? That's the question we must ask ourselves,' muses Father Franz Damen, who runs the Catholic Church office dealing with ecumenical matters. He says that a scarcity of priests and the rigidity of Catholic dogma have alienated native congregations. Those on the bottom rung of society are in search of a warmer, more personal faith which offers emotional release, participation and a concrete answer to their problems. 'The new sects seem to be offering something we aren't able to give,' admits Father Damen. 'Our Church ought to be what many of the sects are now: the religion of the poor.'

Mother tongue, fatherland

Why many Bolivians feel like strangers in their own country.

'Why do some children have mummies and daddies who speak the same language?' mused Amaru one day when I went to pick him up from a friend's house. It seemed a natural question for a three-year-old who has spent most of his short life speaking English with me and Spanish with his father. The two languages and cultures are constantly interspersed in my children's lives, though both offspring insist that

Bolivia is their country and mark their identity by speaking English with a Bolivian accent.

Being bilingual is no rarity in Bolivia. Over half the population speaks a native tongue as well as Spanish, the official language. It is not uncommon for Bolivians to speak even three languages if they live in areas where one ethnic group borders on the territory of another, or if they migrate to another part of the country. Amaru's godmother Angelica, for example, is fluent in Quechua, Aymara and Spanish. But her introduction to the 'official' language was far from easy.

'I was born in the mining town of Potosí, and we spoke Quechua at home. When I was six, my family moved to the Yungas valleys, where the people are mainly Aymara. That was where I started school. Our teacher spoke only Spanish and he used to get out a leather belt to threaten us if we whispered together in our own languages. "Just watch it ... the next one of you I catch will get this," he would say.

'It was a very tense situation. I didn't understand a word. It was still the system of rote-learning in those days. They made us repeat and copy things down, and bit by bit, I picked up Spanish. I learned Aymara too, through friends and work – so now I use three languages.'

None of Angelica's three boys speak an indigenous tongue, though she would like them to. They have little practical need for it in their daily lives. They can speak to their relatives in Spanish, so why learn Aymara or Quechua? Schooling, books, popular music, TV, cinemas, public functions and formal life all make Spanish essential for integration in the city.

Those who speak no Spanish at all live in ethnic communities of Quechuas, Aymaras, Guaranis or one of over 40 lowland peoples, each with their own language. It is more common for women to speak only one language; monolingualism is associated with isolation, poverty and lack of education, and has come to be taken as a mark of 'backwardness'. The children of such women are more likely to be malnourished and die young than those of Spanish speakers.

Many women in La Paz were brought up speaking only a native language but most now speak Spanish too. The mother tongue is often abandoned by the next generation who drop Aymara and Quechua to 'get educated' and join the urban, Spanish-speaking world. Indigenous cultures are stronger in Bolivia than in many other Latin American countries but still the tendency among the growing ranks of city-dwellers is to leave their ethnic roots behind in their rural communities.

One friend of mine, 45-year-old Bertha Quispe, has never been inside a school. She learned Spanish when she was growing up by playing with other kids. Only one of her children, Estefania, is fluent in Bertha's native Aymara language – and she is the least educated of the children. 'Estefania went to primary school for two years, but her aunt said to me: "A girl! What does she need education for? Just to write letters to her boyfriend? All she needs is to be able to sign her name".' So Estefania left school and went to live with her aunt as an apprentice *pollera* maker (polleras are the thick wide skirts worn by indigenous women).

'As for my other daughter, Maria Eugenia,' says Bertha, 'she finished secondary school and all, but she can hardly speak any Aymara. She doesn't want to learn. She says it's a twisted sort of language, she can't get her tongue around it. When my husband and I argue in Aymara, she complains because she can't understand what we're saying. I have to explain to her in Spanish.'

Bolivians from the countryside get treated like foreigners in their own land when they come into town. The nearer the city they get, the fewer the people who understand their language. They have to struggle with Spanish and get pushed aside for being 'ignorant' of city ways.

My kids, on the other hand, constantly get praised for speaking English as well as Spanish. Teachers get them to 'perform', schoolmates ask for help with homework, taxi drivers, shopkeepers and passers-by stop to listen to them, encourage them and tell them how useful it is to be bilingual in the colonizer's tongue which has now become 'universal'. Meanwhile Bolivia's original languages are relegated to an inferior status. People take little pride in being bilingual in a land where indigenous cultures predominate numerically – but Spanish rules.

Becoming a person

Stone throwing in Bolivia gives sex a whole new meaning.

It may not be your idea of romance to have a pebble chucked at you from over a wall. Nor to have the sunlight flashed in your face, caught by a mirror two fields away. Or a hat snatched away and hidden, or a shawl roughly tugged by a passer-by. Courtship rituals in the Andes are a far cry from the 'hearts and flowers' approach favored by Mills and Boon.

But these brusque gestures are loaded with meanings derived from the deepest cultural roots of the Aymaras and Quechuas. Bolivia is a land in which God is the earth mother and the sowing of seed in the Pachamama's belly is a ritual act, performed jointly by men and women. In the Andes farming, survival and human fertility are bound together with natural forces in a silent pact which has the potential to bless or destroy crops and communities.

'In this world, everything comes in pairs,' goes an Aymara saying. Even rural villages on the high plateau are divided into two – with the upper half being male, and the lower half female. Ritual fights between the rival portions can end in death.

Meanwhile adolescents are not deterred from curiosity about the opposite sex. Exchanging furtive glances, they embark upon the courtship game. Desire and repression, pursuit and escape can prolong erotic play for weeks or months. Although direct contact is taboo, stones leave the hand to touch the beloved's body, and outer clothing may be snatched and taken home in the hope that a visit will follow to recover the purloined garment.

It is often at fiesta that the game reaches its climax. Alcohol mellows constraints and social prohibitions relax. The girl is 'kidnapped' by her suitor, who takes her home for the night. The next day his parents visit the girl's family and begin negotiations which usually lead to the regularization of the relationship.

Marriage may not follow formally until the couple have lived together for some time and already have children. 'Trial' marriage, or *sirwiñacu*, is traditional, allowing the young pair to prove their compatibility and capacity for hard work on the land. Youngsters are allowed two tries at establishing a couple – the third would be seen as bordering on promiscuity.

By uniting as a couple, the man and woman acquire adult status in the community whether they are legally bound or not. In Aymara, the verb *jaquichasiña* – to join together or marry – means 'becoming a person'. Together the pair form a cultural and social unit which emulates the dualism of the opposing forces in nature: night and day, hot and cold, light and shadow. The man is fire, lightning, heat, power and order. The woman is identified with all that is dark, negative, archaic, hidden and wild. According to Aymara symbolism, it is only through motherhood that she acquires a magical force which channels her potentially malignant energy into the creation of new life.

Myths are like the pull of a strong, underground stream which vibrates under the thin soil of everyday life. But what happens on the surface? Descriptions abound of harmonious domestic and social relations in native societies and rural homes. It is said that women and men in the countryside have complementary roles. Personal desires are largely sublimated to community needs. Defenders of indigenous values swear that machismo arrived with the Spanish, to contaminate the natural balance which reigned before the Conquest.

Today's Aymara women have their own tales to tell. 'My story is sad, but funny too,' ponders Doña Ema as she sits twisting her spindle in a local meeting turned chat session. 'At least you lot had a chance to get to know your partners. But I was only 14 when I got married. I didn't know what love was all about.

'One night the man who is now my husband took me by surprise. He had a few words with my father, saying he was in love with me. It would have been all right if we had been courting, but I hadn't even known him a day. My parents believed that you shouldn't turn down an offer, so they accepted.

'The next week, they got together with a band and lots of beer and they made me drink. By the time I left I was completely drunk, and I still didn't know my husband. They took us off to his room and left me in there, all alone with him. His aunts were saying: "Just go to bed lass, don't be afraid". That's how it is in the countryside.'

Calling the spirit

When Susanna's baby falls ill, she resorts to traditional magic.

My ten-month-old daughter lay soundly sleeping, tightly swaddled, on the bed. An orange and an apple were bound against her, inside the striped woven blanket. On her head, still damp from fever, was the woolen bonnet which minutes before had been used to summon back her spirit. 'Come, Nina, come,' Mami had called, waving the baby's knitted hat from the back door until the child's *ajayu* or spirit had returned, restoring wholeness and health to her body.

Although I was relieved to see Nina so tranquil after days of fretful illness, the hairs on my arms stood on end as I listened to her grandparents whispering and moving downstairs. A pungent smell of burning herbs and incense wafted up from the yard. No-one was allowed outside now, until the offering to the Pachamama – the Andean Earth Mother – had been consumed.

Had I been an anthropologist, I might have been eager to witness the ceremony and record the muttered Aymara prayers. As it was, I felt panicked, completely foreign to this world of magic where sickness is believed to come from supernatural causes, and healing is an intimate affair, closer to religion than to medicine as I know it. I kept out of the way, partly out of fear and partly hoping that the rituals would have a better chance of taking effect without the interference of my modern-day skepticism.

Like most 'educated' city-dwellers in Bolivia, I turn to herbal or ritual healing only when 'modern' tests and remedies have failed. For

Aymaras of Mami's generation, traditional cures are the first resort, and doctors, laboratories and pharmacies the last. Talk of analyses, bacteria and viruses make little sense to someone who is convinced that the air, wind, fright or the evil eye are really to blame for sickness.

When my children got ill, Mami would always give me a few days to try out my version of healing, nodding silently as I showed her the latest prescription. Then she would summon relatives and scan market stalls for herbs, waiting for the night that I would seek refuge in my room and allow 'la familia' to take over responsibility for my children's health.

Their father was caught between two worlds and so kept a foot in each, alternately chasing laboratory results and making a fire in the yard for the Pachamama's offering. According to Mami, he was living proof that traditional remedies succeed. At three years old he had been cured of a severe wasting illness, by being buried up to the neck in fresh cow dung at the slaughterhouse. 'Larpha, we call the illness,' said Mami. Modern pediatricians call it malnutrition.

On my parents-in-law's farm in the Yungas valleys, I experienced natural healing for myself after a troop of red ants marched into my gumboots and started biting my legs. I screamed with shock and pain. As I ripped off my trousers, el Papá grabbed my straw hat and started calling my frightened spirit back, a much more urgent matter than dealing with a few carnivorous ants. Later I was washed in a hot bath of quinine bark, and made to drink the bitter liquid.

Every year after that, Mami came to treat my winter cough which reappeared with the first gusts of dry, cold, mountain air. Putting on a large kettle of water, she put me to bed and rubbed my chest and back with a sticky ointment. Then she ironed brown paper, stuck holes in it and pressed it warm against my skin. As I itched and crinkled under the blankets, she would wrap a woolen shawl around the hot kettle and refasten it tightly around me. Finally, having watched me sip her sharp herb tea, she would firmly turn off the light and order me not to move until morning.

More than anything, I felt soothed by her confidence, her caring, the warmth and rest. To me, Mami's remedies embodied an equal dose of herbs and Tender Loving Care. But she confided one day that she had special healing powers because, as a young girl, she had been almost struck by lightning. Having been brushed so closely by death, she kept in her hands the power to call back the spirit and mend the imbalance between body and soul.

Shaking the sorrows away

How the living say their final goodbye to the dead.

It's been a year, full circle, since La Mamá died. Time for the 'Soul's Mass', a ritual re-encounter of relatives and friends with each other and with the deceased. Time for a fresh exorcism of grief, as sorrows are physically shaken away with each garment of mourning dress and the bereaved don bright clothes to dance and drink themselves into release from pain.

Spanish and Indian blood, Catholic and Aymara rites merge and give birth to a mestizo ceremony in the backstreets of La Paz. Hierarchy dictates that the dominant religion's god should have first say. Black suits, wide skirts, shawls and bowler hats file respectfully into the whitewashed church and sit, Aymara style, women in the left-hand pews, men on the right.

Kneeling on the hard pew under a bejeweled Virgin's gaze, I clutch Julia's plump arm as she shakes and sobs, pulled back to the sharp edge of her mother's loss. 'HELL!' warns the grey-haired priest, his eyes narrowing as he focuses on this unseemly spectacle of grief. 'That's where unbelievers go. Those of little faith. Those who think that God is BAD. Who cry for the dead, when they should be GLAD that their loved ones have been taken to God's side!' The rest of the family shoot disapproving looks at Julia for bringing Aymara wailing into the house of the Spanish god.

Eternal life is left inside the church, for outside again, the mourners are on the Pachamama's soil. The Earth Mother swallows up her children and their end is final. 'She's gone, she'll never come back,' go the Aymara condolences, as each guest embraces the family members. 'No more sorrows. You just have to accept it. Mami is dead, what can we do?' But with this stoical belief goes the recognition that grief must be expressed and ritually shaken away. A cycle of mourning and joy is imperative, life and color must return.

As we enter the dance hall, La Mamá's table makes her presence tangible among us. Her skirt, woven shawl and best hat sit stolidly under a faded photo and the plaque with her name. Coca leaves, flowers, fruit and bread have been placed as offerings to welcome her to the celebration. A year after the first farewell at the wake, we have another chance to say goodbye to Mami, to ask for her forgiveness, to feel the roughness of her shawl against our faces.

Suddenly the table is cleared and all its contents are bundled into the shawl. Amidst hushed whispers, male relatives abruptly pick up the table and carry it out, taking with them the illusion of La Mamá's fleeting presence among us. The spot is swept, there's nothing left. Mami has really gone and you can see the gap which marks her absence, her disappearance from our lives.

Grief must subside. A mood of excitement takes over as La Mamá's relatives start piling into a tiny room to change their clothing. I wait for some of them to come out but no-one does. I'm pushed in to join them and find myself in a musty, windowless box, where 19 people are struggling to remove their mourning gear and dress in bright colors.

El Papá is the main object of attention. He's still wearing his black shirt and another one has to be improvised. He glows with pride as his sons do up the buttons on the scarlet shirt. His daughter ruffles his scant white hair: 'Now you go out there and get yourself a nice young girlfriend.' Teasing and whistles greet each show of new garb.

Finally each black garment is shaken to release the woes of a year's mourning. All the clothes are bundled into a black bag, which is doused with alcohol from each glass in a ritual blessing. 'No more sorrows! Let there be joy!' is the toast. Firecrackers burst in the yard outside and it is time for us to emerge, a motley crowd in rainbow colors, pushing each other and giggling like so many children.

The band starts to play and the dance begins, stiffly at first and then more wildly as alcohol loosens our limbs and spirits. El Papá jumps around like a colt, to the encouragement of whoops and cries. The formidable aunts shuffle back and forth in their massive skirts, children weave in and out of the rows of dancers. Julia is still sobbing as she sways and turns but the family push her to keep dancing. 'Today I'm here, tomorrow I'll be gone,' goes the lively popular rhythm, as all are swept into an affirmation of life flourishing in the midst of pain and deprivation.

'That's enough, Julia, no more grieving,' insists a neighbor as we recover our breath between dances. 'Cheer up, think how happy La Mamá must be to see everyone here enjoying themselves in her name.'

'And she's here, isn't she?' whispers Julia. We all look towards the door, out through the stone courtyard.

'Yes, she's here...'

'And her heart must be in flower', says Julia, wiping her eyes and going back to the dance.

Letters from Tamil Nadu (India), 1991-1992

Mari Marcel Thekaekara

Mari is an independent writer focusing on social issues in magazines and newspapers which include *The Hindu* and *Infochange* in India, and the *New Internationalist* and *Guardian* in Britain. She is also the author of *Endless Filth*, a book about *safai karmacharis* ('manual scavengers' or people condemned by caste to remove human excrement from dry toilets) which triggered off a huge campaign within India to abolish manual scavenging work. In 2005, she co-edited an issue on caste for the *New Internationalist* which was shortlisted for an Amnesty International award. The issues in the magazine were raised in the British Parliament by MP Jeremy Corbyn and used as an advocacy tool for the rights of *dalits* (people beneath the caste system, formerly known as 'untouchable').

Mari was part of an independent women's commission to document the atrocities against Muslim women during the 2002 Gujarat riots. She is a co-founder of ACCORD (an NGO working for indigenous rights in the Nilgiris Hills of Tamil Nadu, where she still lives), Just Change (an international co-operative linking producers and consumers) and is also a founding member and vice-president of the National Centre for Advocacy Studies in Pune.

She is currently a visiting fellow at the Skoll Centre for social entrepreneurship at the Said Business School, Oxford University. She is also a member of the steering committee of the Planning Commission of India for women and child development drafting the 11th five year plan.

Changes in India

In retrospect India made a landmark political and social choice at exactly the point when Mari Marcel Thekaekara was writing her series of letters for the *New Internationalist*. Following its independence from Britain in 1947, the country maintained similar economic policies through multiple political administrations – the state played a strong role, protecting domestic industries against international competition and controlling imports. In 1991-92, following the assassination of Rajiv Gandhi, the new Congress Party leadership made a drastic shift towards the 'liberalization of the economy' – opening up the Indian market to foreign investment, allowing the rupee to float against the dollar and removing import controls. The role of the state was reduced not only in the economic arena but also in healthcare, education and utilities such as water and electricity.

The significance of this shift was not lost on Mari, who campaigned against it in her letter 'Restructuring the poor' (included here) and in another on the implications of free trade. Economic development in India in the ensuing years has progressed apace, with growth rates eclipsed only by those of China, and a particular boom in the IT industry. The rich and the middle class have benefited substantially from this growth and from the Westernized consumerism it has made possible. But the vast majority of Indians are no closer to attaining such a lifestyle than they were when Mari was writing. A 2007 report by the state-run National Commission for Enterprises in the Unorganized Sector found that 70 per cent of Indians, or 800 million people, lived on less than 20 rupees per day, with most working in the 'informal labor sector with no job or social security, living in abject poverty'. Caste continues to delimit the horizons of the majority of people – another of Mari's main campaigning concerns over the years.

The economic liberalization has been maintained despite the replacement in government of the Congress Party by the Hindu nationalist Bharatiya Janata Party (BJP) between 1998 and 2004. The BJP's period in power signals that tensions between religious communities in India continue to run high – in 2002, for example, more than 2,000 people were killed and 15,000 made homeless in a wave of violence against the Muslim community in the state of Gujarat, ruled by the BJP, which attempted a cover-up of the massacre.

For decades Mari has made her home in the Nilgiris Hills of Tamil Nadu, living and working alongside some of India's indigenous people, the *adivasis*. And the most striking and memorable of her letters convey insights that their very different way of looking at the world have taught her over the years – timeless in a way that political events and eruptions can never be.

In silence and in shame

Lectured about financial honesty, an old man bites back at the ways of the West.

Nestling amid the forests and rippling streams of the Nilgiris mountains of Tamil Nadu, south India, are little settlements of indigenous people. They are the Todas, the Kotas, the Irulas, the Paniyas, the Moolakurumbas, the Kattunaickens and the Bettakurumbas. They have lived here since time immemorial. Today they are termed *adivasis* by the Government, meaning the first settlers or original inhabitants.

The philosophy of these people has remained unchanged for centuries. It is similar to the sentiments expressed by Chief Seattle when he asked the President of the United States in 1855: 'How can you buy or sell the sky, the warmth of the land, the freshness of the air or the sparkle of the water?'

The adivasis passed this reverence for nature down from generation to generation, from grandparent to grandchild – until various 'civilized' people entered the indigenous stronghold: ruling British rajahs, the Indian Government and marauding pioneers came to stay. Homelands were bought and sold over adivasis' heads: no-one even thought it necessary to consult them. And so they lost their land while they lived on it, just like the Red Indians in the US, the Aboriginal people of Australia and other indigenous peoples around the world.

On the indigenous project where I work with my husband Stan, we decided to encourage the younger adivasi leaders to start asking: 'Why?' 'Why are we poor people, malnourished, ill? Why have we lost our lands, our forests, our pride, our culture? Why?'

We came across hundreds of cases where people had signed away their land having been misled into thinking that the paper they were signing would give them ration cards, government pensions or title deeds. Very few had documents to show possession of their lands. Their logic was simple: It is my land. Why do I need a piece of paper to prove it? Is my word not enough?'

Slowly we realized that the adivasis were totally uninterested in literacy.

At the time the Government and various voluntary agencies were trying to popularize a literacy drive. And we ourselves were forming work co-operatives or *sangams* in all the villages.

One day we held a meeting at our office to teach a group of Bettakurumba people how to keep the sangam accounts and write their books. Stan set up blackboard, chalk and duster. But when the group of 50 had finally settled down, he realized with a shock that only two people were literate. Hastily he put away chalk and papers and began a general discussion on the state of things in the local villages.

This group of adivasis lived deep in the forest and their simple way of life had remained intact for centuries, uncorrupted by outside values and standards. Gradually the discussion veered towards money and accountability. Stan tried to explain gently that many sangams had been utterly ruined because of unscrupulous leaders misappropriating official funds. This had led to chaos and the destruction of the villages concerned. The hard work of months could be destroyed by one crooked leader if the people were not vigilant. Thus he argued the case for literacy.

Mathan, an old Bettakurumba man, turned. His skin was parchment-like and weatherbeaten. He looked Stan full in the face and spoke deliberately and gently, as to a little child:

'The chief is my leader. My people and I have appointed him our chieftain. Could he have achieved this position in our society if he were dishonorable? Are we fools to elect a thief as head of our people? And is he an imbecile to throw away the honor, prestige and dignity of his chieftainship, the respect of his people, the veneration of the young ones, for a hundred rupees? You attach so much to written figures. Do people lack honor in your world that the spoken word has so little importance? Why so much value, so much worship for the same words merely because they are transferred to a slip of paper?'

We could not answer him. In silence and in shame I wondered how I could convey his wisdom to our literate millions.

People and other pests

Visitors to the indigenous people's project run by Mari and her husband can be a pain – but they can also be an education.

In recent years, indigenous peoples have become a 'fashionable' group to work with in development circles. And in the Nilgiris, south India, our physical remoteness from the rest of the country makes us especially attractive to a wide range of visitors.

Before we were married, Stan and I belonged to an internationally affiliated Catholic student group. Our homes were open to students from all over the world and this gave us the opportunity for cross-cultural exchanges which have influenced us ever since. Our closest friends came from different continents. And early in our marriage we decided to keep our house open for young people in search of different options. After a while, however, the battery of visitors has begun to seem too much even for us.

The visiting legions belong to two categories. The first are people with a genuine interest in development and adivasis: concerned, sympathetic and sensitive. These we welcome for their intelligent exchange of ideas, for we have neither the time nor the inclination for normal socializing.

And then there is the second kind. They come in all nationalities, shapes and sexes. Instantly recognizable. Obviously obnoxious. Self-termed charity supporters, they generally arrive unannounced, apologizing profusely on behalf of the Indian postal system for the telegram which didn't arrive. This group believes in project-hopping, which is a useful way to see the Third World at someone else's expense. Hospitality is an Indian tradition. And rarely does anyone mind hosting people. It is considered part of life. But people do mind being unfairly used.

Conversely, I have been embarrassed at 'radical activists' (Third Worlders) unashamedly leeching off Western friends in Europe and the US. The Westerners have guilt complexes about our suffering masses, and unquestioning admiration for the activists working towards revolution. So where they would have kicked a fellow country-person in the pants, they acquiesce abjectly to the most unreasonable demands.

Anthropologists of course, descend on us in hordes. The majority regard the adivasis as interesting subjects, not people. They arrive armed with paper and pens, research paraphernalia and not an iota of sensitivity or human concern for the people. They charge into their subjects' homes obsessed with their questionnaires, oblivious to people's objections and with no respect for their privacy. 'Would you allow these people to invade your home and ask you what you eat at each meal?' I asked a researcher. I was answered by a blank, uncomprehending stare. 'But I need the information for my thesis,' was his reply.

Recently, an avalanche of anthropology students from neighboring Kerala University descended on an adivasi village. They camped nearby and besieged the poor villagers mercilessly for days on end. Their questionnaires needed embarrassing details of the most intimate kind. One ridiculous young girl questioned an old Moolukurumba woman about the details of her wedding night. Annoyed, the old woman retorted, 'Get married and you'll find out'. A younger woman, similarly harassed, retreated embarrassed to her husband. Laughing, he replied: 'Send her to me and I'll show her.' The student hastily moved away.

The majority of adivasi people, however, are guileless, defenseless against the thick-skinned academics who come to question them. These academics seem oblivious to the fact that mere friendliness would obtain more authentic research material. Take the British anthropologist who spent a year living with local people. She was sensitive and won the people over. Consequently, our exchange with her was fruitful and rewarding. She gave us a number of insights which opened up whole new perspectives we had missed.

We had observed that most of the adivasis found it impossible to fit in with the local plantation culture which involved a fixed six-day week, an eight-to-five routine. They opted out of the system even when their children were starving, preferring their freedom to the shackles of permanent plantation jobs. Locals tended to dismiss them as lazy even though adivasis tackle some of the most thankless jobs around.

The anthropologist observed the adivasis' work patterns over some months and pointed out that these people were still adhering to their hunter-gatherer traditions. The theory made sense. Suddenly our entire perspective changed. For years we had been puzzling over the adivasi four-day week. And suddenly we understood it. This influenced our planning and helped us to accept a way of life that had until then seemed frustratingly unreasonable.

So now, when the going gets rough and we have had a surfeit of freeloaders, alternative tourists or just plain pain-in-the-anatomy types, before declaring a blanket ban on all visitors, we just stop and tell ourselves that this person might just belong to the right category. With this firmly in mind, we pause, breathe deeply. And take a chance.

Born to shovel shit

Caste is causing a stink in India. But who cast the first stone?

In thousands of towns all over India, human beings still carry night soil on their heads. Night soil? What's that? you may ask. It is the Indian Government's euphemism for what ordinary people call shit – or in more polite circles, human excrement.

The 'privilege' of carrying night soil is accorded to a segment of our society by virtue of their birth; their caste. And the babies born to the people of this community have it ordained that they shall spend their entire lives carrying human excrement on their heads, cleaning public and private lavatories, handling rotting carcasses and sweeping our city streets. That is the birthright of these children; their privilege. By divine ordination. And human concurrence.

After independence, when our constitution was being written, people at the helm of affairs in the country talked about justice, equality and fraternity for all. Especially for the downtrodden. They spoke of righting past wrongs and liberating people who by virtue of their caste had been oppressed for centuries. A special policy of positive discrimination was drawn up to bring the lowest castes into the Indian mainstream.

Over 40 years later, a new commission produced the Mandal Report which declared that the spirit of the policy had not been observed; the status of people from the lowest castes had changed only marginally. It recommended that more low-caste people should receive positive discrimination. And that they should have a larger percentage of jobs in Government. The Government – led by VP Singh – announced that it was committed to implementing the Mandal Report: two of its prominent ministers were themselves from the lowest castes.

There was uproar. The media in general and the English (language) press in particular launched a scathing attack on the Government and the Mandal Commission. Most vitriolic was the *Indian Express* with its upper-caste editor spewing venom every day in front-page editorials. Upper-caste students were incited by the press and joined the campaign. There was violence in the streets. Buses were burnt. Traffic immobilized. And worst of all, a host of young students proclaiming themselves martyrs for the anti-Mandal movement set fire to themselves in public. They were egged on and made heroes by the media and upper-caste mobs. The outcome was inevitable. The VP Singh Government fell. And the Mandal Report was consigned to Government files to accumulate dust like many of its predecessors.

The *Express* editor demanded to know why lower castes should suddenly be given 'special' rights after the country had been independent for 40 years. He argued that this would necessarily imply a promotion of all that was sub-standard and shoddy, and prove a disincentive to merit and talent.

That the newspapers shouted about the need for merit is something of a joke. For in India – as in most countries – there is a system of privilege which works quietly, efficiently and with the tacit understanding of the privileged. Those in the élite invariably think of themselves as the cream of the nation and consider it their divine right to corner the most lucrative jobs going. Nepotism inevitably plays its role. There is the discreet phone call, the letter of introduction, that little extra push which makes the crucial difference.

The waste of real talent is tragic. In the Nilgiris, our entire field team consists of adivasis – a fact which stuns outsiders because most people consider adivasis 'fit' only for specific jobs like clearing forests, or acting as guides in the wildlife sanctuary. That our team is capable of social analysis which would – and often has – put social work graduates to shame, astonishes people. Yet if our young people had competed with city graduates for social workers' jobs, they would have failed. Because the criteria used to judge people in the normal interview are based on Western, urbanized, often totally anglicized élitism.

Undoubtedly there are a few institutions in the country where merit is the sole criterion for entrance. But in the majority, entry depends purely on the economic status of the students' parents. In colleges of medicine, engineering and so on, apart from the fees, there is a prohibitively expensive 'capitation' fee which ensures that only the offspring of the rich get in. What price then, merit?

The system of privilege is not uniquely Indian. We inherited many of our peculiarities from the Empire: the old school tie; the right accent; even, amazingly, the privileges which accompany an Oxford or Cambridge degree. It is not dissimilar to the WASP syndrome which occurs in the US; meaning you can go places faster and better if you are white, Anglo-Saxon and Protestant.

Everywhere the merest mention of rights for the poor brings forth torrents of protest, while the rich and mighty continue their power games.

But then, the story tells us, it is the meek who will inherit the earth. Never the poor or downtrodden.

Meat matters

Temptation or greed? Mari extracts her pound of flesh.

The New Internationalist issue on Animal Rights caused an outbreak of warring emotions and thoughts in my once-contented brain. Having been reared in a strictly non-vegetarian home, I learnt the rule of survival as an omnivore from childhood: avoid the link between meat on the table and all thought of the terrors of the abbatoir.

A Christian education indoctrinated me with the belief that all living creatures are made for humans to enjoy, and helped assuage doubts about the morality of killing animals; paradoxically Western culture preaches kindness to animals except when they are being slaughtered for food. Similarly in India, the land of *ahimsa* (a philosophy of nonviolence), it is not unusual to see a farmer who would die rather than eat beef, whipping his bullocks with impunity to get them to move faster. Or shoving a rod up the wild-eyed, half-starved animal's anus to get it to the marketplace on time.

Rarely are children chastised for teasing animals. During Diwali – a festival of fireworks – it is common to see a pack of brats amusing themselves by tying firecrackers to some helpless mongrel's tail. Adults smile indulgently at them, the rare exception being the English-speaking, reared-on-a-diet-of-Kipling kind of person.

Soon after my marriage I considered the question of vegetarianism seriously for the first time when my husband's Brahmin teacher, a person both of us revered and loved, asked: 'How can you kill an animal and eat it?' He spoke with so much passion and emotion our only response was a weak: 'it's a difficult habit to break'. Intellectually and emotionally we agreed with him. Several times we discussed the possibility of turning vegetarian. But finally we relapsed into orgies of meat-eating, pushing those uncomfortable feelings to a safe distance in the recesses of our minds.

Then the NI arrived. And with it the reopening of an unfinished chapter. Pangs of remorse, guilt.

Yet even now there is conflict. For ourselves it makes sense to turn vegetarian. The only obstacles are inconvenience and habit – surmountable barriers that simply need will-power to overcome them.

And I have another incentive – a vivid childhood memory of my grandmother feeding bread and precious milk to the cat and dog. Outside children played in the dirt while their mother, Shanti, swept and mopped our homes and cleaned our bathrooms. These kids never got as much milk as our cat. And they would have snatched the bread and milk from the animals' dishes if they could have. The thought always made me sick, even as a child. The only solution Shanti's employers could suggest was that she should get herself sterilized. As for her eight malnourished children – too bad – we couldn't possibly feed all the starving children in Calcutta. So that was that.

Today the same issue torments me. The money we spend on our Doberman's food would set a hungry child on the road to health. Every time I pour milk into the dog's dish, the unbidden image of a rickety, starving child looms reproachfully before me. So what is the answer? Don't feed the dogs? Obviously not. It would be ideal to have no starving children. But the kids are there in every village I visit. And though I wish to God they wouldn't haunt me, they do.

Protein deficiencies are a major problem here – especially severe anemia. Traditionally indigenous peoples got most of their protein from wild boar, deer, birds and fish. But hunting is now forbidden. And people are dying in huge numbers as a result. Women suffer most – many young girls die in childbirth.

Our doctors examine many poor, pregnant women and the healthiest are Christians and Muslims because they eat beef, the only affordable meat, at least once or twice a week. This takes them over the brink of anemia. And in the hope of preventing more deaths from anemia we are promoting the rearing of rabbits, fish and chickens.

'How can you raise these animals with the sole objective of killing them?' a friend shuddered recently. And I share her revulsion. A few years ago I would not have. But now I am plagued with doubt.

The solution would be for our country to be self-sufficient in protein-rich foods like pulses and soybeans. But everyone is growing cash crops, the only profitable crops to grow. In India no-one grows cattle for meat. Only old, tired animals past their prime end up as beef. Even many wealthy Muslims and Christians shun this as the food of the lower castes. Which is not so bad, because a bit of beef makes all the difference to a poor, pregnant woman.

So could one ever ban animal slaughter in India? For myself, the aroma of a succulent kebab wafting on the air is a temptation. Pure greed. Something I could do without. But I could not make the moral decision to take away a bit of meat which might make the difference between life and death to a child. Should I?

Killer drugs

Babies are being born deformed while Western companies boost their profits.

Bommi, a young adivasi girl from a small village near here, had a problem that millions of young girls like her have faced before. She was pregnant and unmarried – and the father of the child didn't want to marry her. After a month of agonizing she asked a friend to get her an 'abortion drug' from the local chemist.

Ketan, the friend, can neither read nor write. But he asked the chemist for a drug to 'get rid of a pregnancy'. The chemist obliged with an estrogen and progesterone (EP) drug which Bommi took. The next day she was rushed to the doctor with severe stomach cramps and vomiting.

Deva and Roopa – two young doctors who are part of our team – were appalled. Abortion is frowned on by *adivasi* society. But more than this, by taking the drugs Bommi could have irreparably harmed her unborn child.

The incident recalled an interview I did some years ago with Dr Vincent Pannikulangara, a lawyer fighting a mammoth battle against Indian and multinational pharmaceutical giants producing and selling banned drugs in India – especially the EP drugs which Ketan had bought so easily. The companies repeatedly procured stay orders to thwart Pannikulangara.

Finally, in 1986, weary and dispirited after four seemingly futile years, he made an impassioned plea to the Supreme Court. He informed the bench that for four years he had been fighting in the highest court of the land what he considered 'a patriotic battle for justice against the criminal use of harmful drugs whose presence violates the fundamental right to life guaranteed to every citizen in India by our constitution.'

Pitted against him was the might of pharmaceutical giants that had succeeded in ensuring that the drugs remained on the market even though they endangered the lives of millions. Pannikulangara declared that he had expected the Government of India to respond in a spirit of justice and concern but after four years he had achieved nothing. He had reached the end of his tether and was ready to step down defeated.

Moved by the sincerity of his plea, Justice RN Mishra – in a landmark judgment – criticized the Union of India, the Indian Medical Council and State Governments for their indifference to the cause of public health. In unusually strong language for a Supreme Court judge, he pointed out: 'So long as you were not aware of the harm to public health it was excusable. Thereafter it was murder. '

Pannikulangara was elated by the victory but was quick to point out that for effective implementation, women and concerned health action groups must take up the struggle to keep EP drugs off the market.

Two years later, the Drug Action Forum Karnataka (DAF) a voluntary health vigilance group, proved the banned EP drugs were still around by producing sales receipts from local chemists.

EP drugs were still being routinely prescribed for women's menstrual problems. For example, a woman comes to a doctor complaining of a delayed period, anxious in case she is pregnant. The doctor prescribes EP drugs supposedly to regulate her menstruation. But if she is already pregnant this is very dangerous, for the drug contains an abortion agent, not usually strong enough to induce abortion but definitely strong enough to cause irreparable damage to the fetus.

The DAF approached the State Drug Controller with their evidence and were assured that action would be taken. The Controller then issued a press release instructing chemists not to sell the drugs and people not to buy them. He also sent a circular to drug inspectors throughout the state with orders to seize the drug from chemists stocking it. Even after this, DAF volunteers bought EP drugs from three different chemists and mailed the receipts to the Drug Controller for action. But nothing seems to have happened and the drug is easy to procure.

Governments of developing countries would do well to take a leaf out of Bangladesh's brilliant National Drug Policy which ordered the withdrawal of nearly 2,000 dangerous drugs and emphasized the manufacture of essential ones.

On the international front, developed nations must be pressurized to stop their multinationals from dumping killer drugs on Third World populations, in connivance with corrupt bureaucrats and health authorities.

Last week Bommi lost her baby. But millions of young women like her will not. Their babies will be born deaf, blind, deformed or mutilated. And all so that the drug companies can make a few dollars more.

The time trap

Indigenous peoples question whether racing to meet deadlines makes us happy.

A delightful old Simon and Garfunkel lyric popped into my head recently: 'Time it was and what time it was, it was a time of innocence...' It came back to me when Roopa, a young doctor working on the project that my husband and I run for adivasis, remarked: 'Whenever I go to the villages I realize we are working with two time frames. Ours, where we are always in a tearing hurry, and the adivasi time zone where everyone has all the time in the world.'

It always requires a mental switch to adapt to the adivasi concept of time. Without it you get irritated, completely fed up. With it your whole perspective alters. You realize how enjoyable life can be when you give yourself time to stand and stare. Of course this is not conducive to meeting deadlines or hectic work schedules. But it is good for building relationships with people. It is also useful for picking up pointers about the adivasis' lifestyle – which for outsiders is not always understandable.

For two years we lived on a farm run by adivasis. The farm manager used to go berserk because people simply did not turn up at eight o'clock in the morning when they were supposed to clock in. Later we realized that their unpunctuality was due to a simple fact which did not occur to the manager – or to us. None of them owned a watch. They were gauging time by the sun. So during the monsoon and in winter when the nights were longer, people assumed that it was not yet eight o'clock because it looked earlier.

Likewise, adivasis rarely work the mandatory six-day week demanded by tea estates, despite the wages being the highest in the area. We were bewildered by this at first, until an anthropologist pointed out that they were adhering to the food-gathering patterns of their ancestors. The pattern? To forage for food from the forest and when they had found enough, to relax until the next hunter-gathering trip was necessary.

Neighbors condemn this attitude towards life and consider the adivasis to be lazy. Yet if more sophisticated urbanites suggest that a short-day week is necessary to relieve stress, they are not dismissed as shiftless or feckless. Neither are the people who clock into work on the dot – and then waste government time and money with innumerable extended coffee-lunch-tea breaks, gossip sessions or radio cricket commentaries.

I don't want to romanticize the adivasis' lifestyle. Yet it did work well before the outside world caught up with them. The forest provided most of their limited needs. The unhurried pace of life was gentle.

Today there are still a few unspoiled villages in the heart of vast tracts of forest land. Entering them is always an enchanting experience. There is a quality of timelessness and tranquility which is impossible to convey. Quickly you feel the strains and stresses of your normal work day falling away. The air is cleaner, fresher. Unpolluted. And so is the atmosphere.

But now, with the 21st century creeping up on them, cutting the earth beneath their feet, felling the giant trees that provided them with their protective, giving environment, any adivasi who wants to survive has to compromise. There is no choice.

Probably the hippies had the same experience in the 1960s. The break with established systems was utopian – a necessary and wonderful experience which enabled them to stand back and observe a lifestyle they had rejected. But when you need the establishment and its systems to survive, in the end you are forced to work with it.

Try to change it. Try your hardest. And make sure you never give up.

But you can't live in a prehistoric time zone no matter how wonderful the experience. The reality of ordinary living brings one down to earth with a resounding bang. I think the trick is to keep a perspective ... always.

The wisdom of sages

If the indigenous peoples of India have such an idyllic way of life, why do they need outsiders to help them?

Our work – which includes teaching local people about their land rights – is frequently attacked by those who push for 'preserving the pristine purity of primitive people'. This is a quote from a former Minister for Tribal Welfare who declared publicly that he believed adivasis should be put into reservations à *la* America – pretty much as a nearly extinct species ought to be preserved, to create a museum for the rest of the world to enjoy.

Another visitor was appalled because many young adivasis who worked with us were clad in jeans and sneakers. This guest was disgusted by the 'modernization' process that had taken place since her visit in 1980. Then she had revisited the adivasi hamlet she had first surveyed in 1970 and returned shaken and distraught because half the young people who ought to have been in their twenties and thirties had died – mostly of malnutrition.

Of course the adivasis must have access to education and modern amenities. But even as we try to introduce these people into 20th-century mainstream India, we recognize that the process of transition, inevitable though it is, contains all the elements of a monumental tragedy.

Had the adivasis been left undisturbed, their environment would have provided everything they needed to live comfortably. Now they are forced to adapt and change their ways, to come to terms with a lifestyle they don't even begin to comprehend. The rules are dictated by an alien culture.

Take land. The adivasis never saw the need to own land. Now an alien government decrees that people must possess pieces of paper to prove they own land they have lived on for centuries.

Of course adivasis must learn to read and write, but the reason behind their need for literacy is tragic; they must arm themselves with the weapons of 'civilization' which will otherwise destroy them. This happened to the native peoples in the US, to Aboriginal peoples in Australia and South America, and all over Asia where indigenous peoples are victimized.

The same process is also happening in housing. A Moolukurumba house is a beautiful piece of architecture. Made of mud, bamboo and timber, it is invitingly cool during the hot summer and warm and welcoming during the winter. Yet the people are clamoring for the ugly, concrete box-like structures that the Government gives them. Modernity implies status of a sort. And the grasses and timber used to build traditional dwellings are less available since forests have shrunk. In one village the juxtaposition of modern and traditional houses is startlingly jarring.

A well-constructed modern house would be a blessing for any family. But adivasis are exchanging beautiful, graceful houses for sub-standard monstrosities. This is tragic. Our struggle is to find viable alternatives which combine the best of both worlds. Not an easy task to be sure.

In the course of it we must take care not to adopt the role of messiahs and conclude that we have all the answers. Our challenge is to continue the questioning process and know when to learn. Especially by listening, really listening to the people. Ordinary people everywhere can display enormous elemental wisdom.

Years ago an old West Virginian farmer in the US said to me: 'If Russia dropped an atom bomb here, there'd be nothing but charred earth. Any farmer can tell you that such earth would be no darned good to anyone, man nor beast. So why do their government and ours continue making bombs? Instead they could try to feed the poor in their countries. There's a lot of poor kids in West Virginia, I can tell you.'

Old Eddie Gillenwater will never be nominated for the Nobel Peace Prize. He was apologetic about his lack of education and that he couldn't 'talk fancy', as he explained to me. But statespeople and scholars could learn a thing or two from him, just as they could learn from the Betterkurumba people. Which is the point I was trying to make in the first place.

Restructuring the poor

India is poised to take a big step which will change everything.

As we enter 1992, the Indian Government threatens – our politicians use the word 'promises' – to take the country away from socialism, independence and sovereignty. Everything in fact, that our foreparents fought for as they tried to free India from colonialism.

We are about to sign ominous agreements for yet another round of International Monetary Fund (IMF) loans. By the time we sign on the dotted line we will have sold our souls to the IMF. Already they have started to 'advise' us about our economic policy, telling us gently what we can and cannot do.

The structural reforms will involve a three-pronged attack. First, there is the inevitable devaluation of currency; we have complied twice in the last year, since the loan negotiations began.

Next there is the liberalization of the economy. For this read: 'Encourage free trade. Allow in multinationals. Let growth begin.' Our Government is already busy assuring everybody that India wants to welcome foreign investment with open arms.

The third and most lethal demand is to cut subsidies. This hits the poor where it hurts most – in the stomach. India has what is known as a Public Distribution System: ration shops where poor people buy rice, sugar, wheat and a minimum supply of kerosene oil at a subsidized rate every month. The rice is of such poor quality that no-one except a very poor person would eat it. Yet the Government has announced that the ration shops are to be 'reformed'. Although our Prime Minister claims to be committed to looking after the poor, he defends the 30-per-cent hike in the price of rice and wheat which are the staple and often only diet of the poorest of our poor.

It is not as if we are stepping into unknown territory. All countries that have liberalized and followed IMF and World Bank orders for structural adjustment have landed themselves in an even bigger mess than they were in to begin with. Unemployment, debt and crime have spiraled frighteningly in a host of African countries which have undergone adjustment. Yet we have chosen to follow the same path.

Not everyone is pessimistic about the direction the country is taking. There is a consumer boom, and proof of our thriving middle class is that everyone who can is visiting TV and video parlors, or buying washing machines and electronic appliances. Indians who return from the West remark at the number of new cars on our roads, and the improvements in our supermarkets. Our major cities have a plethora of fast-food eating places. A whole lot of people out there are spending more money than they have ever done before.

But what these people do not see is that 80 per cent of people in India will never use a washing machine, a food processor or a computer; will never see the inside of a burger joint or an ice cream parlor; will never own a video recorder.

For these people life has become worse, not better. They do not have a one-room hut of their own, their kids will never go to school. And even more crucial, their children may not make it to adulthood.

The nutritional intake of the poorest segment of our society has dramatically declined as prices of basic foods have rocketed; the poor person's only protein base are pulses and *dals*, the cost of which have trebled in the last couple of years, as have edible oils. This means more malnourished children, more health problems and a worsening of the quality of life for the major part of our population. Yet the country is said to have 'progressed'.

It is fashionable at the moment to nod wisely and pronounce that the country's economy made IMF negotiations inevitable. However a host of Indian economists have demanded to know why we, one of the world's poorest nations, are currently importing over three billion US dollars' worth of defence equipment annually when our annual budget deficit is up to five billion dollars. Couldn't we reduce our defence expenditure to help our economy?

The last decade has seen a great deal of pandering to the middle class in order to buy their votes. This is why we are experiencing a consumer boom even though the economy is a shambles. Of course, everyone emphasizes that the poor cannot afford to become victims of any new belt-tightening measures. This point has been reiterated by pro- and anti-IMF advocates, and by politicians of every party. But the New Year starts with a bad omen. Rice and wheat will cost 30 per cent more. For the poor, it is belt-tightening time again.

They're singing our song

The peace of southern India is shattered by ethnic unrest.

The south of India has always been known for its stability and its general atmosphere of non-violence and serenity when compared to the turbulent north. So the outbreak of frenzied violence which came around Christmas 1991 took everyone by surprise.

Tamils who had for generations lived in Karnataka state found themselves the targets of criminals and thugs on the rampage. The issue at stake was a historic feud over how the waters of the Cauvery River should be shared between Karnataka and its neighbor Tamil Nadu. Agriculturalists from both states regard the Cauvery as their lifeline. So when the tribunal which had been appointed to look into the dispute proclaimed its judgment, all hell broke loose.

The people of Karnataka claimed that Tamil Nadu had been favored. 'Those Tamils in the Thanjavur region get three crops of rice while we have to struggle for one measly harvest. Our people don't even have drinking water,' was a popular Kannadiga complaint. Meanwhile, the Tamils grumble that it's their hard work which makes them so prosperous.

However the violence was not whipped up by farmers, but by politicians and others with vested interests. In this part of the Nilgiris, half the population has never been anywhere near the Cauvery River. What happened was a local brawl between two people who happened to be Tamil and Kannadiga. The Tamil set fire to the Kannadiga's hut and the latter ran away to a friend's house. A local newspaper so exaggerated the incident that in a couple of days there was looting and mayhem across the border in Gundulpet, a small town 50 kilometers away.

The Kannadigas in Gundulpet swore they were avenging the attack on their kinsfolk in Gudalur. But at the root of this dispute were local jealousies and petty grudges which were rekindled and encouraged by individual government and police officials. Ironically, half the farms and houses that were looted and burned were not even Tamil. They belonged to people originating from Kerala whose families settled in Tamil Nadu.

The violence in Karnataka was on a larger scale than in Tamil Nadu. And the press reported that while the capital Bangalore burned, the Chief Minister was far away in another state at a musical soireé.

The fear has been that these events portend worse to come – fanatical ethnicity, communalism, regional chauvinism (call it what you will). Many of us see ourselves simply as Indians. We have no other primary identification. Our families have migrated from one state to another, from the north to the south. There has been intermarriage between men and women of different communities, religions and castes. And we have transcended many of the barriers that might previously have divided us.

The theory of sons (never daughters, please note) of the soil – otherwise known as regional differences – is floated up whenever politicians find it expedient to create a diversion from a flagging economy, unemployment and poverty. Their intention is to channel anger at 'safer' targets – safer for the politicians that is. Not for the terrorized Tamils.

There are echoes everywhere of this phenomenon which is sometimes called 'ethnic unrest'. The war between Serbs and Croats, for example. Or the emergence of neo-Nazism in Germany, whose targets are the immigrants who have done the dirty jobs Germans stopped doing a decade ago. In the US, Afro-Americans have street battles with Hispanics: 'We were here first. Go back to your country. This land is our land,' is the refrain.

In France, the Prime Minister and President are politely reiterating that they don't dislike non-white immigrants. They merely don't want too many of them. None of these sentiments are viewed as fascist in the new climate of the 1990s. There is a recession. There is economic depression. And some heads have to roll. Naturally, loyalties are to the sons of the soil. For the others, too bad. You served your purpose. Did a good job. But surely you see our people must come first.

In Karnataka and Tamil Nadu, in Punjab, in the US, in Germany, France and Britain, they are singing the same song. The refrain is frightening. But it is a popular tune.

No requiem for Rajkumari

An Indian woman who lived and died without recognition.

I heard about Rajkumari's death the day after Princess Diana's.* The coincidences were so remarkable. Rajkumari was about the same age as the Princess. She was married in the same year; her two sons were similar ages.

But she was not born into a noble family. She fell in love at 18 and ran away from her average working-class Hindu family to marry a Christian motor mechanic. Her family disowned her. She was inordinately proud, so she didn't go back to them to beg pardon or to ask permission to return to the family fold. Later, after the children were born, they relented and relations improved.

When I met Rajkumari her arm was in a sling. I gathered – although she was too proud ever to admit it – that her husband, in a drunken temper, had shoved her and she had fallen down and broken her arm. Although he was a wonderful mechanic, they had been cheated by a friend with whom they had planned to start a business. They left Bangalore to escape their creditors and we found them living in a corner of someone else's one-room tenement, homeless and totally down and out.

* This letter was written well after the others, in 1997.

They joined our team. He fixed the Jeeps. She cooked for our meetings and training programs. There were days when she started preparing for 150 people and 250 showed up. We'd creep into her kitchen and ask, embarrassed: 'Should we send them to the corner café to eat?' She'd grunt and reply: 'No. It's OK. I'll manage.' I never once heard her complain about the numbers. She had one person to help her cut and chop the mountains of vegetables. She could be rude, overbearing and insulting. But she managed, always guarding her family fiercely and protectively.

She was making money, cooking for our sessions. She became bloated and took on the look of an Amazon queen. He started drinking.

Our team was launching an anti-liquor campaign, so alcohol was strictly prohibited. We told Rajkumari and her husband, and she turned on us ferociously, determined to defend her husband. 'He works all day, doesn't he? Fixes your Jeeps at any time of the day or night, doesn't he? So what's your problem? You don't own him body and soul. If he wants a drink in the evenings it's his business, not yours.'

We were taken aback – given their past history, her defense of his drinking seemed bizarre. Yet that was typical of Rajkumari.

They went rapidly downhill after they left us. He looked dissolute and decrepit, in an alcoholic haze often, even in the daytime. He started beating her again.

She became half the size and it suited her. I'd always thought her beautiful – she had the looks of an ancient, classical, Indian idol. Taller than average, when I first saw her she was slim and graceful, always with flowers in her hair, a brilliant smile and the dark, flashing eyes of a dancer. Yet she was dark-skinned, not fair. So her beauty was discounted, debatable.

For a long time she stuck it out. Sometimes he would send the kids to ask us for money. 'There's no food,' they'd say. It was difficult to refuse them. She looked slimmer and younger, but her spirit was taking a beating. Begging was not her way. She started a tea shop, but it failed – the location was not right.

Finally, a couple of years ago, she left him. He'd humiliated her, beating her in broad daylight, in the center of town, tearing her sari, leaving her in rags. In a small town the news spread rapidly. People loved gossip. 'She's left him finally,' they'd whisper. 'Run off with another driver. Abandoned her two boys.' That, to the Indian ethos, was unforgivable.

No-one gave her credit for the fact that she'd always been a wonderful mother, slaved to feed her family; worked incredibly hard, always; kept an array of gleaming pots and pans in really difficult circumstances; carried water up the hill to scrub them and wash the clothes; put up with drunkenness and debt for 14 years. She was condemned. No-one looked at it as a last-ditch attempt to find happiness and love.

The details of her death were fuzzy. A telegram arrived telling her former husband that she had died in Bangalore, six hours away. He had a new wife and didn't really care what happened to her. They didn't know where to go, anyway – there was no proper address. There was speculation. She was young, so it must have been suicide. Was she pregnant, perhaps? Was she with the other man, or had he abandoned her too?

She might have got a pauper's funeral, unclaimed in the large city. No-one was sure. No-one really cared. There was no requiem for Rajkumari.

Letters from Lahore (Pakistan), 1992-1993

Maria del Nevo

Maria started her working life as an office worker in the New Internationalist co-operative in Oxford. She then went to Lahore, Pakistan, in 1986 to work for the local church. She lived for two years within a small Christian community in a walled compound housing a cathedral, a school and a hostel for church workers. She found life within the compound restrictive and frustrating – she was not encouraged to mix with the wider Muslim community as it was regarded as unsafe to do

so. Despite such attitudes, she managed to make friends beyond the compound walls and to explore life in Pakistan. She began to share her experiences by contributing short features to *New Internationalist*.

After a spell back in Britain, she was offered a job as a journalist on the *Frontier Post* and jumped at the chance of going back to Pakistan. This time she lived independently in Lahore and worked on a number of daily newspapers, writing mostly about issues related to women, minorities and rural communities, but also contributed her 'Letters from Lahore' to *New Internationalist*. She married a Pakistani, though the marriage did not last.

Returning to London, Maria worked for a national charity for people with disabilities, for the World Association for Christian Communication and then for Hammersmith and Fulham Council before suffering a devastating stroke in April 2007. Sadly, as this book goes to press a year later, she remains in hospital undergoing intensive neurological treatment and is still unable to communicate normally with her partner Martin and her daughter Jasmine.

Changes in Pakistan

Pakistan's political history since its independence from Britain in 1947 has been dogged by periodic crises and military coups. Its own birth involved nightmarish Muslim-Hindu violence as India was partitioned, and there was full-scale civil war in 1971 leading to the independence of the former East Pakistan as Bangladesh.

Maria del Nevo's first stay in the country in the 1980s was during the military dictatorship of General Zia ul-Haq, who had executed the democratic leader he deposed, Zulfiqar Ali Bhutto, in 1979. Her second period in the country was during the prime ministership of Bhutto's daughter, Benazir, who became the first woman to lead an Islamic country when she took office in 1988. Maria's writing always homed in on the dramatic stories concealed by everyday life, and particularly explored the restrictions faced by women within families. But the changes instituted for women during Benazir Bhutto's first term of office were disappointingly small, and were eclipsed by the introduction of sharia law under Nawaz Sharif in 1991.

The democratic period of the 1990s was far from a golden age, dogged as it was by ethnic violence and accusations of political corruption, not to mention confrontation with India over Kashmir and nuclear testing. General Pervez Musharraf seized power in 1999, claiming that this would be a temporary measure but carefully accruing power, including the presidency. The West was initially disapproving but following the 9/11 attacks in 2001 Musharraf became a key US ally, supporting the military intervention in Afghanistan that deposed the Taliban Government.

Musharraf thereafter walked a tightrope: support for al-Qaeda and the Taliban runs high in many quarters of Pakistan, and there has been significant growth in Islamist political parties, but he sought to keep a lid on this and retain Western support.

In 2007 Musharraf faced a constitutional crisis as he suspended the chief justice as part of his maneuvers to secure a new presidential term. The decision caused widespread protest and was eventually overturned by the Supreme Court, but Musharraf still managed to secure his own re-election (by parliamentarians) as President and imposed a state of emergency in the run-up towards long-promised parliamentary elections. Benazir Bhutto, who had recently returned from exile, was assassinated while campaigning in December 2007. The elections finally took place in February 2008 and saw the defeat of Musharraf's party, though he remains in place as President.

The enduring appeal of Maria del Nevo's letters, however, is that they chart – with microscopic intensity and keen human sympathy – the fortunes of ordinary people whose stories would never appear in the headline news.

The sari's curse
The terrible burden of daughters' dowries

When I became a friend of Saleem Farhat's eight daughters, I was not to know that I had been unofficially adopted. But it didn't take me long to find out, and after a while I couldn't conceal my pleasure whenever Saleem Farhat introduced me as his ninth daughter. Alone with him I used to tease him about it. 'Don't you think you have enough to cope with, Farhat Sahib?' We would laugh together as if he really were my father.

Saleem Farhat was a tall, distinguished man who had served in the Pakistan Army for 35 years and afterwards worked in government offices. He earned 1,500 rupees a month – the standard wage, but still a small amount for a man who had no sons to contribute to the family earnings. Yet on my frequent visits to the small, overcrowded house I detected no hint of stress: instead there was always that infectious 'Farhat laughter'.

When Nasreen, the eldest daughter, was married, Saleem Farhat relaxed visibly and for a while there was an expression of self-satisfaction on his face. I and the six youngest sisters all turned to Kesra, whose turn it was next. At our hinting and giggling she would turn away shyly, hiding her blushing cheeks.

It was several months before I noticed a quiet change of mood and a year before I was told of the concern about Kesra's future. A boy could not be found, or at least not a suitable one. Saleem Farhat seemed to be ageing before my eyes. There is always anxiety when parents are searching for their child's life-partner. But it was not until Saleem Farhat came specially to visit me that I realized how serious the situation was.

'Kesra is ill,' he began, and dropped down in the chair across from my desk. 'She has a rash on her scalp and her hair is falling out.'

I didn't have to ask the cause and anyway Saleem Farhat talked on. 'She is 26 and not yet engaged. She believes she is doomed to be a spinster. Oh, my poor Kesra. It is a terrible situation. Even if I find a boy and his family make a proposal, I cannot see how we could accept.'

Saleem Farhat raised his eyes to meet my puzzled expression. 'Ah no, my daughter,' he continued, 'you know little of our real troubles. But you must know. For 35 years I served my country. I fought in two wars and received these scars which are a reminder of the horrors I witnessed. At 54 I was nearing retirement and my wife and I looked forward to receiving a good pension of 75,000 rupees. It was a time free of worries. Yes, we had longed for a son in the old days but instead God had blessed us with eight beautiful and obedient daughters and, after a lifetime of hard work, I was to be in a position where I could prepare them, materially, for marriage.

'My oldest and closest friend visited us a lot in those days. He would come every couple of days and eat with us. I always welcomed his visits – 'another man in a house full of women!' I would say. Azad Hamad had set himself up in business. He was an agent for people who wanted to work in the Middle East. These people paid him to arrange their visas, travel and contacts at the other end. It was a lucrative business, he said, and he felt he was helping the Pakistani people.

'Azad Hamad asked me to recommend him to my relatives who had sons wishing to go overseas to Dubai and Kuwait. Because these families respected and trusted me, they followed up my recommendation and in total Azad Hamad received 60,000 rupees from three families. But the weeks went by and Azad Hamad didn't come. Yes, you may guess the rest: we never saw him again.

'Well, my pension was due and I had to repay all the money that the families had lost.' Saleem Farhat covered his brow with his hand. 'All that money, for 35 years' service and for my daughters' dowries. What a fool I was. So you see we were still poor and knew we would stay that way. My wife would go and eat dust outside the mosque believing that when God saw her He would take pity on us. I had 15,000 rupees left and that paid for Nasreen's dowry. Now there is nothing left.'

I sat silently, and so did Saleem Farhat, shaking his head slowly until he continued. 'I am a victim of poverty, corruption and the desperation which causes friend to steal from friend. And the dowry, that is my curse. But I cannot ignore it. Who am I to make my daughters social outcasts, and who am I to leave them unmarried, unprotected and scorned?'

I had no words of comfort or encouragement. It was too late for that. And it was almost too late for Kesra, who in anguish saw her one option rapidly drifting away from her. She would soon be labeled unmarriageable. Saleem Farhat's pension had been tragically lost and seven dowries remained. A curse, and there was no way out. No escape from the price that had to be paid to dress a daughter in the red and gold wedding sari.

Heavy shadow

Rani went into hospital to have a baby; she emerged feeling she had been punished by God.

I was at Rani's house when she was admitted into hospital with labor pains. It was the third time I had stayed at the house and formality had been slung aside so that I was sprawled across a bed, Rani's in-laws surrounding me, watching the gore of an American video which they had hired in my honor. On the wall above the television was a large silver plate with the typical inscription engraved across the middle: *Allah Ho Akbar* (God is great). It was a more comforting focal point than the horrors on the screen.

The room was still filled with sounds of gunfire and obscenities when Shamim walked in. She stood looking pale and tired. Someone eventually turned the television down and Shamim told us that Rani's child, a girl, was dead. Silence followed the news. Her mother-in-law was sitting cross-legged on a chair, a *chadar* draped carelessly around her head; she didn't stop chewing her pan. Her three daughters, all huddled together, made meaningful eye contact while their father did not take his eyes off the action on the television. Rani's husband was away working in the Middle East.

As suddenly as silence had fallen, noise returned. The mother-in-law launched into a long, expressive speech, earnestly swaying her head from side to side, waggling her finger for further emphasis and curling up her top lip to expose the pan-stained teeth. Everyone in the room listened without interrupting and I too was enthralled, though her rapid Punjabi was beyond me.

Two days passed by and we continued to sit in the room watching endless horrors on the television, not even moving to eat as Shamim always served us right where we were. Rani stayed in hospital because she couldn't stop bleeding. No-one went to visit her and although I thought this strange I didn't feel my questioning would be appreciated. Even once she was home I had no chance to offer any words of comfort because the family put her in a separate room and I was warned not to enter or even pass the door.

Several hours after Rani's return there was a knocking on the adjoining wall. The family rose from their seats, Shamim took my hand, and we all went up the stairs to the roof. There we stayed for some 20 minutes. I asked Shamim what was going on. 'Rani needed to go to the bathroom,' I was told, 'and she would have to pass us to get there. But she has a heavy shadow now, and the family are scared that it might pass over their faces. For if it touches them then bad luck will come their way. She cannot work, as no-one could eat the food if her hands had prepared it. Nor can she wash the dishes. Rani has been punished by God – and that makes herself and her shadow unclean.'

Later, when I had thought on Shamim's words, I questioned her further. 'Throughout her pregnancy Rani kept saying that she wished the child to be a boy. She said that if she had a girl then her life would be ruined. The family even suspected that she tried black magic to make this wish come true, so obsessed was she to have a boy. But the child was a girl and she was dead. That is God's punishment on her because she tried to determine the sex of her child.'

I asked Shamim if she believed Rani was involved in black magic.

'No, not really. She only used to talk about the sex of her child because she is always frightened her husband won't come back to her one day. She thinks if she gives him all boys then he is tied to her and she will gain more respect from him and his family. But she wouldn't go so far as to interfere with nature.'

So Rani stayed in isolation and not once did I even hear her. Whenever she had to leave that room we would all traipse up onto the roof until we were safe from her shadow. I delayed my departure for some time because I couldn't make up my mind whether to go and see her. The family's behavior and superstitions made me angry. Rani had no comfort, no love, no husband by her side, and was led to believe that her shadow carried God's punishment. Yet I was the family's guest and I didn't wish to offend them by blatantly acting against their wishes.

When I eventually got up to leave I happened to pass Rani's open door for the first time. In the corner of my eye I saw a figure lying on a bed but I didn't stop to look. I said a fond, but rather strained, farewell to the family and walked from the house along the narrow lane to the main road.

Suddenly I wanted to rush back to the house and go to the room where the figure lay and take her in my arms. But it was too late. I had stayed on the side of the majority and, anyway, Rani had already seen me pass by with my bags and heard me leave the house.

Caught in the web

Bonded laborers held in the grip of debt, beyond the reach of the law.

The tall chimneys of the brick kilns, rising above flat, barren land, are the symbol of bonded labor here in Pakistan. There are some 10,000 kilns in the Punjab alone, and many more in the northwest and south, with 50 to 60 families working per kiln, modern-day slaves to a close-knit and élite group. Most of the workers have been born into bonded labor – tied to the kilns by the *paishgee* (loan) system – and the majority will grow old having seen or known nothing else. Earning no more than $4 per 1,000 bricks – which an average family of five would find difficult to complete in a day – they find it impossible to make ends meet and survive on advances from the owner, which are then deducted from their earnings with interest.

The workers, being illiterate, are unable to keep accounts and continue repaying long after their debts have been cleared. Children are forced into labor to assist their parents in completing the required amount of bricks, the families are denied sick leave or public holidays, and the owner has no regard for safe working conditions.

The families are watched over by the owner's *jamadars* (supervisors) who are notorious for using physical violence and rape as a means of punishment for those who try to escape. Should the owner decide capture is no longer profitable, he may sell his workers.

The kiln where Bilquees used to work outside Lahore is strangely quiet, with no black smoke rising from the chimney. The owner closed it down three months ago because it was making a loss. And today the workers walk four kilometers every morning to another of his kilns, returning late at night.

Like the other workers, Bilquees' family lives in one of many one-room hovels made of mud which run in a row either side of a narrow, dusty lane. A hole in the ground at one corner of the compound serves as a latrine for both men and women and another area has been surrounded by a waist-high wall where the families bathe and wash their clothes and dishes. There is no running water and the women have to carry buckets from a handpump which is situated beyond the walls of the quarters.

Bilquees has ten children and is pregnant again. She doesn't know about family planning, contraception or about the risks to her own health if she keeps bearing children. Her only concern is that with more hands more bricks will be made and hence more money earned.

She goes to work with her husband, her sons and her elder daughters at four in the morning, after eating a piece of roti and drinking a cup of tea. They return at night-time when, if they have the money, they may eat roti and chilli. Most days however, they cannot afford lunch and dinner. They cannot remember when they last ate meat. Her children are thin and weak; their hair, streaked with golden tints, betrays signs of malnutrition.

The family owes $760 to the kiln-owner and each week an installment is deducted from their already meager earnings. They have no idea how much has been paid so far. They also owe $100 to the shop-keeper who has refused them further credit. When Bilquees opens her flour container it is empty; God knows how or when it will be filled again.

When does Bilquees have time to attend to her household chores? I ask. 'What chores?' asks Bilquees. 'What is there to clean?' She looks down at the floor of mud and dust. 'And we don't have to cook because we have no food.'

Last week the National Assembly passed a Bill abolishing bonded labor, making the loan system a criminal offense, and providing for the rehabilitation of the laborers. There should have been a mass exodus of hundreds of thousands of men, women and children. But there was not. The workers did hear about the Bill but when they questioned the owner he said they were mistaken. They do not dare contradict him. When the new law, which vaguely promises them freedom and rehabilitation, is explained to them, they look disbelieving. 'But where would we go?' they ask. Rehabilitation for the workers has not been specified, so what can they look forward to even if they are released? And the confusion is intensified by the fact that although under the Bill the *paishgee* system is abolished it does not clarify the matter of existing loans which the workers are continuing to pay off.

The kiln-owners are pleased with the many loopholes in the Bill which will permit them to evade the new law. Eight of the Punjabi kiln-owners are members of the Provincial Assembly with immense power and political clout, while the laborers have no access to information regarding changes in the law. They remain unaware of their basic legal rights and even if they do hear of the Bill by word of mouth their hopes will soon be quashed by the owners, who are powerful enough to somehow keep them in isolation and ignorance – caught in the web of bonded labor.

The burned bride

Even a generous dowry does not protect some young wives.

Nosheen was getting married and I'd been invited to visit her before the day to see her dowry. She led me into a room crammed with huge trunks and boxes and one bed where her many silks and jewels were laid out for me to admire.

I looked wide-eyed at the velvet boxes containing heavy gold necklaces and earrings, dripping with pearls and emeralds. I was dumbstruck as she displayed quilts, blankets, sheets, dinner sets, crystal glasses and every kind of modern electrical kitchen appliance. In another room stood a huge double bed, a sofa set, dining table and chairs.

Nosheen's mother stood in the doorway, her face alight with pride, and when eventually I was left alone with Nosheen I asked how her father could possibly have afforded such lavish expense for I knew he was only earning 2,500 rupees per month and had a family of six to support.

'I collected most of this myself,' she said. 'I've worked for five years and bought it with my salary. My father borrowed the money to buy the rest.'

Shocked, I remembered a conversation when her father had expressed strong opposition to the dowry system. For this practice is the root of prejudice against girl children, the cause of endless poverty and debt, and incites terrible greed in the families of boy children.

Quickly, however, I realized that her father is locked into a cultural tradition which faces him with two options: debt or the shameful burden of a spinster daughter. Very few families in Pakistan manage to arrange marriages for daughters without providing dowries, for if the girl goes empty-handed to her marriage there is the constant fear that the in-laws will mistreat her.

Sending a daughter to her husband's family with a full dowry wins respect for her from her in-laws and brings honor to her own family, even if they spend the rest of their lives repaying the debt. The dowry also pays the husband's family

for the girl's keep. But the system has gone far beyond any traditional agreement between two families.

Farhat, a young girl in her early twenties, went to her husband's house with a dowry which left nothing out. Her in-laws welcomed the addition to their household and all the valuable items she brought with her. But after the birth of her daughter, Farhat's married life took a turn for the worse. Javed, Farhat's husband, dreamed of going abroad, but needed money in order to fulfill his dream. His parents asked Farhat's family to give them money. They gave 20,000 rupees, but Javed's parents demanded 30,000 more, a sum which they could not afford.

One day last August, neighbors heard terrified screams coming from within the house. They banged on the doors but were told to mind their own business by Farhat's sister-in-law, who promptly bolted the gates. As the screams continued, a boy from the neighborhood jumped the walls. He found Farhat in an undisturbed room, sitting on a stool in the corner. Fully 97 per cent of her body was covered in burns and as he carried her out of the house chunks of her scorched flesh fell from her body. On her death bed in hospital, Farhat accused her husband and sister-in-law of throwing a burning oil stove at her.

In 1990 there were a recorded 1,800 deaths caused by burns from oil stoves, 85 per cent of the victims being females aged between 18 and 30. A more recent report claims that every six hours one lower-middle class Pakistani woman dies in this way.

Dowry deaths occur for many reasons. Some marriages are arranged with the girl's family promising to provide the dowry after the marriage has taken place. But when the time comes they can't provide all that they promised and the girl falls victim to the wrath of her in-laws. Alternatively the son may be married to a girl who can provide a full dowry so that his family can kill her, have the boy marry again and so receive another dowry. Often, the in-laws feel that the dowry is not enough and after the marriage they demand more: when payment is denied they take the girl's life.

I remember Nosheen, who I have not seen since her marriage, with that magnificent dowry which she courageously collected herself to save her father from debt and poverty. And I wonder how she is, knowing that all those jewels and gold, which were supposed to guarantee her safety, in fact exposed her to as much danger as if she went to her husband's house empty-handed.

Wretched of the earth

Dishonor makes Pakistan's poorest women desperate.

Every morning at dawn Qulsom, Bhagan and Sardaran walk the city streets with sacks slung over their backs, and pick up litter – paper, leather, copper and plastic – which they sell to intermediaries who then sell for a far greater price to recycling factories.

They are three of the thousands of women who walk the streets of the suburbs to clear away debris from the streets. They are notorious for stealing and the *chowkidars* or nightwatch people eye them very suspiciously. Although they are Muslim, these women are regarded as social outcasts, along with Christian road sweepers and sanitation workers.

Qulsom stands arrogantly in the doorway of my office. 'Give me a cigarette and I will tell you about myself,' she says. I give her the cigarette and she inhales deeply, filling the room with smoke before walking away without a word to join her friends.

'Come to Begum Court,' she says over her shoulder and I watch them walk away, their deep, coarse voices and their raucous laughter drifting on the chilly morning air.

Next day, intrigued by the name Begum Court – Begum meaning 'grand lady' – I take a jeep with a colleague and travel far beyond the city. Thin, scantily dressed children tiptoe barefoot through muddy narrow lanes. Women peep through cracks in doors and window shutters. I feel as if I am standing on the edge of the world.

We ask after Qulsom, but no-one recalls her. 'Cover your head,' my colleague snaps at me as he tries to control a crowd of men which has formed around us. Everyone is talking, laughing. I feel exposed and uneasy, until at last someone leads us to Sardaran's house.

We sit in a neat, but sparsely furnished room with Qulsom, Sardaran and Bhagan. 'We earn one rupee for a kilo of paper,' Sardaran tells us, 'four rupees for a kilo of copper. And we're lucky to collect even two or three kilos a day.'

'My husband is in prison,' she continues without regret. 'He was such a criminal I took him to the police myself.' Doesn't she fear what he'll do when he comes out? 'No,' she says, 'he's not capable of anything. Most of our husbands are drug addicts, and they never do any work.'

She talks as if discussing a delinquent child, yet with a strong undertone of loyalty. Perhaps she is the only one who understands her man.

Meanwhile Qulsom stares at me challengingly. 'She's been divorced three times,' someone explains. 'She can't have children.'

Qulsom pulls a nonchalant face, then smiles, sarcastically, as if laughing at the world. 'You want to know about us? We are not Hindu, Christian or Muslim. We can't read and we don't know anything...' A trail of smoke comes out of her nostrils and she looks away in disgust.

The stories of abuse continue: the woman who was raped by a depot *chowkidar* while she squatted between the seats, picking up paper and anything else she could find; the nine-year-old girl who was molested by police after being arrested for stealing.

There is no-one to help these women. They have been dishonored by society and then stigmatized as 'immoral'.

'And now,' Qulsom says, her voice breaking though the chatter of the other women, 'we have found another way of making money.' There is an uncomfortable silence before the other women begin to giggle and I realize what they are talking about. Qulsom raises her head and stares at me with the same expression of challenge.

Disillusioned with the city's so-called middle-class morality, Begum Court and the surrounding colony exists as a separate state, with its own rules and regulations, its own culture and lifestyle. If a woman can seduce a male neighbor and earn a hundred rupees then she will. 'We do it in the fields, or an empty building,' says Qulsom with a twisted smile.

I leave Begum Court totally drained. I feel like I have traveled many continents, yet I have only driven about 20 kilometers. And, ever since, when I see the paper women sitting on the roadsides resting, or bending down to pick up pieces of paper, I can't help looking out for Qulsom who, although she remains detached, has managed to tell me so much.

A lesson too late

A boy's life shows the gulf between Christian rich and poor.

I met Putras during my first stay in Pakistan, when I lived and worked for two years on a cathedral compound in the heart of the city. This place seemed to be a perfect haven of peace and tranquillity, and initially I imagined it as a kind of Garden of Eden. But once I met Putras I soon realized how superficial this image was. Indeed, the better I got to know him, the more the compound came to symbolize the gaping divide that exists within the Pakistani Christian community, between the small number of privileged church clergy and their flock, the two or three per cent of Pakistani people who are mainly sweepers, sanitation workers or bonded laborers.

Putras was six years old, the eldest son of a sweeper who had to keep a family of seven on the meager monthly salary he earned at the church school. The family lived with the other sweeper families in a small area at the back of the compound which was surrounded by a high wall and a gate.

Each family lived in one room no bigger than three meters by four, with a narrow verandah at the front where they cooked their food. In the center of the quarters stood a communal hand-pump and near the gate a communal latrine was hidden behind a torn old curtain. With no school to attend, the children sat throughout the day, listless, naked and grubby, surrounded by piles of rubbish where flies swarmed. It was difficult to imagine that only a stone's throw away, wealth and magnificence sheltered the families of bishops and padres.

Then one day Putras walked through the main gates of the compound, sobbing. He had been working with a car mechanic: 13 hours a day, 7 days a week, earning one rupee a day. And now he was crying because the other boys in the shop, all Muslim, had been bullying him. He was tired and hungry and didn't want to go back to work next day.

When the wives of the clergy realized that the children of their sweepers were either spending their days idle or working in places where they were being exploited, they opened a school in the church hall. The sweeper quarters remained squalid, dirty and diseased. But the children came out in little groups each morning and walked across the compound, neatly dressed, books under their arms, talking and laughing. Enthusiastically they sat on their mats on the floor, balanced their books on their laps and recited the Urdu alphabet in loud unison.

Soon afterwards Putras was sent to me every morning for an hour, when I taught him the English alphabet and counting. He was slow but he never missed his lessons. And when I left Pakistan a year later, Putras, then eight years old, was still attending school.

When I eventually returned to Lahore I made it a priority to visit him and his family. Putras was 11 and as tall as I. I couldn't wait for his mother to finish her welcoming chatter, so I could enquire how he was getting on.

'Oh, Putras left the school,' his mother said.

I looked questioningly at Putras. And he stared steadily back. His mother explained that he had struggled at school; couldn't concentrate and was restless; wanted to go out to earn money to help his parents feed his brothers and sisters, and provide medicines for the youngest child, a victim of polio.

Then Putras himself spoke: 'I'm an apprentice for another mechanic. I earn two rupees for a nine-hour day, six days a week. When I've learned more then I'll start my own business.'

The chance of education had come just too late for him, he said. The family walked back out with me into the fly-infested quarters. A child was urinating into the drain beneath the handpump.

'They haven't done anything to improve things here then,' I said, referring to the church leaders.

'They don't care,' Putras's mother said bitterly. 'They never even come here to see how we live.'

I looked at Putras, less dreamy than I remembered. And I realized that for him, like so many other Christian children in Pakistan, education had never been a right, but a privilege for those who had the time to learn.

A suitable arrangement

Why it's not always just the family that wants to arrange a marriage.

In early December Farah finally received the news she had been awaiting for almost two years. She was to be married.

She had been in love with a boy some years earlier. They used to meet in the park every other evening, where they would sit on the grass, hidden by tall flowers, hedgerows and trees, and Khashif would confess his undying love for her. Farah had just turned 24 when she finally decided to speak to Khashif about their future together. But he only mumbled and made quick arrangements for their next meeting before rushing home.

The next day he didn't turn up. She went to the park every evening and stood by the gates waiting, but she never saw him again. Her sister-in-law Mira told her that boys rarely marry the girls they have dated on the grounds that if they can go out with one boy they can go out with others.

But it wasn't until Farah heard through a mutual friend that Khashif had married his cousin in the traditional manner that she really began to understand. And it was then that she turned on her parents.

'It was awful,' Mira said. 'One evening she started screaming at her parents. She said that they had better do something soon. She also said that if they didn't have the money for her marriage she'd make them sell the house.'

After that day Farah never gave her parents a moment's peace. Haunted by their daughter's threats, they went to the best marriage bureau.

'There was one other problem,' Mira went on. 'Farah didn't want just anyone. She was after the film-star type. Tall, handsome and rich.'

Prospective in-laws could not be entertained at the family house, which only had three rooms and was situated along a lane so narrow that even a rickshaw could not enter. Other arrangements were quickly made. Rashida, another sister, had married three years previously. She was the second wife of an entrepreneur who set her up in a spacious and well-furnished flat in a good area, where he visited her once a week. It was decided that Farah's mother and sister would receive interested mothers at Rashida's flat, which they would claim belonged to the family.

Sometimes an entire female clan would turn up – aunts and daughters – eyeing the flat, the furniture, the curtains, the carpets, the neighborhood. And eventually Farah would be called in from the bedroom and asked to walk around the room a couple of times so that the women could inspect her. They waited for a proposal. None came.

A year went by. Farah's mother became visibly exhausted. Ramadan came. Farah went into near seclusion. She fasted every day and said her prayers five times a day. Whenever I saw her, it seemed she was bent towards Mecca with her head covered in a long scarf, or standing on her prayer mat with her eyes closed and her palms held upwards. It was the first week of December before Saleem's mother and sister turned up at Rashida's flat. Saleem lives and works in Dubai and they were over in Pakistan to look for a wife for him. The women took an instant liking to Farah. The wealth that Saleem's mother displayed, together with her charm and promises, impressed Farah's mother and sister. They saw a photograph of the boy, whom they said looked very pleasant, and accepted the proposal without hesitation. Farah was overjoyed.

I went to congratulate the family. But I couldn't help noticing that Mira was holding something back. I prodded her until she finally opened up and spoke in a whisper so that the family in the next room couldn't overhear.

'He's been married before. The wife was in Dubai with him. The family haven't really explained what happened. They just said that she ran off one day, leaving behind two children. She hasn't been seen or heard of since.'

I gaped at her, stunned and horrified. 'But aren't they worried, sending Farah to Dubai without knowing the full story?'

'They don't want to think about it. This is their only choice,' came Mira's reply. 'It was the only proposal they received which Farah would accept.'

You can fly it !

Two kite-flying parties and two very different worlds.

With springtime comes the kite-flying festival of Basant. A cold winter is behind us and the city of Lahore is alive, bathed in sunlight. Men and boys of all ages climb onto flat rooftops and the sky is full of bobbing multi-colored kites.

There is extensive preparation. From the crowded narrow alleys of the Walled City and the vast sprawling slums of the suburbs to the most exclusive and affluent neighborhoods, Lahore-dwellers spend thousands of rupees on kites.

But it's more than simple kite-flying: it's fierce competition. The kite's string is covered with crushed glass and once the flyer has his kite up, the objective is to cut down a kite being flown from a neighboring rooftop.

It is my favorite season, a time when I savor most the experience of being in Pakistan. The excitement is infectious. Although every year the authorities try to prevent the celebrations on the grounds that it is un-Islamic (it is celebrated throughout predominantly Hindu India) they fail miserably every time.

On the eve of Basant, parties are held and even in the dark kite-flyers exhibit the most amazing skill. But it is on this night that the police come out in force. A party I went to, hosted by a member of Pakistan's Liberal Party, was raided by police just before I arrived. It was hard to believe it though, as I looked at men and women mingling, sitting around small circular tables eating and sipping soft drinks. On a higher terrace, fashionable young couples stood talking and laughing, boys flew kites and older men gathered around a low table, guarding a crate of whisky. 'How did they manage to keep this?' I asked. My husband laughed and told me that the hosts had 'got heavy' with the police.

I looked around me – this was perhaps the most liberal gathering I had ever been to in Pakistan. There was none of the usual formality and self-consciousness which all too often causes me to decline invitations. And I was relaxed because no-one looked my way. As a foreigner – so often the focus of inquiring looks – it was a relief to be able to blend in for once.

'See the difference?' said a man standing next to me. 'These people are not used to segregation. They know how to socialize, how to interact freely.'

The next day I experienced a very different Basant at my in-laws. The men of the family had been up on the roof since dawn, competing with their neighbors. Cassette players blared out Hindi film songs, while some families had hired *dholis* (drummers). The smaller over-excited children ran here and there with sticks, trying to retrieve kites which had fallen and were stuck in the trees. Moni – my husband's eldest nephew – and his friends were concentrating on keeping the kites up. I went and joined them, but only for a few moments. Eventually I was called back downstairs where

the women of the family were gathered. I wanted to ask them if they minded having to stay indoors on such a lovely day and whether they wished that they too could fly kites.

'Women don't go up much,' my sister-in-law said as if reading my mind, 'only the men can enjoy themselves. We have to cook special food for them,' and she went to the kitchen where she stood in her fine dress, preparing huge pots of *haleem* (rice and chicken).

Nevertheless, a couple of hours later she accompanied me back to the roof. Moni was in the middle of a fierce battle with another kite-flyer. We watched as he maneuvered his string around that of his neighbors until the other fell from the sky and we laughed as he danced the *bhangra* (a Punjabi folkdance) and roared with the pleasure of victory. My sister-in-law and I stood against the wall, talking, looking up as the sky filled with millions of bobbing kites. Then Moni suddenly came up, gave his mother the kite string and she exercised the same skill as her son.

'You can fly it!' I exclaimed, and she laughed and said that she used to fly with her brothers when she was small. Some boys on a roof opposite began looking our way, showing off and giggling.

'Let's go down then,' she said passing the kite back to Moni, and my heart sank. I desperately wanted to stay up there with her sons, where I could relish their enjoyment and the atmosphere of fun and frivolity which only comes once a year. But instead I quietly trailed after her.

Sperm in the market

Being a working mother can be frustrating – even in a progressive household.

Nusrat and I were sitting on her bed with her two-month-old baby daughter, Umrao, who lay between us. Nusrat's husband, Imtiaz, lounged in a chair across the room. It was early evening.

'I've been sitting on this bed for two months without a break, attending to my child,' Nusrat said. 'This little baby needs my constant attention.'

She looked up then at her husband, who was gazing out of the window. 'And what's his role?' she asked vehemently. 'His sperm only!' Umrao began to cry. 'I wish,' said Nusrat as she took the baby to her breast, 'that I had got the sperm from the market. At least I could then say that the baby was all mine.'

Imtiaz chuckled. And so did I, simply out of pleasure at listening to such frankness, something which is quite rare between husband

and wife in Pakistani society, especially in company. Such talk was in fact one of the things which had drawn me so often to Nusrat's home, a place where I felt anything could be discussed without reservation. They had known each other for many years. Imtiaz, the former leader of the Pakistan Communist Party, had been jailed for six years during President Zia's martial law, and he had turned to Nusrat, a psychiatrist, for treatment. A friendship had developed. Non-practising Muslims, they were always known as a couple with strong progressive ideas, ideas which they tried to put into practice by not succumbing to social or family pressures.

Eventually, in their late thirties, they married, and a year later Umrao was born. Although parenthood came as a real joy, as professionals they are also finding it difficult to adjust. Both have demanding jobs, and their work has always come first. Nusrat is about to finish her two-month maternity leave from the Lahore Mental Hospital. Ever since she gave birth she has worried about her patients. In addition there is the Hamara Ghar (Our Home), a halfway house for destitute women who have been mentally ill, set up by Nusrat and which she helps run with a group of psychiatrists and social workers.

'I can't survive without my work,' she said. 'But what to do with this child? It's so difficult to find help. I'll probably have to leave her with my mother during the day, but she's elderly and it'll be difficult.'

I asked her about Hamara Ghar, where she used to spend several hours in the evenings. 'I visited the other day,' she said. 'The women there need me. They need me like this baby. But when I came back Imtiaz shouted at me. He said: "Do you want to kill my child?" And I was only gone for two hours!'

'Okay, okay,' said Imtiaz, with a demonstrative wave of the hand. 'I swear on my daughter's head that I will give her her mother's name. Satisfied?'

'In Pakistan,' Nusrat said, turning to me, 'working women get no help when they have a child. We just get maternity leave. In China they have crèches. Here there is no concept of such a facility. Why? Because it is not considered important. Professional women are simply not valued.' Hospitals, Nusrat told me, regard women doctors as a waste of time because once they become mothers they will have to give up their work completely. And those few doctors who do manage to keep their jobs are forced to put their babies on formula milk.

'This is why we need the support of our husbands,' she said. 'Besides practical help we need their emotional support. They have a good role to play. But they do nothing.'

Imtiaz had heard enough. 'No woman can be happy even if you try to fulfill all feminist demands,' he stated with another wave of the hand. 'Why? Because she wants to play the male role. She aspires to be a male. If she was married to a real patriarchal, feudal man, then she would realize!'

'He has only exposed himself,' Nusrat said condescendingly. 'Men are all alike. In Pakistan we have a saying: *baccha mera khoon hai* (a child is my blood).' I asked her what this meant.

'Pakistani men,' explained Nusrat, 'often don't have a good relationship with their wives. But they develop a good relationship with their children because, they say, those children are "of their blood", whereas their wives are not. So you see,' she concluded, 'men are all alike. Whether they are liberal or not.'

Dupatta or not dupatta

What happens when Pakistani women dress in a non-conformist way.

My husband didn't take me to meet his mother until after we had married. This was rather unconventional and I was very nervous about the whole thing. But I needn't have been in the slightest bit worried. She greeted me warmly, smothered me in kisses and continually blessed me throughout the evening.

'I am glad to see that she is wearing Pakistani dress,' she murmured to my husband, and she adjusted my *dupatta* (long scarf), which was the largest one I owned and which was draped rather untidily across my chest.

'Did you ever wear mini-skirts in England?' she asked.

'No,' I said emphatically.

'Good girl,' she said with a fierce nod of the head. 'My own daughter.'

At the time I had thought it a harmless lie. My acceptance into the family had, in fact, depended a lot upon it. But ever since, that lie has continued to niggle at me and the dress which I had always loved and found comfortable yet elegant has begun to seem increasingly less so.

Now that summer has come and tempers are prone to fly, I realize that I am not alone in this discomfort. Beena, a 30-year-old journalist, comes striding into the office every morning, her face flushed and her eyes flashing with anger. 'This damned thing!' she curses loudly, and ripping off her dupatta she flings it over the back of her chair.

Our male colleagues glance up from their work for a moment and I murmur sounds of sympathy. We frequently share our experiences – the frustration of walking on the roads in Lahore where men whistle, blow kisses, stick out their tongues and occasionally move just a little too close for comfort. There must be few women who don't have similar stories to tell.

'Things are getting worse here every day,' Beena declares when she has caught her breath. 'It never used to be like this. Men just don't want us to come out of our homes.'

Memories of General Zia's Islamization, when the idea of barring women from driving cars was even discussed, are still vivid. But on the surface things do seem to be changing for the better. Women are no longer restricted to 'acceptable professions' like teaching. They are appearing as lawyers, doctors, in banks, in the media and in big business.

But, as Beena frequently points out, women still can't walk down the street to work without being harassed. They still have to conform by wearing the dupatta.

Neelam, another colleague, often does leave hers at home. But as a result she faces numerous unpleasant situations when moving around Lahore. She is from a more conservative home than Beena, who was brought up in Karachi and did her higher education overseas. And unlike Beena, who chose her own husband, Neelam's parents would like to arrange her marriage for her. 'But,' she states, 'I don't want to live a life of slavery like my mother. And if I ever do get married it'll never be to a Pakistani man.' But Neelam has to have a lot of courage to live the life she has chosen for herself.

'One day,' she tells me, 'I was walking to work. This man – I think he was a *maulvi* (priest) – was cycling by. He stopped when he saw me and shouted: "Woman! Where is your dupatta?" I was so angry, I asked him why he was even looking my way. Then he was embarrassed. "No, no," he said, "I am only saying this because I am like your father." So I told him that one father was enough for me, and he cycled away!'

The dupatta is in fact an integral part of a Pakistani woman's dress, and even in the confines of their homes, women can be seen adjusting it, slipping it over their heads at prayer time or when a man enters the room, without even a second thought. Most women would not feel fully clothed without it.

But essentially it is the symbol of modesty and this is why, in a society where a family's honor is dependent upon a woman's virtue, the dupatta has become an issue for women like Beena and Neelam, who see it as fundamental to their struggle for emancipation. Last year in nearby Faisalabad the Education Department advised young girls and women to cover their heads when traveling to and from schools so as to prevent sexual harassment on the roads. There was an uproar when the news reached our office. 'See what we are up against!' cried an outraged Beena. 'If we are raped or assaulted then we are to blame for not covering our heads!'

I think I realize now how women are the victims of a cruel, yet very subtle, form of emotional blackmail, and how a virtue like modesty is used against them to reinforce the indestructibility of a patriarchal system. Perhaps this is because I am no longer standing as a spectator on the periphery of a culture.

Letters from Lagos (Nigeria), 1993-1995

Elizabeth Obadina

Elizabeth began her long love affair with Nigeria in 1974 when an engineering company sent her road building in the north of the country. In the late 1970s she retrained as an English teacher and, after a spell teaching in the East End of London, she renewed her love affair with Africa, married journalist Tunde Obadina, and embarked on a new life in the then Nigerian capital, Lagos.

She was initially a features writer for the Lagos *Punch* group of newspapers and magazines, then the first women's editor on a new Nigerian newspaper, *The Guardian*. Over many years in Lagos, she also corresponded for *The Times* of London, the BBC, Radio Deutsche Welle, Radio France International and, of course, *New Internationalist*.

A quarter of a century and three children later, life has turned full circle and she once again finds herself teaching and writing, this time in the English Midlands. Liz and Tunde's children have grown up and flown the nest to settle in Norway, Tokyo and Manchester and have taken partners from Norway, Japan and France, but they all remain close, with happy memories of growing up in Nigeria.

Changes in Nigeria

The 1990s were a tumultuous time in the political life of Nigeria. The country had been ruled by military regimes for most of the years since independence from Britain in 1960 but elections in 1993, when Elizabeth Obadina began writing her Letters from Lagos, were supposed to bring a return to civilian rule. Instead the presidential elections in June were invalidated and the apparent winner, Moshood Abiola, disqualified from standing in a new poll. Massive protests broke out in Lagos but the replacement election never took place; instead, power was seized by General Sani Abacha, who dissolved Parliament and banned political activity. Abacha took the country into the international wilderness – the execution of nine members of the Movement for the Survival of the Ogoni People, including the poet Ken Saro-Wiwa, in November 1994 caused many countries to withdraw their diplomats in protest.

Abacha's death in 1998 eventually led to the restoration of democracy, though the winner of the 1999 presidential election, Olusegun Obasanjo, was himself a former military ruler. Nigeria is a vast federation, involving 250 ethnic groups, of which four predominate – the Hausa and Fulani in the north; the Yoruba in the southwest; and the Igbo in the southeast – and around 250 ethnic subdivisions. The country is also broadly split between a Muslim north and a Christian south. These faultlines were a major preoccupation of the Obasanjo presidency, which faced many violent confrontations on ethnic and religious lines and saw 12 northern states introduce an extreme version of sharia law in 2001 and 2002.

Resistance to the Government was at its fiercest in the Niger Delta region, source of the country's oil wealth, where rebel groups continue to fight for the resources to benefit local people instead of disappearing into the coffers of transnational corporations or the national élite – Nigeria was rated as the world's second most corrupt country by Transparency International in 2001. Obasanjo reluctantly ceded the presidency to Umaru Yar'Adua in 2007, and the new leader has broadcasted his hope that Nigeria can ride the whirlwind of high oil prices to become one of the 'top 20 nations' in the world by 2020.

Elizabeth Obadina's letters reflect the tumultuous political life of modern Nigeria. But they also show a family grappling with the myriad demands of everyday life in the chaotic sprawl of Lagos, from a nightmarish banking system through hospitals ravaged by public-spending cuts to a bizarre array of beauty aids.

What's in a name?

What a Nigerian baby is called reflects not only its place in the family, but also the circumstances in which it is born.

My newest neighbor, little Oluwatosin, was named yesterday on the seventh day of her short life. Like most Nigerians, she will grow up answering to a much shorter name, Tosin, but to her parents she will always be 'Oluwatosin' meaning 'God is worth worshipping'.

Unlike her brothers and sisters, all born in easier circumstances over ten years ago, Tosin was the product of a troubled pregnancy. Her first breath was drawn not in the well-equipped private hospital where her siblings first saw the light of day, but in the local general hospital where a lack of drugs, dressings and equipment are the norm. Luckily for Tosin and her forty-something mum, God had heard the family's prayers for safe childbirth: hence the newborn's heartfelt name.

Africa is a land where names mean something and parents, grandparents, aunts and uncles will all bless the new child with names appropriate to the circumstances of her or his birth. Tosin's brothers and sister were born in a comfortable era, before the Nigerian middle class was annihilated by the reforms wrought by an economic restructuring program. Their names are celebratory. The first-born son's name, Olumide, proclaims that 'God has arrived' to bless the newly married couple. His sister's name, Olajoke, means 'an adorable girl bringing wealth'. Then came Biodun, the 'festival child', born in the Christmas season.

After this my neighbors felt too 'sapped' – Nigeria's IMF-approved economic reforms rejoice in the name of the Structural Adjustment Program, or SAP – to have any more children. So did I. I ignored the constant hinting from my mother-in-law.

'Ah Mummy,' I would frequently explain, 'times are changing. People can't afford big families any more. Look at Mama Olu next door. She also stopped at three.'

'I suppose it's sensible,' my mother-in-law would sigh. 'Everything needs so much money nowadays. School fees, hospital bills, food, transport... I don't know how anyone manages at all.' Indeed since Mama Olu and I had our first-borns the value of the naira has slipped drastically. The resultant inflation has done more to promote the cause of family planning in Africa's most populous nation than any amount of moralizing over the perils of overpopulation. Nowadays the average family size amongst the Yorubas is six children. A decade ago it was nearly nine.

Then Mama Olu dropped her bombshell. Little Tosin was on the way. What with biological clocks ticking away and winding down, next door went for their 'quota'. Four children is the officially recommended maximum family size for Nigerians. Mother-in-law and sundry aunties fired a few more salvoes in my direction.

'It's not too late for you either,' they chorused. But what to call a 1993 child? My eldest, Adenike, grew into her name, 'one needing petting and constant care'. Nike developed diabetes when she was 11 years old. She has a quicksilver temper, arising from a finely honed sense of justice. There was little choice about Babajide, my middle child's name. He was the first son to be born into the family following his grandfather's death. He was 'father who had woken up'.

Today's babies' names carry more pointed messages. Ireti, 'Hope', is enjoying a revival, but more common are names which combine prayer tinged with desperation such as Oluyomi ('God save me'), or Oluwasanmi ('Maybe God will favor me').

Little Tosin's naming ceremony was a simple affair. Nowadays guest lists are pared to the bare bone; spring water replaces the alcoholic drinks that were freely offered to guests a decade ago, and a goat is killed instead of a cow. But at least Tosin's arrival and naming was celebrated.

As I crossed the gorge separating our estate from Lagos' five-star Sheraton Hotel last week I stopped, always nosy, to investigate the cause of a large crowd gazing over the bridge into the bush below. Two young men were bringing up a baby someone had noticed dumped with the rubbish. She was alive and seemed well. Amid the murmurs of concern and voices raised in indignation that Nigeria has come to such a pass that mothers throw away such 'fine babies', the little girl had a most unorthodox naming ceremony. One stout matron insisted, 'Such a child can only bear one name. She must be called Ebunolu.'

It means 'gift from God'.

A way with waste

In Lagos even knickers and nail-clippings may find themselves recycled.

Nigeria is a nation of hoarders and savers. As someone who compulsively squirrels away rubbish I have found my spiritual home. I spend my life surrounded by clutter. Empty jam jars and sauce bottles weigh down kitchen shelves, cardboard boxes are kept 'just in case', stacks of 'rough paper', used on one side, litter my office. Although the world's worst seamstress I find it hard to part with any old clothes which might be, but never are, made into something else.

Occasionally storms hit the household, forcing a bout of spring cleaning. Usually it's an impending visit from Mother, but the recent stay-at-home pro-democracy protests whipped up a hurricane of activity and bad temper as I fought to work at home under a deluge of children's books, toys, videotapes and grown-up debris.

I sold off the jam jars to the 'glass-jar woman'. A young man reeled out of my house under a meter-high stack of old newspapers. I sold the stack for 30 naira and made his morning. He will resell them at twice the price. Assorted plastic bottles and plastic cooking-oil cans went to the man who collects such stuff. Old clothes I considered beyond redemption made a miraculous reappearance on the backs of the neighborhood's squatter children. The local 'bender', or welder, came to take away any old iron.

We carefully stored away old wood. In these days of perennial kerosene and bottled gas shortages and a looming power-workers' strike, no-one knows when they will be reverting to wood fires for cooking.

A man with a bicycle collected what would have gone in the dustbin, piling all before him in a swaying basket-tower of Pisa. I tried to help him by taking the overflow down to the local dump by car. The help wasn't appreciated and I soon found out why. I had hardly drawn to a halt before three young men bore down upon the boot of my car, wrenched it open, unloaded the contents and fought over the spoils. They fought over the kitchen-bin contents, broken polystyrene packaging, old lightbulbs, torn and mauled old lino, and various spoilt car parts which even the ingenuity of the local mechanic had been unable to renovate. Clearly I had deprived our regular waste collector of unappreciated valuables.

One has to take care that nothing of a 'personal' nature ever goes into the dustbin. I once caught my next-door neighbor burning her old knickers to prevent them turning up elsewhere. Hair and nail-clippings are always flushed down the toilet for fear of them ending up on the fetish stall of the local juju market.

There is very little about waste recycling that the West can teach Nigerians. Poverty forces people to find a use for virtually everything. Little wonder that Lagos State's most spectacular white elephants, three American-designed, state-of-the-art waste disposal plants could never be used because the volume of appropriate waste was so low. After a dozen years standing idle they were recently decommissioned, stripped for scrap and sold off for alternative use.

You might imagine then that Lagos is one of the cleanest cities on earth. It isn't. The waste that absolutely no-one can use masses in infrequently cleared dumps blocking roads and marketplaces. The smell is appalling. Everywhere in Nigeria the last Saturday morning of every month is compulsorily devoted to an 'Environmental'. Movement is prohibited and anyone found out and about doing anything but cleaning up courts arrest and a stiff fine. But when the public sanitation exercise is over, after the scavengers have worked over the rubbish and gutter slops have been piled along the roadsides, there still remains the final disposal problem. A problem tackled by desultory public authorities.

Public carelessness and the creation of rubbish on a massive scale contrasts sharply with the values of the people who have next to nothing. The paper-feed from my computer printer went mysteriously missing for months until it turned up posing as an ornament on my housemaid's shelf. 'I liked its shape,' she said, adding, 'I thought it was a broken toy.'

'It's a real shame,' said Aji, my lawyer friend, when I told her the tale, 'because for most of our people that's all life in the late 20th century means: a collection of alien artefacts. Some can be found a use for, but most are simply ornamental curiosities.'

No hair for Josie

The raw deal that widows get in Nigeria.

My friend Josie had the most beautiful waist-long black hair imaginable. But that was a year ago, before armed robbers cut short the life of her young husband. Josie, a part-Yoruba from the west of Nigeria, had married an Igbo, from the east. According to Igbo custom the widow must shave her head after her husband's burial. Josie and her husband were thoroughly Westernized Nigerians. Out of pity her husband's people decided they would let her off lightly.

Josie told me that she believed the old village women were just going to take a symbolic snip of hair which wouldn't show. But just as she thought they were untying her pony-tail she heard a tremendous scrunch and her hair, still tied up, was chopped off. They stopped short of shaving her bald. She left her appalled mother-in-law and sister-in-law, who had no more anticipated the savage cut than she had, and high-tailed it out of the village and back to Lagos.

Her first call was to the hairdresser to have her ragged bob recut into a style her husband would never have recognized. But Josie ranks among the luckier of Nigerian widows. She wasn't forced to wear black for a year, not wash for a month, drink the water used to bathe her husband's corpse, maintain a dusk-to-dawn curfew or submit to any other distressing practices often inflicted upon widows in the name of tradition. She was not inherited by her husband's brother or nephews. Nor did her husband's family storm the family home to make away with the couple's property.

Her worst experience was to arrive home after the harrowing three-day funeral to discover that the electricity had been cut for three days, leaving her freezer in a stinking mess. Well-provided-for and with supportive in-laws, she now has 'only' to cope with raising her two baby daughters by herself – and with her grief.

Most Nigerian widows have very much more to bear. Just over a year ago a military transport plane carrying around 200 officers and schoolchildren dropped from the skies into an inner-city swamp. Everyone on board died a horrible death as the plane became entombed in the ooze. Nigeria's military rulers promised the victims' families heaven on earth.

A year later the widows of the officers publicly challenged the military to make good their promises. They said they had been forgotten; that only well-connected relatives of the victims had managed to receive any compensation. Compensation hadn't reached the immediate families of the deceased. They said their children were yet to receive the promised bursaries for their education.

The army waded into the controversy. With some truth, the army maintained that compensation had been paid to the officers' next-of-kin.

It was just that very few of the men had named their wives as next-of-kin. In Nigeria it is an unusual man who declares his wife to be next-of-kin. Those who do, and let it become known, endure serious pestering from relatives who attempt to convince him that he is courting death through poisoning at the hands of a wife intent on realizing her inheritance.

Under most customary laws the wife cannot inherit land or property. Under Islamic law the wife is entitled to only a quarter of her husband's estate. Under common law, inherited from the British, everything depends on whether the man has made a will or not. Most don't. If they die intestate, many widows will opt for the crumbs they can grab from the customary carve-up of the man's estate, knowing that the legal fees and bribes necessary to secure their just inheritance would probably swallow it entirely.

There was one widow I knew who left her wealthy husband's body to lie for months on ice. There had been no love lost between them as he had taken younger wives in later years, leaving her unhappy and hard up, but with the family house as a roof over her head.

'Let him rot there,' had been her response when charged with the responsibility of burying him. 'He chose to die without leaving a will. This is his house and his people are trying every day to throw me out. His bastard children are claiming what should belong to my children. And you tell me, my sister – what money do I have to bribe the judge to rule that we get our fair share?

'No, let his brothers and sisters bury him. I'm keeping my money for living.'

Siren values

The only children in Nigeria who learn practical skills at school are the ones who don't need them.

'Would you believe it Mum? Mum! Listen now! It just blew up!'

At last Nike, my 13-year-old daughter, has my undivided attention. I stop trying to force my way into the unending stream of traffic at the crowded junction by her school and park by the roadside to wait for the road to clear.

'What blew up, Nixie?' I ask.

'Don't call me Nixie! And Muuuuu-um how can you stop just here? What an embarrassment! Please I beg you, don't TALK to ANYONE! I'm going to DIE! Please Mum, MOVE!'

Nike is cringing in the back seat willing the earth to crack open and swallow her up. Even her much less sensitive 12-year-old brother Jide shows concern. 'Look Mum, the "yellow fever" is sorting out the jam. Let's try to get out,' he pleads.

Obligingly I start up the car and nudge my way forward. I set all my flashers flashing, a signal to the orange-shirted traffic warden – the 'yellow fever' – that I want to go straight across the junction and not turn right into the heart of the traffic chaos. Helpfully he forces a Mercedes to back up and a BMW to shift forward and ever so carefully I squeeze between their gleaming bumpers through to the empty road ahead.

'Thank you,' I call to the saluting 'yellow fever' before accelerating away with a tractor-like roar and a clatter of dangling exhaust pipe.

'I'm dead,' moans a little voice from the back seat.

'What blew up, Nix?' I return to her first concern. 'Have you been hurt?' I strain into the rear view mirror to see if I have missed evidence of a terrible injury. She seems intact.

'I'm destroyed! When are you going to get a new car? This one's beyond a joke. I've never been so EMBARRASSED.'

Ah, my poor rust-ravaged, much-dented, hardy little 1979 Toyota is going to be verbally savaged again. It's just one of many equally decrepit old wrecks out on the highways of Lagos. But there is a better class of traffic jam around Nike and Jide's school. Most pupils are picked up by their parents' drivers and most parents are 'made-it' politicians, bankers and sundry professionals. Army 'made-its' have their own military schools. There is no kudos at all to be had from being collected by one's mother in a jalopy.

'Most children in this country have to walk to school. You are both lucky...' I stop my well-rehearsed diatribe as I catch sight of Jide sawing away at an imaginary violin. 'So what blew up?' I ask yet again.

'My technology project,' wails Nike.

'What? A bookshelf?' I am puzzled.

'No! No! No! We're not doing carpentry any more. I told you ages ago. It's my SIREN that blew up. We all have to know how to build a siren, and mine blew up when I switched it on, and now I have to go to school on Saturday and start again.' Nike is fuming.

On the list of skills important for survival in Nigeria, teaching teenagers from the country's élite how to build their own siren is probably one of the more important. Anyone who is anyone – or any bank clerk shifting cash between banks – is accompanied on their way by official cars with sirens blaring and police hanging out of car windows thrashing motorists who don't move aside quickly enough with a koboko, a form of cat o'nine tails.

What other practical skills could wealthy teenagers learn? My mind leaps to laundering. My first 'laundering' thought was prompted by the acres of crisply starched robes worn by both men and women of substance which get changed at least twice daily – and more on special occasions when one changes for every stage of a social function.

Laundering of the other variety might also be a useful skill to learn. Nigeria must be the only country where the disgraced Bank of Credit and Commerce International, BCCI, continues to flourish under a changed name.

But let me not pillory my poor children's school. Ironically I sent them there precisely so that they would experience a full curriculum, especially the practical aspects dropped from the overcrowded, underfunded state school curricula. In addition to siren-making, my children have hoed up a productive little farm, learnt chicken- and rabbit-keeping, made concrete blocks, and learned a range of skills from cooking and cleaning using traditional methods to computer technology and *adire* cloth-dying. The irony is that the Nigerian secondary curriculum, meant for all and emphasizing the vocational practical skills desperately needed for development, is only enjoyed by children of parents with enough money to pay for the better private schools.

Vanity Fair

Hair and skin become victims in the battle for beauty.

Midweek. Midmorning. A time when I should have been working. A time when visitors rarely call. But I'm not working. I'm lurking furtively around the remotest garden tap. My hair appears to have had an affair with the compost heap. It is full of green bits and every now and then a trickle of rust appears on my neck and face to dry like blood on my skin. I am not a pretty sight. I am undergoing a beauty treatment.

At forty-something, and greying, vanity has got the better of me. It was a chance encounter with Ilona, my Hungarian friend, at the school gate that began my transformation into a mildewed vision from hell. 'Eleezabetta. Oh Eleezabetta,' she warbled. 'Why you no look beautiful any more? Why you let all this grey come? Don't you know we married Nigerians eh? So you want to let a young and beautiful second, perhaps third, wife to come and share your husband now? Yes? No: you must get rid of the grey. Yes.'

Now my husband had never mentioned my grey hair or much else for that matter about my appearance. Maybe he was quietly casting a roving eye elsewhere. Ilona was positive he had to be. She arrived

that evening with a 'nearly-black' wash-out-in-six-shampoos hair color. It was past its sell-by date; common enough for Nigerian imports which range from British right-hand-drive cars which have failed their roadworthiness tests – Nigerians need left-hand-drive cars – to Italian toxic waste and ancient EU beef surpluses.

That night I had nearly black hair. My husband didn't notice. However, he did notice my purple hair the following night. I don't know whether it was the out-of-date chemicals or the tropical sun that achieved the purple look but my husband waxed scornful about people – like me – who risk their health using lead-based blackening pomades (another British export) to destroy the 'distinguished' look of grey hair. He's getting grey hair too.

I told him I hadn't used lead, arsenic, asbestos or any other poison or carcinogen as a beauty aid. He said the results spoke for themselves and, lapsing into sarcasm, said I was clearly the sort to try out a skin-lightener to restore my weather-beaten white skin to a pink and creamy childhood complexion. Mercury-based bleaching creams, another British contribution to the dermatological health of African nations, were banned by the Nigerian Government in 1988, but are nevertheless freely available and used by many Nigerian women who believe that black is not beautiful. 'Fanta faces,' the local kids call them, after the fizzy orange drink. 'Fair-skinned' is how the consumer sees herself, and mercury-poisoning and taut, paper-thin, permanently ruined skin seems a small price to pay.

By the same token, visiting whites sacrifice themselves to melanomas, despite vastly superior European health education, by sunning themselves under the scorching tropical sun – and all for a more beautiful brown skin.

But back to my purple hair. My kids thought the purple was deliberate; a calculated act designed to embarrass them by adopting a pathetically dated punk hairstyle. I was ordered not to show my face near the school gates until 'something had been done'. There was only blond hair-color left on the supermarket shelf. I balked, fed up with out-of-date beauty aids from a bottle, and went to the market in search of something 'natural'. The herbs and spices trader didn't speak English. So a lot of people volunteered to explain my need for something to turn my hair another color, preferably brown.

She understood and shoveled a medium-sized plastic bag full of crushed leaves I took on trust to be henna. She mimed that I should mix them to a green gunge with water and plaster this over my hair. I got the message and headed home. I went to the bathroom first but soon discovered that henna leaves a trail like the aftermath of a chainsaw massacre.

Out in the garden I thought I would never wash the gritty green particles from my hair. It didn't help that the government water tap ran dry halfway through the palaver. But I did get rid of the grey and the purple. My natural brown looked browner, and the grey...

'What do you call that color?' asked my youngest. 'Autumn leaves,' I said, pleased with myself. 'What's autumn?' he said.

'A time when Europeans become senile and their brain cells die off,' said my husband, who at last has begun to notice my appearance.

Blood money

Elizabeth's night guard is attacked and wounded.

It was three in the morning when the doorbell rang and rang with frantic urgency. There was the sound of a commotion in the compound and my husband and I woke up, scared stiff. 'Armed robbers.' The thought passed silently between us and fear rose from our stomachs to gag in our throats.

Whoever was ringing the doorbell couldn't be seen from the window. 'Come to the back door,' we shouted, and breathed a sigh of relief to see Amina, the young and very pregnant wife of the night guard. She was wielding a bloody cutlass.

'Thieves murdered my husband,' she wailed. Sick at heart, we unbolted the back door to face whatever was there, armed only with another cutlass and a golfing umbrella. We tried phoning the police but the line was cut off with each attempt. In any case we had found out once before that the police only come when you go and fetch them and pay them something for their trouble.

Our relief upon seeing the 'murdered' man stagger around the corner drenched in blood was profound. He thrust his head under the garden tap to wash away the blood but this was no scratch on the head. I had no idea how high blood could spurt until I tried to staunch the wound on Zachariah's skull. Towel after towel was pressed down on the wound. But the bleeding wouldn't stop and it became obvious that he would bleed to death if we waited for morning.

Collecting all the money we could lay hands on, my husband and I set off with Zachariah and Amina to seek help. We made one last nervous patrol of the compound to check that the thieves had gone and found trails of blood over plants and paths. Amina had certainly left her mark with the cutlass. Slightly reassured, I bolted myself into the house and waited. Not once did my three children stir from their sleep.

As dawn broke Tunde, my husband, returned. It had been a long night. The night watches of the private hospitals had refused to open their gates to a 'police case'. The doctors in the public hospital were sympathetic but had no tools to work with.

Leaving Amina with money to register Zachariah as a casualty patient, Tunde had embarked on a search for all-night pharmacies. He had to buy cotton wool, surgical tape, bandages, suture thread, surgical sewing needles, syringes, paracetamol, disinfectant, surgical spirit, iodine, blood plasma, intravenous drip solutions, needles and tubes. Only the anti-tetanus vaccines and antibiotics could be bought from the hospital pharmacy but first he had to find the cashier to issue an official receipt to exchange for the drugs. The cashier was asleep somewhere. The pharmacist wouldn't issue the drugs without the receipt and in casualty Zachariah was lying on a bench, bleeding to death.

But he didn't die. Tunde got what he could from pharmacies open at that ungodly hour of the morning. What he couldn't find, the doctor fetched from his personal supplies at home, kept for 'real emergencies'. Zachariah was sewn up without a local anesthetic and Tunde was sent back to the slumbering cashier to pay for a week's admission to hospital. He then went next door to the police headquarters to report the incident.

In the morning I took my turn on the hospital shift. Linen had to be taken in to cover the filthy plastic mattresses upon which patients lay. X-rays had to be purchased from the radiography department. Blood tests had to be bought from the private labs clustered around the hospital gates. Zachariah needed blood. I set off to buy some from the AIDS-infested blood banks which feed from the people passing through the neighborhood bus- and car-parks. I was told to come back later. Was the blood really necessary? I pleaded with the doctor – still the same man who had been on duty throughout the day and the night before. Well, he said, maybe Zachariah could manage, just. He was young and strong and yes, the blood might leave him with more problems than he had now.

As I left casualty, a formidable Sister and hospital security staff were in hot dispute with a taxi-driver who had brought in an unconscious and bleeding road-traffic victim. The boy was left on the hospital trolley to roast in the car park under a blazing mid-morning sun. His penniless friend pleaded with staff to release the taxi-driver, who had only acted as a Good Samaritan. They were implacable. The taxi wasn't moving until the driver paid for the boy's treatment.

I left, amazed that the world monetary authorities could still be demanding cuts in public service spending from a government which has all but abandoned any pretence of providing public services.

Your money or your bank

Why saving in Nigeria is such a hazardous business.

It is 8.30am and the air over the breakfast-table is blue with domestic tension. My husband has delayed me and he knew I had set aside today to go to the bank. Now it's too late. Unless I join the small army of customers waiting for the bank gates to swing open at eight o'clock sharp I have no chance of withdrawing any money in less than an hour.

By 8.30am the banking hall is full and not even soldiers from the local army cantonment, who bring all the military menace they can to bear upon the bank cashiers, can cash their pay checks in much less than three hours.

We bank at one of the 'old' banks. You can count their number on the fingers of one hand. But our money is as safe with them as anybody's money can be safe in this crumbling economy. If they fail the country is truly finished. A few years ago the antiquated methods of our bank drove us to open a new account with a 'second generation' bank. In 1986 the introduction of the Structural Adjustment Program (SAP) meant financial deregulation, which led to a host of new banks. With their computers, marble counters and canned classical music, these were like a breath of fresh air to those of us tired of and fed up with the old ones.

Here were banks where you weren't forced to forge intimate physical relationships with other hapless customers wedged into the scrummage round each cashier's post. Here were banks which didn't exchange your check for a plastic disc which, hours later, at the bank's convenience, you could exchange for cash – assuming the man with the keys to the bank vault had turned up for work.

The post-SAP banks were lovely. Clean, cool, short orderly queues, no discs and smiling staff. The new banks were also mainly for the rich. They demanded opening balances far beyond the means of the ordinary men or women who were still forced to spend hour upon hour in the savings halls of the old banks. Major banks aren't interested in small savers and the Government, under pressure from various international development agencies, has fostered the establishment of 'people's banks' and 'community banks' to serve the poor with varying degrees of success.

But let me not deviate into the role banks could play in nurturing development. This is Nigeria. What other role could there be for banks in Nigeria if not to allow important bankers to lead a 'London today, New York tomorrow' lifestyle?

Ever alive to the possibilities of realizing easy access to the international jet set, Nigerians took to the newly deregulated banking environment like ducks to water. International monetary experts pronounced the nation 'underbanked'. True. And busy as the proverbial beavers, Nigerians set about remedying the situation.

Over 200 new banks were set up during the seven years of SAP. Intended to spread the reach of banking to all of Nigeria's nearly 90 million citizens and to release long-term loans for national development, Nigeria's new banks did nothing of the sort. Many were one-branch operations concentrated along particular streets in Lagos. All of them were looking for quick returns on their capital. Some, it was said, were just fronts for laundering illicitly gained money.

They fought for depositors by offering 20, 30 and sometimes even higher percentage-rates on savings. They raked in the money and speculated heavily on short-term investments, mainly foreign-exchange trading. They had a ball. Then the 1994 budget re-regulated the foreign exchange market and interest rates were pegged at 12 per cent for savers and 21 per cent for borrowers. Inflation galloped away at 100 per cent. Suddenly depositors wanted their money back from the new banks, which had to face the prospect of collapse.

My friend Aji has been to her new-breed 'merchant' bank every day this year in a vain attempt to claw back a fixed deposit. Inside their prime-site headquarters the pot plants have died. The chrome fittings have tarnished, the carpets are muddied and the haze of sweaty palm-prints over the glass separating cashiers from their angry customers shows all too clearly that the modern banking party is over. Going to the bank in Nigeria was, is and seems set always to be an unmitigated nightmare. And Tunde and I have still to settle our domestic dispute.

Shadow boxing

How the ethnic card is being played by those in power in Nigeria.

As an academic, as a journalist, and as a foreigner, I have commented on difficult situations with an ethnic dimension. I have met with people who for one reason or another are deeply afraid. Sometimes I cried and felt sick – but I would edit out the tears from a broadcasting package or written despatch. I never internalized those outrages – they weren't my problem. I could only ape Solomon and attempt balanced and unprejudiced comment, often coming down firmly on one side or another after weighing up all the facts.

Recent events in Nigeria have changed me. They have given me the unpleasant experience of being a player rather than a mere spectator. At the time of writing nothing too terrible, measured on the scale of human dreadfulness, has happened. For a military regime, the Nigerian Government's reaction to week upon week of pro-democracy strikes and demonstrations has been quite mild. In the south a handful of demonstrators have died in scattered protests. Some opposition leaders have been imprisoned but most were quickly released. The Nigerian 'soldier-boys' seem not to be cast from the same mold as Latin American military dictators or sergeants-turned-despots like Idi Amin, Bokassa and Samuel Doe.

Both the northern Hausa-backed military élite and the largely southern-based pro-democracy campaigners appear to be mindful of the Biafran war. It is nearly 30 years now since that conflict claimed a million Nigerian lives and introduced the world to the now-familiar imagery of starving African refugees and children. No-one wants to commit the first atrocity, to risk a repeat of that terrible ethnic bloodbath.

In late July, the ethnic card was played. Moshood Abiola, the Yoruba winner of last year's canceled presidential elections, was arrested by the police. It was a time of shadow-boxing for most Nigerians. Lagos's six million inhabitants held their breath expecting the worst, but no catastrophe occurred.

Last year, when the military annulled the elections, everyone dashed fearfully back to their 'ethnic' home areas. This year they sat tight. 'Who has the money to go home for holidays, let alone to pack out and pack back every time there is trouble?' said my friend Noney, who comes from the eastern Igbo city of Emugu.

For myself, I felt profound relief that my husband's veins are half-full of Yoruba blood and my children's therefore a quarter-full. Most importantly in Nigeria, as that blood is paternally inherited and therefore significant, they are considered to be entirely Yoruba. Lagos is a Yoruba city and so they are safe, ethnically secure.

Ethnic security has become a factor to be dealt with in our family life. I could never rest easy if my children should choose to go to school or university or to work in northern Nigeria. Ironic, really, since my first love for Nigeria was born in its northern states in 1974, where I worked as an expatriate. I loved the whole area. My husband too, after years of living in London, preferred to holiday in the north with Hausa friends rather than face the drastic pleasures of his Lagos home.

Now an evil ethnic wedge is being forced between Nigeria's 200-odd ethnic groups. Ties of inter-ethnic friendship, preferences for environments other than your ancestral ones, and the urge to better your employment wherever the job may be, are being perverted by ethnicity. Unfortunately this is partly due to some well-intentioned Government schemes to provide equal educational opportunities throughout Nigeria. Public services and government-sponsored employment are ethnically balanced. This has nurtured ethnic sensibilities which might otherwise have been subsumed by a wider identity as a 'Nigerian citizen'.

At the root of current concern for ethnic identity lies, inevitably, the desire for power and money. Political power in Nigeria was vested by British colonialists in the hands of the feudal northern aristocracy and 90 per cent of Government income comes from southern oil sales. It is an explosive combination exacerbated by worsening poverty. No ruler wants to lose their hold on the purse strings. Every poverty-stricken area feels hard done by. Ethnic blame is easy to apportion. But as greedy politicians and generals heighten ethnic awareness, Nigeria's 90 million ordinary citizens quake in their shoes.

Bello, the technician at my husband Tunde's workplace, discarded his Hausa-style clothes in late July. He now sports Western or Yoruba-style dress. When teased about this, he replies: 'You may laugh but this may become a life-or-death-issue – sooner rather than later.'

Phoning for democracy

Mobile phones in Nigeria are the playboy's toy – but they have other uses.

The ragged youth stood center-stage on a traffic island in the middle of the Lagos morning 'go-slow' – elsewhere known as the 'rush hour' – and held an animated conversation on his mobile phone. He chuckled. He struck aggressive business poses. He whispered and laughed and slapped his thighs. His left hand traced expansive projects in the sky. His whole being was concentrated on his never-ending telephone conversation.

Would you dare interrupt such intense conversation? He'd be delighted. For with acting skills which would do a national drama company credit – if Nigeria had one – this young boy, straight from the village, is avoiding destitution by selling the latest hot item to be sold through the Lagos traffic jams: a fake cellular phone.

Telephony in general is still strictly for those with money. Cell phones are for businesses and for the super-rich, but for a fraction of the price you can now fool your friends and pose as one of the élite. In many ways mobile technology is the ideal means of providing a telephone service for Nigeria's 90 million people. They live scattered in towns and villages which spread from the vast desert expanse of the Sahara's southern fringe, southwards through savannah and the virgin rainforests across the mountains of the Cameroon borderlands to where Nigeria meets the Atlantic Ocean in a morass of inaccessible mangrove swamps and deltaic lagoons.

Nowhere is very suitable for the laying of telephone land lines. The latest colonists of the southern swamplands, the oil companies, use radio communication. How wonderful cellular telephone networks would be for reaching the villages that few other services can reach. As it is, mobile phones are merely the ultimate fashion accessory in the few major Nigerian cities covered by cellular phone networks. The

phones lie concealed in the voluminous starched gowns worn by both men and women without ruining the fashionable cut of the cloth.

In recent months the cellular telephone has begun to rehabilitate its playboy, drug-dealer image and carve for itself an heroic role as a key tool in the pro-democracy movement. The mobile phone shot to prominence when we listened, rapt, one evening to the blow-by-blow account of the arrest of a former state governor recorded live by the BBC's *Focus on Africa* radio news program – via the politician's mobile phone.

The ex-governor, Chief Segun Osoba, a one-time BBC correspondent, knew the value of international news media broadcasting in a country where local media are severely restricted. He had phoned the BBC as soon as he was arrested. The military Government chafed at Western media imperialism but there were few Nigerians that evening who remained unaware of the arrest of one of the country's leading pro-democracy activists.

After that incident the security police learned to search the robes of political detainees for their cell phones. The mobile phone was also the glue which held the pro-democracy oil workers' strike together from June to September. The strike leaders played cat-and-mouse with Nigerian security operatives and co-ordinated the strike by phone.

They weren't a natural tool for the cash-strapped trade unionists. Journalists phoning one prominent strike leader would have to have their questions well prepared and brief, as he would only allow two minutes for each interview. The union couldn't afford to pay the exorbitant charges for receiving calls charged by the telephone parastatal.

It is unfortunate, but trifling, that one by-product of the end of the pro-democracy strike is that mobile phone-users in Nigeria will once again run the risk of being identified as fraudsters and drug barons instead of men and women of political principle. Those involved in the political struggle have had their bank balances drained by months of activism. They can't afford to use mobile phones even if they had them. Sad really that such a useful technology may once again become identified with the affluence that accompanies such dubious lifestyles.

A gust of pure evil

Servants who are witches; sorcerers in the office.

It's the Sunday evening prayer fellowship at a neighbor's house. Against a background of sympathetic murmuring from a dozen or more shocked matrons and young evangelists, Auntie Vee is testifying how a commonplace enquiry over a plot of land turned into a trip to the fringes of the spirit world.

'I just wasn't sure about the plot Mama Olu was offering me,' began Auntie Vee. 'Mama Olu said she would swear on a bible that there was nothing wrong.'

So Auntie Vee took Mama Olu to a reputable reverend gentleman nearby. Both ladies were attended by their housegirls. The reverend gentleman greeted Auntie Vee and Mama Olu but found himself unable to pass by Kudirat, Auntie Vee's 10-year-old housegirl.

'This is serious. Come with me,' he said. The two ladies and Kudirat trailed after him. They emerged two hours later. The land issue had been forgotten, overwhelmed by far greater concern about Kudirat. The reverend gentleman had been hit by a gust of pure evil when he first walked past her. Close questioning and prayer revealed her to be a witch and just coming into her powers.

Kudirat's induction had taken place some time during her last visit home. Her grandmother had been the one to introduce her to the coven which met, as covens usually do, at night, under the broad fronds of the plantain groves. Auntie Vee had attributed Kudirat's lean and troubled looks since returning home to poor feeding whilst away.

Now she knew better. Every night, while Auntie Vee's household slept in Lagos, Kudirat had been flying off to meet and play with her coven brothers and sisters under the plantains a hundred kilometers away in her home city, Ibadan. Deeply distressed, Auntie Vee decided that Kudirat would have to go.

Kudirat wept and wailed. She didn't want to leave Auntie Vee, who had been more of a mother to her than her own. She was strong-willed. She could disobey her mates in the coven. She hadn't done a fraction of the evil deeds she had been told to do. The recitation of these turned Auntie Vee's blood cold.

Friends and neighbors who had assembled to hear Kudirat's confession and help Auntie Vee with the crisis were agreed that she must leave. The trouble was that no-one was brave enough to take her home. But witch or not, no-one was going to put a child on a bus to travel the hundred kilometers alone.

A week passed. Kudirat spent every night sleeping at the foot of Auntie Vee's bed with CNN blaring out its world news loudly through the dark hours to drown out the phantoms of her coven mates who crowded the walls calling to her. Only with Auntie Vee did she feel safe. When power cuts silenced CNN Auntie Vee would beseech Jesus's protection. At the end of the week they were both worn out from keeping the witches at bay.

Kudirat decided to confess the source of her power. It was a charm that was hidden in her family's house in Ibadan. In the end, Auntie Vee took Kudirat home. Her 'power' was discovered and despite being a Muslim she began a 40-day fast at a church which specializes in the exorcism of witches.

Friends assure me that more and more children are becoming witches nowadays. With the economy and education lying in ruins and individual lives and aspirations destroyed, increasing numbers of people are asking themselves questions. Not: 'Why is this happening and what is the political solution?' but 'Who would wish this evil upon me?'

Ask the question 'who?' and individuals immediately come to mind. A good friend, a senior executive in one of the most corrupt parastatal

corporations, has been trying to clean up operations at work. He returned from his annual leave to find loyal staffers begging him not to enter his office. His immediate subordinate had employed the services of a powerful sorcerer, a *babalawo*, to cast evil charms about his office. My friend, a devout Christian, had no fear of them. He believed himself protected by the far greater power of Jesus Christ and reprimanded his staff for allowing their minds to be chained to the superstitious past when the 21st century is almost here.

'You can't protect yourself against poison, Liz,' advised my mother-in-law when I told her about Auntie Vee and my friend. 'That's why it's good not to let the children eat outside. You don't know what evil they might swallow. But Jesus protects against all witches. Why do you think the churches are so full nowadays? Only God can save us now in Nigeria.'

Letters from Russia and Chechnya 1995-1997

Olivia Ward

I'm an inveterate traveler, and lucky enough to have a job that accommodates it. But it was a great surprise to me when the *Toronto Star* appointed me bureau chief for the Former Soviet Union, a daunting sweep of territory. From 1992 to 1997 I was based in Moscow, reporting on Armenia, Azerbaijan, Ukraine, Georgia, the Baltics, Belarus and Tajikistan as well as Russia. Unexpectedly, much of my time was spent at wars, including the devastating conflict in Chechnya.

Working in this area was more than a job, it was something that got into the bloodstream. I was privileged to be there at a historic moment of hope, chaos, freedom and tragedy that was extraordinary and unique. After leaving Moscow in 1997 I continued covering the region, as London-based European bureau chief. Now, as the *Star*'s foreign affairs writer, my scope is even wider, and includes most of the world. But Russia is very much on my mind.

I was born in Scotland but grew up in Vancouver, Canada. After university and freelance writing I joined the editorial board of the *Toronto Star* and became foreign correspondent at large, based at the United Nations in New York.

Now, in my 'spare time', I work with the Bishari Films company headed by Shelley Saywell. Her documentary *A Child's Century of War*, based on my stories from Chechnya, was shortlisted for an Academy Award. One of my **NI** columns became the text for a war requiem titled *Chechnya Story*, by the British composer Clement Jewitt. It was premiered at the Birmingham Conservatory.

Changes in Russia (and Chechnya)

The 1990s were one of the most tumultuous decades in Russian history. The collapse of the Soviet Union and of Communist rule in 1991 brought sweeping changes. A society that had been unchanging and arthritic for decades plunged to the opposite extreme as state controls were abandoned for the whirlwind of the free market. Under the negligent presidency of Boris Yeltsin, whole state industries were given away to individuals who made fortunes, and gangsterism flourished while the poor found themselves in welfare lines. It was into this maelstrom that Olivia Ward landed in 1992 and her letters to the *New Internationalist* from 1994 onwards conveyed a vivid picture of a people in painful transition.

The end of the Soviet Union was also, though, the end of a form of empire. And while many countries wriggled free of control from Moscow – from Estonia in the northwest to Kazakhstan in the southeast – other peoples found it much less easy to assert their independence. Olivia reported from many of the Russian republics that are little mentioned in the West, such as Daghestan and Ingushetia, but found herself preoccupied by the war in Chechnya. The people of Chechnya have battled against Russia for centuries, under the leadership of Sheikh Mansur in the 18th century and Imam Shamil in the 19th. The country was finally annexed by the Russian Empire in 1859 but the resistance continued – Tolstoy's novella *The Cossacks* is drawn from his own experiences as a Russian soldier occupying Chechnya. In the wake of the Soviet collapse, Chechnya declared its independence in October 1991 but the Yeltsin Government rejected this and from 1994 invaded the territory, bombing the capital, Grozny, to ruins. By 1996 at least 40,000 civilians had been killed and 300,000 uprooted from their homes. A peace agreement was signed in 1997, allowing Russia to reopen the vital Chechen section of its oil pipeline, but war restarted in 1999, with the Chechen rebels clearly stating that they were fighting for an Islamic state.

When Vladimir Putin, a former KGB operative, succeeded Yeltsin as President in 2000, he took the opportunity to redefine his war against the Chechens as an 'anti-terrorist' operation in the wake of the 9/11 attacks on the US. Putin also played the anti-terrorist card at home to consolidate his own power and exert greater control, but proved popular with many Russians for reasserting a level of economic stability derived from soaring oil and gas prices. In 2008, unable to stand for a third presidential term, he nominated his own replacement, Dmitry Anatolevich Medvedev, and agreed to become prime minister.

The honest colonel

Traveling south with a soldier who paid the price of exile for his honesty.

The Colonel was proud of his American tape-player and he hummed to it softly as we lumbered along the dust-choked roads to a village not even the locals could identify. He spoke no English, but something in the song on his tape appealed to him. Above the wheeze of truck engines, a gritty American voice sang about freedom, the loneliness of the open road and the courage to strike out for the unknown.

In profile, the Colonel's rugged tanned face with its jet-pilot sunglasses was a mirror-image of the US military officers who inspire troops and win invitations to run for Congress. Their sports-clad blonde wives look at them with unflagging admiration. They live in glass houses and throw no stones.

Life has not worked that way for the Colonel. His home is half a one-roomed flat in a sleepy provincial town, his wife struggles for survival in another country and his only brush with politics was at the sharp end of a Russian Government tank.

It was there that the Colonel and I met, or narrowly escaped meeting, in October 1993. We stood on the embankment facing the Russian White House as tank fire blasted blazing holes in the masonry and bullets whined in the bushes.

I was waiting for the inevitable surrender of the rebellion leader to round up a long day's story. But the Colonel had come too late for the hopeless task of saving the Parliament, and was waiting for nothing.

Now, a year later, by a quirk of fate the two of us were face to face in the south of Russia in the Colonel's sturdy Lada. The officer who had commanded soldiers in every hot-spot of the former Soviet Union was driving a journalist to visit a remote army settlement for more money than he had ever seen in a military pay check.

Three years after his discharge, one month short of his 25-year service, the Colonel was still wearing military fatigues. He could not separate himself from the institution that was his pride, his shame and his torment.

'One tried to be honest but honesty is not a requirement,' he said quietly. 'When they told me to take charge of a unit, to impose order, I thought they meant to apply human standards. I was always wrong.'

In the corrupt military establishment the Colonel, then a rising officer, refused to close his eyes to the bribes, the arms sales, the drunkenness and barbaric cruelty. He joined the Communist Party in the vain hope that tapping the ideological source would give him strength. When he found out the truth he was expelled for insubordination.

But he paid his dues to a system that existed as a shimmering mirage, always beyond his grasp. His honest reputation worked against him. He was thrown from the deserts of Mongolia to the barrens of Siberia. To Afghanistan, Central Asia, then Moldova, where his family was stuck with no money to move and nowhere to go.

The wounds of his service still smarting, the Colonel felt a great rage wash over him. Democracy had solved nothing. The days and months spent alone in the southern backwater, patiently waiting his turn for a military flat that always went to somebody with better connections, exploded inside his head. He still had his strength, and a gun.

'I thought the country would have one last chance for justice,' he said. 'But when I looked into the faces of the people who were trying to take over, I saw the same old chronic sickness.'

Now he has locked up his gun. There is nothing to save or defend, he says. But his name has been put on a list of enemies of the Government and he is regularly questioned by local police.

'I'm fooling myself that I'll get an apartment,' he says with a wry smile. 'The only way is bribery and I wouldn't pay if I had the money. All I have left is my honor, the honor of a military man.' That, he said, is worth the dust that was seeping in through the car windows. He twisted the switch of the tape deck.

'Do you mind if I play the song again?' The American voice rose. 'Nobody understands me bein' so alone, but I know I'm headed home. Somewhere's the freedom road.'

We all sang.

Walnuts and sunflower seeds

Searching for signs of rebirth amid the ruins of the Chechen capital, Grozny.

Mud again. Muddy skies, muddy buildings, mud underfoot. The endless misery of it penetrates to the bone, as the dirt invades every exposed core of the body.

I've learned that living in the ruins of a city requires a special kind of endurance, the sort the great Russian poet Anna Akhmatova knew when she wrote: 'So much to do today: kill memory, kill pain, turn heart into a stone, and yet prepare to live again.'

I would like to look for signs of spring in this trampled place without heat, light or water. Instead I watch the people I know by sight, by name, in their bomb-blasted apartments. They are moving toward nothing. Everything is behind them. Each night of the war, as the rockets exploded, their reward for survival was a black hole in their lives.

Last Fall we used to chat in the central square where the men leapt and whirled in their wild Muslim dances, gold teeth gleaming and Chechen knives flashing in the frost. They were defiant, but I was afraid for them. Watching the Russian war machine cranking up in the distance, I could predict what was to come.

'Hello, have you eaten?' old Magomed would ask, pressing some walnuts and sunflower seeds into my hand no matter what the time of day.

'What she needs is real food,' Rosa would scold. 'There's no point hanging about here talking to you without some good *shashlik* under her belt.'

Guests in Chechnya are part god, part captive. To refuse hospitality, no matter how inconvenient or unaffordable, is an impossibility. A guest who is not fed within 40 minutes knows she or he is unwanted, I was regularly reminded. That, in any decent household, was a disgrace.

But as the weeks wore on, and charred Russian corpses replaced the lively crowds in the square, the people in the center depended on the hospitality of others. I retreated with them first to the outer edge of the center, then to the suburbs. The foibles, the vanities, the flamboyant humor began to fall away. Stripped of their eccentricities, people began to resemble each other. Life at the cutting edge of necessity peeled away individuality in a way that surprised me. Even I felt myself reduced to a body with freezing feet.

But I had money that would allow me to drive away, and no lifetime of possessions to abandon in the city. Visiting those who had no choice but to stay, I watched the daily routine become smaller and more desperate – a battle against hunger, cold, homelessness and the omnipresent mud that sucked at our boots as though trying to pull us down into some foul pit of Hades. Magomed and Rosa went to a village with relatives but the war found them there too. Their punishment for heaven knows what imaginary crime was to move from house to house in their old age, adding to the burden of poor families.

Mine was to watch ordinary people mutate into survivors. Each morning there was the trek to the reservoir and the usual rumors that the Russians had poisoned the water in some final, genocidal gesture. At noon perhaps the trucks of free bread from the villages would arrive. Women who were used to shopping had learned to beg.

'As for me,' said language professor Tatyana, 'I learned to loot. It really doesn't take much skill. You just have to swallow your code of ethics.'

She faced me squarely, her watery and bloodshot eyes locked on mine. 'What do you think? Is it better to ask for handouts, or help yourself? What would you do in my place?'

But there are no answers here in limbo, this place of being and non-being, where happiness, in so far as you can remember it, is the absence of pain. As Tatyana lost her morality, so the normal boundaries of civilized life have collapsed. People weep in front of strangers as they would ordinarily be ashamed to do, their heads thrown back, their mouths open in a mask of misery. Like lunatics from an old bedlam scene, they wander aimlessly, accosting unknown people in the street, telling them stories from the depths of their anguish.

In a city without calendars, we have forgotten spring. Traces of green nibble at the fringes of the mud. Rebirth and hope – one day they will mean something to us. A day when flesh prevails over bone. When the skin has grown back over the exposed nerves. When Magomed finds me in the square and holds out his hand, full of walnuts and sunflower seeds.

Love and pies at the Usinsk Cafe

Two bears are embracing on the dance-floor. Olivia comes in from the cold and discovers a sanctuary in the Russian Arctic.

The air had a clammy chill, though the small space of the room and its wood paneling made for an illusory coziness, like a welcome bomb-shelter in a time of heavy siege. But the smell in the air was of pizza, noisy Western rock music overwhelmed the conversations, and a bar lining one wall was glittering with bottles of imported wine, beer and liquor.

After days in this remote Arctic oil town that made the eyes water with bitter cold, smog and sheer ugliness, I had somehow found its hidden heart.

Each day I had talked to embittered oil workers, ruined fisherfolk and suicidal pensioners who could neither live in nor leave this land that communism built and fickle fate abandoned.

Returned to my bleak hotel after those interviews, I chopped stale black bread with a blunt knife, drank my precious supply of packaged orange juice, and wondered that all life in the town didn't end on some interminable night when the dawn carelessly forgot to pull aside its curtains for even an hour.

'What you need,' chuckled a Norwegian friend, 'is the Usinsk Café.' Without argument I followed him through long, featureless blocks of high- and low-rise buildings until at last we shoved our way through a doorway marked only by a light-bulb.

It was too cold to remove our coats and I wondered if my colleague, an experienced northerner, would be embarrassed at the sight of me eating pizza in gloves.

'Pizza, or pizza?' joked the waitress, a cheerful young woman who doubled as a disc-jockey and bartender. Some clever Arctic entrepreneur had nabbed a fast-food franchise and proudly transported the frozen pies direct from cosmopolitan Moscow.

Expecting the worst, I nodded. But, as my teeth did battle with the crust a few minutes later, my spirits unaccountably rose.

Through the smoke I squinted around me. There, on the tiny dance floor, two large bodies – were they bears or humans? – lumbered together to the trilling tunes of 'Lady in Red'. Their faces, round and androgynous under fur hats, were blissful. They were, it was obvious, very much in love.

Another couple joined them. The female partner had left her head recklessly bare to show off a mass of dyed blond curls. But her companion stared at her with undisguised adoration, ignoring her lined and weathered skin.

Behind me in the corner, yet another stolid couple sat oblivious of all around them, his hands grasping her wrists under the sleeves of her heavy coat.

Never impressed by public displays of affection, I felt a lump in my throat. None of the lovers here was young, none was beautiful by the Hollywood standards that now obsess Muscovites. And they were not casual pickups that would finish the night in my hotel, where the vicious arguments of the sex trade echoed into the wee hours.

I was transported back in history to the desperate days of Stalin's camps, where many of the wilderness settlements had their beginnings. Places where brutality and starvation were the daily fare, and survival meant sinking to the lowest common denominator.

But there too human affection survived. Women spoke of fingers touching through barbed wire, moments stolen in the shadow of guardhouses. 'The most important thing was exchanging words to affirm that we were still human beings,' said one.

Poetry was written and love letters carefully buried. And friendship too managed to survive, with astonishing bursts of compassion appearing like flowers from the frozen tundra.

'People come here to celebrate,' said the waitress, snapping me back to the present with amusement. 'Yes, even here we remember an anniversary or a birthday.'

She was laughing without rancor. This was an oasis, not a place to talk about the realities of life. Unpaid wages, burgeoning pollution, declining prospects, were all left behind at the door as those terrible conditions were blotted out for a minute or two.

Hardship was a condition of life, so what was there to discuss? In moments like these, however stark to an affluent outsider, the spirit was somehow restored.

Then the lights flickered discreetly and a kind of shock ran through the fuggy dimness. Eyes came back into focus and a look of hard awareness returned, identical with the expressions I had seen on the streets. Shoulders squared, the guests filed out into the breathless cold to face what had to be faced.

Closing time at the Usinsk Café.

The future is rising

Visiting a state farm to find things haven't changed since Soviet times – or have they?

Pink petticoats are flying and the gold-threaded felt coats of the men raise dust as they dip and swing to rollicking folk tunes.

It's the perfect Middle Russian scene: happy peasants dancing and singing while a benevolent farm boss looks down on them, beaming, from the steps above.

It is also the perfect vision of how things work in Russia, how they have always worked, and how, regardless of politics, they are changing against all odds.

'Of course you turn out and support the administration, whoever they are,' chuckled elderly Fama through her few remaining teeth. 'A boss is a boss.'

Yet a few meters away from her, on the fringes of the crowd gathered for the state farm's rally, were younger people who were less amused.

'You couldn't say things are ideal here,' said Grisha, who looked nervously over his shoulder as he gave me his first name and withheld his last. 'People try to make you fall into line. They want you to believe their lies. They try to force you to vote their way.'

As he spoke, a clean-cut young man with short blond hair elbowed his way toward us, smiling purposefully as he kept my tape-recorder in his sights.

'Things have never been better for us,' he enunciated clearly for the benefit of my readers. 'We have lots of housing, good food to eat, whatever we need to live. Nobody should complain.'

Grisha got the point and moved away, glowering. As I followed him, a few weary dancers, plump women with the strong calves of dairymaids, watched my investigations with interest.

'Why are you interested in our views?' said one. 'We're not here because we are political enthusiasts. We wouldn't be here at all if we weren't told to come and perform. All of us are in the same boat.'

Life simply went on as it always had, she said. As for freedom, who needed it when there wasn't much to do with it?

But even as the Russians disparage their new-found freedom – which has little to do with the democracy that is still an illusion – they are quietly, gradually, absorbing it into their pores. It's from this small personal reservoir, which few even acknowledge, that the future is rising.

'In the old Soviet days we'd be lined up like cattle and given our order,' chuckled Vladimir, an oil worker. 'Support X for head of the co-op, put your mark there. A bottle of vodka would go with it, or maybe a bit of meat. We'd all obey.'

Now, he said, that's all finished for most people. In five short years the dictates of decades have vanished like invisible writing. It was the industrial bosses and their bosses in local government and the bosses of the bosses in Moscow who carried on as though nothing at all had happened. They, seemingly, were the last to get the joke.

'Tell me to do something and I'll go out and do the opposite,' said the ebullient Vladimir. 'I don't know who they think they're impressing these days.'

Fear and control still remain, of course. For the refinery workers, whose perks and work hours depend on the co-operation of authority, and the farmers who wait in frustration for hand-outs of housing. They still turn out on parade when asked, tug their forelocks and give their superiors a tight-lipped smile.

For centuries Russians have not known freedom, either in the days of the Tsars or of their Soviet successors. Now many rank it with banditry and rampant crime. They mutter about the need for order, and their deep-seated anxiety about anarchy which can only be smothered by a strong hand.

But here, even in a sleepy provincial town, I can see the strength of the opposite pull in this constant tug-of-war between two fears – one of oblivion, the other of authoritarianism.

Young people stroll through the leafy, dandelion-strewn park smoking foreign cigarettes and kissing passionately on benches.

Their parents, wearing the generic uniforms of any Western city, window-shop and bargain. It is only the old, disenfranchised and without a future, who appear like specters, their presence shadowy and fading.

A few kilometers away, on the state farm, the director is still grinning at the crowd and the band plays on with its feigned gaiety. Some of the dancers are not dancing. Some are edging away.

Mountains and miracles

Returning to Chechnya with friends in search of their home, Olivia understands at last why they love their country.

The scribbled sign on the city gate still says: 'Welcome to Hell'. And I can read a pathetic note painted on an empty doorway in the pulverized city center: 'Lyosha, I'm still alive. Where are you?'

We drive swiftly because we don't want to look at the wreckage. It's too painful to remember that last winter of purgatory, to catch a whiff of the corpses that have merged with the sludge of scrapheaps and basements. The unidentified remains that just a year ago were the life and breath of the city.

On the eastern side of town I feel my hands clenching. My battered but stoical friends are returning for a look at what is left of their home. We have all been through the war, from the plains to the mountains. We expect the worst, and now hope is too violent to entertain.

But we find a miracle. There, surrounded by a shattered metal gate, is a neat brick house. A few late-blooming flowers sprout around the door, as though casting a fragile vote for life in the overwhelming presence of death. The youngest children tumble out of the car, eager to find their rooms and play. But Hussein holds them back. 'There might be mines.' Gingerly he sweeps the pathway with a long-handled broom.

The house is windowless, as are most houses in Grozny after the reverberating blasts of the Russian bombs. But the bare interior is almost as it was, save for the droppings of birds. Gleefully we begin the cleaning operation. But as I throw my arms around Hedi her muscles tighten and I can sense the underlying anger she feels, the grief and futility of it all. In this house, where she spent 21 years building and polishing and raising her children, strangers have pulled apart her handiwork, her peace and her security.

Suddenly I remember my first trip to the Caucasus two years ago, and the look of anger on the face of my Russian guide when I asked who lived in the attractive single family homes flanking her dilapidated Soviet highrise.

'Them,' she said. 'Those people.' Her cold, spiteful eyes spoke volumes.

Russian settlers felt envy when they colonized the supposedly subdued people of the Caucasus, only to find that living well was the best revenge. The sad, sometimes dangerous gap in the two mentalities, played out across centuries of slaughter.

'They have never understood us,' said Hussein. 'These are people who would rather pull down someone else's house than build a better one of their own.'

That mentality, based on who knows what sense of powerlessness and insecurity, was the opposite of a Chechen's head-on approach to life. A philosophy which at its worst led to tribal battles and banditry. At best, a sense of pride, not in towering monuments, but in the way one lived.

'A man deserves the home he has,' said Hussein. As a newcomer in the region I was struck by the welcoming human scale of the buildings. Their essential ingredients were air, space and light – more vital than the luxuries and gadgets which filled far richer places.

Used to the apologetic squalor of dingy Russian flats, I found it a revelation. In this tiny republic where great works of art had seldom sprung, a home was a life's work in progress.

I was also struck by the visceral way in which Chechens were attached to their land, not as an abstract idea but because they saw beauty in it. Sitting on a lush hillside last spring while attack helicopters rocketed the nearby village, I heard a Chechen commander ask, almost comically: 'What do you think of our place?' And, he added, with contempt rather than hatred, wasn't it too good for a people who spoiled and polluted every inch of their own vast territory?

I wanted to argue against this sweeping generalization, seeing the faces of Russian friends, and their struggle against all those centuries-old impulses of national self-destruction. But I could only stare at the hillside, as bees played among the apricot blossoms and rockets blasted away decades of work and care. Later, as I lay awake on the floor of a house under siege, political arguments melted away. In the laser-pierced darkness I could feel each tremor as it was absorbed by the house itself. In my skin and bones, I understood.

Dzhamilla's degree

Traditional values have helped people in Ingushetia resist Russian domination. But they have not helped women.

Like the good host that he is, Moussa is doing everything to put me at my ease as Fatima heaps the table with steaming vegetables and *shashlik*. But I am still uncomfortable, watching the women from the corner of my eye as they hang back in the doorway, waiting for the signal to bring more food.

Young Dzhamilla, who just turned 16, looks back at me and giggles silently. She has dark circles under her eyes. When her father comes in late at night she gets out of bed and begins the arduous process of scraping, washing and polishing his mud-spattered boots. Then she is up early to help prepare breakfast.

As a journalist and a foreigner here, I qualify as a sort of honorary man. Too important to hang around the kitchen with the women, and important enough to carry on serious conversations with the masters of the house. But I listen to Moussa's political discussion with half an ear. I am preoccupied with the lives of the women, the hidden realities of the household that are politely kept out of my reach.

I have to remind myself that this is modern-day Ingushetia, a tiny Russian republic in the Caucasus, whose Muslim population was subjugated by communism for seven decades. The Soviet Government preached the doctrine of male-female equality and pushed women into the workplace but gave them no help in surviving their double load.

As I finish my cup of sweet tea I slip into the kitchen to confront Fatima, a strong solid woman in her early forties. She starts with surprise as I plant myself firmly on a stool among her daughters.

'You should be talking to my husband, not me,' she says, with routine modesty.

I wave her objections aside. How is it, I ask, that after so many years of atheism, Leninism and Stalinism, Ingushetian families still fall into traditional roles?

'Well, we never lost our traditions,' she says. 'When I was married to Moussa 20 years ago we went to the Soviet registry office, then had a quiet Muslim ceremony.'

'Did you know Moussa very well before you married?' I ask.

She laughs again. 'That would have been scandalous. We saw each other at school and our parents arranged it.'

The union was a success, as four healthy children attest. The youngest, little Chingiz, is only three years old, his father's greatest pride. Dzhamilla and her sister are there to serve, and their large dark eyes and gleaming black hair are rated above any academic ability or career ambitions.

I am irritated by this stultifying devaluation of women, and tell Fatima so. Communism did little to liberate women in other parts of Russia. But here in the Caucasus they seemed to inherit the worst of both worlds. The war in neighboring Chechnya has made things even more difficult, with the most traditional religious values seen as a bulwark against Russia's domination.

Dzhamilla nods her head as I speak. She hopes to be a lawyer. But how, I wonder, will she get from this Cinderella life to university? Will she become like her mother, huddled in the 'women's wing' of a spacious home with her daughters and granddaughters? Fatima appears untroubled by a routine so segregated that she does not even eat with her husband.

'Can men and women be friends?' I ask her.

'The main thing is that they work together for the same goals. Men protect women. Women care for their men. But men are friends with other men, and women with women.' Moussa, she adds, is a good husband.

But I look at Dzhamilla, and am troubled. She seems withdrawn, sad. As I stand in the hall later putting on my boots she draws me aside.

'Can you bring me an English grammar book when you come back?' she asks, clinging to me like a drowning woman in a floodtide. 'Everything is going backwards here. I want to learn so I can get away. When I get my degree I'll come and do something for my country. Now I can do nothing.'

Walking through the muddy streets I look back at the house, silhouetted darkly against a leaden sky. In one small room in the women's wing a light is burning.

Stalemate

Olivia finds a gulf growing between her and her friend Galina. And there is nothing either of them can do about it.

I should be looking forward to Saturday, the day when I'll get together with my closest Moscow friend, Galina.

But as the day approaches, I am frozen with embarrassment. Galina and I haven't seen each other for a month, but not because of any bad feeling. We've shared each other's jokes and misadventures since I came to Russia three years ago. There is no-one more warm, perceptive or understanding.

But the thing that upsets me is money. Something that is throwing up bigger and bigger barriers between people in this society, as effective as the walls surrounding the monster homes of the newly rich. In a Western country we would be on an equal footing. In this topsy-turvy place, a simple friendship is an emotional tightrope.

We live 45 minutes away from each other, a wearing trip by cab or bus or metro. And, especially to a Russian, unthinkable without a meal at the end of it.

At first things seemed easy. I was new in the country, Galina pointed out. A visitor. That called for a trip to a concert, and eventually to her small neat apartment where a chicken would be roasting in a sputtering oven. In those days admission prices were cheap, transport costs negligible and food prices affordable though climbing. But over the months inflation exploded, while Galina's salary stayed flat. Even a university department head could not make ends meet without moonlighting at other jobs.

As the months passed, the circles under Galina's eyes grew darker. With a gravely ill mother, an ailing student son, and an apartment that was crumbling by the month, she was like a woman walking through financial quicksand.

I persuaded her to come to my flat for meals, uneasily watching her stare at the pricey ingredients she could no longer afford. Sometimes she would join me for a café dinner or a pastry-saturated afternoon at a glossy hotel coffee shop.

But sooner or later the bill would arrive. When I paid it, as discreetly as possible, there was no point in pretending that the tab was 'absolutely nothing'. Galina knew it was the equivalent of her family's grocery bill for a week.

Soon she told me sadly that she couldn't go on accepting these treats. Arguments about repaying her early hospitality had died of exhaustion. And guilt choked me when accepting her invitations to dine on the high-priced delicacies she believed were staples of the Western diet. Opting for a walk in the woods and a cup of tea only seemed patronizing.

Our friendship was reaching a stalemate. The meals were merely symbolic of the huge division between us, one that showed up every aspect of our lifestyles. It wasn't only the economic effect of inflation but the emotional fallout. Once a member of Russia's urban élite, Galina was used to an equal relationship with her friends. Now, in a city that was one of the most expensive in the world, she could see people like herself begging in subways to survive.

When she got an after-hours job with a Western company, I thought her fortunes would rise. But, she explained wryly, 'they wanted to hire a

Russian. That means they want to pay Russian wages.'

In Russia there is now a three-tiered system – top pay for foreigners who venture into the rugged East. Fractional wages for the Russians who do much the same jobs in joint ventures or new Russian companies. And rock-bottom pay for those in traditional institutional jobs.

But inflation attacks everybody the same way. All that saves many Russians from starvation is their old dirt-cheap state flats. Like many people, Galina could privatize and sell her apartment. But she would end up homeless after a year or two in one of the astronomically expensive flats leased by gouging landlords who know they can always find a tenant to pay their soaring rents.

I think about this as Saturday approaches and I visualize the new stress lines in Galina's face, the deeper hollows in her cheeks. And the inevitable stories of daily struggles that are ageing and breaking down this courageous woman.

I leaf through a pile of economic reports on Russia, trying to find some light at the end of what seems an endless dark tunnel for people like Galina.

'In spite of its problems, the market economy is already a success,' enthused one. 'It has introduced Russians to a concept they never dreamed of under communism: freedom of choice.'

Crystal glasses and kidnapped wives

Sipping champagne and listening to the alarming story of a marriage in the Caucasus.

Midnight, and the hot dusty wind is merging with the muffled blasts of nearby bombing to convince me it is time to slip into the unconsciousness of sleep. But when Madina comes to my room with her best friend and a bottle of champagne, I am startled enough to put off the much-craved rest.

As a good Muslim wife, my host in this spacious Daghestan home officially doesn't touch alcohol. But at midnight, with the children asleep, she needs some courage for the story she is eager but reluctant to tell.

'I was kidnapped,' she declares matter-of-factly after a few sips. 'Fifteen years ago my husband took me to his house and kept me there. I had to marry him. I was so angry and depressed I thought I would never forgive him.'

Madina watches my face as she drops this bombshell, her clear blue eyes defiant.

'You mean that you're held here against your will?'

'Not any more. Now everything is normal. I wouldn't leave – because there's nowhere for me to go.'

I listen with horror coupled with surprise that this capable woman in her mid-thirties should treat such a bizarre fate as merely routine. But in the Caucasus, she says, that is exactly what it is.

'It happens to a lot of women. Men take a fancy to them, carry them off and then they are trapped. That's our life.'

It is difficult to take in what Madina is talking about, here in this comfortable room with shelves of crystal glasses and an enormous television set silently projecting images of scantily clad women gyrating to unheard rock music.

But for Madina and her 21-year-old friend Rosa those are exotic pictures from a world they could only imagine. Rosa too was kidnapped while still in her teens – by a young doctor whose mother made her life a misery of abuse and drudgery. After 10 months she escaped.

'Now I have only one possibility,' she says with little emotion. 'Somebody will want me as a second wife.'

I try to imagine what it is like to live in a culture of kidnapping, where women are traded off by their parents for sums of money. A world almost untouched by more than half a century of communism and atheism. 'The custom is that the village elders will come to see the woman after she's kidnapped, and if she's unhappy they'll send her home,' says Rosa bitterly. 'If not the man pays a dowry and they get married. That's the theory. It didn't work in my case.'

In western Chechnya and Ingushetia, I am told, forced marriage is giving way to mock kidnappings in which women agree to elope with their sweethearts to speed parental consent. But in Daghestan's Muslim communities in the more primitive eastern Caucasus, marriage is often abrupt and unwanted.

I listen to these stories with a sense of helplessness: the normal-seeming home that is my oasis from the war is little more than a prison. But for a Caucasian woman, Madina assures me, the journey from rejection to resignation is often short.

'At first I was furious. I wouldn't even speak to my husband for a year. But once I had children and I got used to the life, things changed. After all, he's pretty good to me, and I've learned to love him.'

I find it difficult to reconcile my ebullient host – a stocky energetic man with a quick sense of humor – with the brute who snatched his unwilling bride from the street. And I puzzle over my own role. For years in this small backwater the women have waited for someone who would listen to them with more than an apathetic shrug. But does my very appearance, the first Western woman they have ever met, make their fettered lives seem more bearable?

Madina laughs and shakes her head. 'You know what I'm really hoping for now?' she says, pulling off the floral headscarf that binds up her sleek dark hair. 'Old age. In the West women would probably find that funny. Here it's a time of liberation. Nobody cares what you do any more.'

She pours another tiny crystal glass of champagne.

'If we meet when we're 70, maybe we'll both be free. Come and see me then. I'll be here. Thinking about it will keep me alive.'

Business as usual

Lunch with a protégé – and a nasty shock.

Behind us, two US Air Force pilots were having a heart-to-heart about hard landings.

Across the way a New Russian mum, her styled-to-kill blond hair flipped over one eye, handed her irritable toddler her cell phone.

Volodya, happy to be part of this happening crowd, was smiling over his Caesar salad, enjoying the buzz and the hubbub of Moscow's trendiest brunch spot.

In the two years I'd known him, he had changed from a shy spaniel of a science student to a confident young executive. When he first came to my office, eyes downcast and badly typed résumé in hand, I doubted he'd get much further than the door of any Western corporation. He seemed so insecure, so unsure of what he had to offer, or what anyone might offer him.

Feeling sorry for him, I made a few phone calls to friends in need of a willing gopher. Within a week he had a research contract and I had become his mentor.

'Is this the right kind of tie?' he would agonize, blushing at an outbreak of acne. 'Can I charge my Metro tickets to expenses?'

Over many Coca-Colas I saw his confidence slowly expand.

Like a proud parent I looked forward to our meetings, noting a sleek new haircut, a briefcase that replaced his habitual plastic bag. His tall frame seemed to have stretched as he strode into the room like a full-blown yuppie.

This, I told myself, is the Russian future. If Russia is to have one, it would need many more young people like Volodya, bright and energetic climbers who were determined to learn new ways of doing business and filled with zeal for a 'normal' non-corrupt, non-mafia state.

Today we are celebrating his first full-time job. 'I'm starting at the top,' he crowed, flashing a new business card: Moscow manager of a European company with a luxurious office overlooking the Kremlin. With the job went perks that would boggle the mind of any Western 24-year-old – a car and driver, European travel, promise of a company flat.

'My first assignment,' he told me, 'is setting up my own division.'

I was all ears. My friend Anya, whose overseas company had pulled out of Moscow, was sinking into despair of ever finding work as an administrator again.

'Volodya,' I urged, 'you must hire her.'

'Can she supervise accounts, handle computers and speak English and French or German?'

She could. And I remembered all too well her depression after throwing her glowing résumé on top of hundreds of others from women decades younger than her. Twenty-five, she was told bluntly, was the maximum for female employees these days. A glance at the mini-skirted and stiletto-heeled applicants who were ushered into the personnel offices and she got the point.

The only 40-or-older women who managed to find paying jobs were ones with connections. Now, to my delight, I could give her one. Jotting down Volodya's business number, I told him she'd call next day.

'Sure,' he added with a shrug, 'but she can't expect big wages. I want to keep down office costs.'

The 'not big' wage would be $500 a month, a third of Anya's previous salary and scarcely enough to pay her apartment costs.

'Look here,' I argued, 'I didn't bring you up to be a killer boss. Don't you want happy and loyal employees?'

'There aren't any happy employees, only happy bosses,' he laughed. 'I learned that from studying Western business. If the staff don't like the conditions you can always find somebody else.'

I pushed away my half-eaten chicken.

'Volodya, this is serious. You have the chance to build Russian business with a human face. Business that benefits everybody, not just the élite. Isn't that what you wanted?'

'You sound just like my mother,' he chuckled. 'She never got over her boring old communist background. Wake up, I tell her. This is the future.'

He glanced around the room restlessly, eager to get on with the afternoon's shopping. His eyes had a new withdrawn look, his mouth a new hardness around the corners.

'It's great to see you,' he said into the air. 'And by the way, this time I'm paying the bill.'

Dust and memories

Remembering two lovers who were also combatants in the bloody war between Chechnya and Russia.

I met Rosa in a friend's house in a village that is now dust and memories. 'I started as a farm girl,' she said with a smile. 'Then I became a nurse. And then...'

She kept her voice low. In a war zone you cannot be too careful.

Rosa was a fighter, one of the many who had taken up the gun against Russia when their homes were destroyed or family members killed. With her creamy skin, soft grey eyes and red hair, she looked more like the milkmaid she had once been. And, she admitted, in the beginning the hardest part was dressing for the job.

'I used to wear a skirt, because I am a devout Muslim. But my commander said I was crazy, this was war.'

She blushed. 'I put on fatigues, just like the men. But at first I wore the skirt over them.'

As we rode into the hills the next day to the dull thud of Russian rockers, Rosa's shyness abated a little. She was married, she told me. But her husband had left Chechnya to earn money in Azerbaijan. In the year he had been gone there was no word, and no money.

I wanted to ask if, as the only woman in a group of 30 men, she had formed any new attachments. But for a strict Muslim woman the question was not merely shocking but insulting.

'Relationships are very different up here,' she volunteered. 'Instead of living completely separate lives from men, as we normally do, here we are all comrades. In war some traditions can't be observed.'

Her eyes glowed with excitement as she explained how she now ate all her meals alongside men, talked to them as equals, and sometimes gave them orders.

As our springless four-wheeler heaved over the steep track, she jumped out and ran to the top of the hill, oblivious to the rocket bursts.

At dusk I sat on the ground with some resting fighters, sipping tea. Rosa had disappeared from view.

Worried, I moved cautiously around the shadow of the trees as fresh blasts reverberated. In front of me was the outline of two people in rapt conversation. They sat side by side, but only their fingers were touching.

Rosa's eyes met mine in the flickering dimness. She smiled.

The next day, as we sat in the jeep, she said simply: 'His name is Issa.'

Their forbidden relationship began six months earlier, when he helped her collect the wounded in Grozny. Then he joined her unit and they were together almost every day.

'I had no idea of what men thought or felt,' she admitted wonderingly. 'Even my husband. In our society men make demands and women fulfill them. It is part of our religion and sense of duty.'

Issa told her his thoughts and feelings. He was eager to understand hers. As the death-dealing weeks passed, a new kind of love took root. Not a physical one, as taboos were too strong and they were never alone. But a bond that made even their daily hell bearable.

'When we die, we go straight to paradise,' Rosa whispered. 'We will meet each other there. It is all we can expect.'

That was one year ago. Since then death has traveled to every corner of the land, feasting on civilians and combatants alike.

Rosa vanished defending a village where her refugee relatives were hiding from Russian bombs. Issa fell in a rocket attack on an ammunition dump.

Now I stood at the edge of a mass grave in Grozny, staring at anonymous mounds of earth, washed over with grief.

I remembered how Rosa and her friends had prayed that night on the hill, prayers for the safety of all of us. As an unbeliever I had only wishes.

Now, looking at the pathetic heaps of earth with their final indignity of fading number tags, I wished from the bottom of my heart that I had the faith to pray for them, even too late.

I knelt in the dry, bitter wind and crushed a bit of earth between my fingers. Was she there, somewhere? And Issa? Lives blocked, cut off, done violence, ground to dirt.

At Jean-Paul Sartre's grave, Simone de Beauvoir had said: 'His death separates us. My death will not unite us.'

But my fingers pressed the earth as though Rosa and Issa were, somehow, brought together there in the palm of my hand.

Thinking, may there be paradise.

May you find it.

Letters from Atlantis, (Colombia) 1997-1998

Jenny James

Jenny was born in 1942 into a communist, atheist family in Dartford, England. She was a member of the Campaign for Nuclear Disarmament and of the Committee of 100, a militant resistance organization advocating civil disobedience instead of the demonstration march as the appropriate method of protest against weapons of mass destruction and the war in Vietnam. Jenny was involved in direct action throughout the 1960s, including a mission to Southeast Asia during the Vietnam War, and suffered six imprisonments in different countries.

She co-founded the Atlantis therapeutic eco-community in 1970, which moved to Ireland in 1974. In 1987 the Atlantis community moved to Latin America, eventually finding a home in the Colombian rainforest, and Jenny began her series of letters in the *New Internationalist* from there in 1997. She has written nine books about the Atlantis community, including *Atlantis Adventure*, *Atlantis Magic* and *Male Sexuality: the Atlantis Position*. You can read more about the Atlantis community at www.atlantiscommunity.thinkhost.net and can contact it via email at atlantiscol@hotmail.com – Jenny says that visitors are welcome any time, at no cost.

Changes in Colombia

Colombia's history is riddled with civil conflict – and its recent past is no less troubled, with paramilitary groups (often associated with the Government), drug cartels and guerrilla forces continuing to protect their various territories and commit atrocities. So when Jenny James's Atlantis eco-community put down roots in Colombia in 1987, it cannot have been an easy choice – and her letters reflect the violence with which Colombians are forced to live, marking the deaths of friends and even her own grandson. The community was then based in the mountains to the south of the country, an area under the *de facto* control of the Revolutionary Armed Forces of Colombia (FARC).

Colombia's politics from the 1980s through to the present day have been dominated not just by conflict between guerrilla groups and government troops or paramilitary organizations but also by the US-led 'war on drugs'. In 1996 the US took Colombia off its list of countries that 'co-operate' in the 'war on drugs' and cut off aid but since 1998 right-wing presidents Andrés Pastrana and Alvaro Uribe Vélez have presided over governments that have sought to enlist US support. In 2000, Pastrana's Plan Colombia sought to eradicate 60,000 hectares of coca crops by employing three anti-narcotics battalions trained and equipped by the US. In 2003 Uribe – who is accused of links with paramilitary groups – requested Washington's direct intervention in the civil war, with the result that US special forces were deployed in the province of Arauca. Some 130,000 civilians were newly displaced by the conflict in the first half of 2007 alone and Amnesty International's report to the UN Human Rights Council in 2008 expressed continuing concern about extrajudicial executions by security forces, guerrilla groups and paramilitaries.

The danger in looking at Colombia, however, is that the violence excludes all else. The natural beauty of the country, for example, is extraordinary. The primary concern of most Colombians, as in any other country in the world, is to pursue their livelihoods as peacefully as possible. And for all the pain they have experienced along the way, Jenny and her Atlantis community continue to experience their home in the rainforest as a magical place – and their lives as an adventure aimed at creating an ecological, organic alternative to capitalism.

An avalanche of love

Setting up a commune in the rainforest – and the death of a former lover who made a difference.

Eduardo Rincón is dead. Murdered on his scooter in San Vicente del Caguán, Caquetá, on 16 June 1997. Just over 40 years old. The first and only Green Party councillor for the Amazonian region of southeast Colombia where we live.

Eduardo was my friend, and, extremely briefly, my lover. But much more important than that, he changed the history of this enormous area; an area controlled by the guerrillas and abandoned by the Government. Unlike anyone else, it seemed, he cared for the trees – and for the people who are felling them at an alarming rate.

When I first heard of Eduardo, I refused to believe that he existed. It was 1994 and two of my young daughters (nine and eleven at the time) were in Guayabal, the one-street, many-shack 'shopping center' of this mountainous area. They had been singing and juggling at a Halloween fiesta with the other members of our small back-to-nature commune called Atlantis.

'It wasn't just a Halloween party,' they said. 'It was a Green Party celebration – their candidate has just been elected councillor for this part of Caquetá.'

'Impossible,' was my reply, in my usual tolerant way. 'There couldn't be a Green Party in this God-forsaken place.'

Then I read Eduardo Rincón's letter to me. I was invited to meet him and he expressed amazement and delight that a group of gringos (foreigners) had landed in the area and were concerned about nature.

We had been here in Caquetá for four months, arriving the day that three children in our nearest hamlet, Rovira, had been killed by a landslide sweeping their shack into the ravine below. We had come on foot, picking our way in alarm over the 300 (yes, 300) avalanches blocking the mud road between Rovira and Neiva, the nearest large town.

It took us two days, but we were happy. We were going to our new home on the edge of cool virgin forest, 1,500 meters above sea level.

We had left Europe seven years earlier. I was 45. My youngest daughter, Katie, was still in nappies/diapers. I had lived with my commune for 12 years on a windswept Atlantic island off the coast of County Donegal in Ireland. We had planned for years to remove to some even wilder, remoter spot. For 18 months we roamed the islands of the Canaries, Cape Verde and the Caribbean. Helped by various men from the commune,

my three daughters and I
lived on beaches and in caves
and even shanty towns with
the poorest of the poor. We
traveled through Venezuela,
Colombia, Ecuador and Peru,
looking for a new home for
our tribe.

We didn't choose Colombia.
It chose us.

'You absolutely must stay
here. Colombia is the most
politically alive country in
South America. And we need
you.' The seduction was too
strong for me. After a miserable look at Ecuador and Peru, I came
home.

For six years I lived in Tolima, where the commune still has a large
settlement. We made friends with the guerrillas. But environmentally
it was never wild enough for us and at best we were an odd, though
thoroughly accepted group. I longed to be more politically effective.

Then one of our men found Caquetá. And the Green Party found
us.

Eduardo Rincón had brilliant blue eyes and grey hair; Fernando
Zapata, his right-hand man, was black, hugely enthusiastic and very
talkative. I was bowled over at what was happening; we were planning a
Green future for Red Caquetá.

'Look, I haven't any money, no power, I'm nobody,' I said. 'But I
tell you what: I can type, I can write, I'm really middle class and I know
what it feels like to be in Europe; to hear about the destruction of the
rainforest and despair at one's powerlessness. I just know there are
thousands of ordinary people everywhere who would love a chance to
help in a personal way. I'll write to the Green Movement over there and
tell them what's happening here and we'll see what happens.'

What happened was an avalanche of love and caring from abroad and
the rise in popularity of Eduardo from local councillor to the obvious
choice for next Mayor. And his death last Monday.

Monkey business

An unplanned adoption brings Jenny much more than she bargained for.

The first time we saw Cirilo, he was chained to a crate of Coca-Cola in a dark shop in the little market center of Guayabal, being fed on biscuits and chocolate. The children gave me no peace from that moment until I gave them the exorbitant 50 dollars to rescue him.

When we returned to the farm, Cirilo took one look at me and leapt onto me, hanging desperately round my neck. Absolutely no persuasion, kind or rough, would loosen him. His instincts told him I was the Mama of the tribe and that was that. He would attack fiercely with tooth and nail and hideous screams anyone who tried to rescue me by unraveling him from my neck.

My life took a hellish swoop for the worse; can you imagine what it is like to dress, undress, go to the toilet, have a shower, go to bed and wake up with a baby *maicero* (maize-eating) monkey wrapped round your head, clinging painfully to your hair if an attempt were made to remove him? I had done nothing to gain his affections and did a lot to earn his rejection. In vain. My anger and distress would reach fever pitch at times, especially on long journeys when he would shit and pee down my back. At night he would clamp himself over my face in bed with his funny little non-retractable penis uncomfortably near my mouth or nostrils. I guess his real mother wouldn't have slept horizontally.

Most bizarre was the fact that I could never see him: everyone would make the most appropriate oohs and ahs but if I tried to pull him far enough off me to have a look, I lost another handful of hair. And if I dared look in a mirror, he would deafen me with hysterical screaming at the imagined intruder.

The weeks and months passed and slowly, painfully, Cirilo learnt to accept our nasty ways: like putting him in his own little compartment at night with a blanket with which he could cover himself when the howls of protest subsided. He also had to learn to sit at the table and not on it and to eat from his plate and not from ours.

He loved gardening. He would watch me carefully as I weeded and then copy me, scrabbling up every plant in sight. And he loved birds' nests, but got into bad trouble for it: the parent birds dive-bombed him while he sat screeching on the roof, wrapping his arms around himself and staring pitifully at all his horrid, unsympathetic tribe who did nothing but kill themselves laughing.

As he grew older, Cirilo became increasingly accustomed to our rules: he knew that during the busiest working hours of morning he simply had to be tied up on a tree, not to keep him from running away but to prevent our ointments, medicines, ornaments and kitchen knives from theft.

Sometimes he escaped. Entering my room one day I did a double-take, not sure what I was looking at. It was very colorful. Every inch of my cabin had been turned into an elaborate spider's web of knitting wools, with Cirilo pouncing around joyfully in the middle of it like a maniacal kitten.

In the afternoon, he knew it was official playtime. The moment I sat on my huge fallen tree-trunk in the sun, he would come bounding over, knowing that at last he could get all the affection he longed for. He would lie on his back in my lap while I tickled him and curl up, laughing. Yes, monkeys laugh, not with noise like we do, but with the same helplessness. At such times I forgot all the tension of having a delinquent child who had to be constantly watched. I loved Cirilo.

One day, the children decided they wanted to go to our other settlement, two days' journey away. 'Not without Cirilo,' I said firmly. I wasn't going to be left holding the baby.

Cirilo went. Forever. Shortly after reaching our farm, he disappeared. I have a gnawing feeling he was trying to get home. He would have died very quickly at the hands of larger monkeys or other forest carnivores. There is a painful Cirilo-sized hole in all of us.

And I nurse a secret. I know that the only way a baby monkey becomes available is when the mother is shot for food or crop protection. But if ever someone handed me one again, would I have the strength to say no?

Natural causes

The life and death of an unlikely environmentalist.

There are no two ways about it: Ricardo was crazy. He was our nearest neighbor and one of our best friends. He was also one of the most successful men around: his tree-felling, opium-poppy-growing lifestyle had enabled him to set up a discotheque in Rovira, the nearest hamlet, where he sold drink and junk foods.

But he was not happy: his even grumpier wife was leaving him. He started spending a lot of time on our farm. He would weed carrots in silence beside me, or play for hours with our pet monkey or simply sit in our kitchen while food was being prepared.

Once he arrived during birthday celebrations: we were putting on quite an elaborate theater show for our own entertainment. He watched reverently, though it was in English, and later returned with a message from the local Community Action Group, of which he was a prominent member: please would we perform for the people of Rovira on Mothers' Day?

I was horrified. We did not consider ourselves professionals and had never done such a thing before. I argued and wriggled. He held his ground. And won – we put on our three-hour theater show in Rovira on Mothers' Day.

Ricardo was a good community leader. He was neither swayed unduly by the guerrillas, nor by empty Government promises. He grew closer to us, not out of any heartfelt environmental concern, but because he was bored and saw us as a possible source of fresh influence (and maybe affluence). Just before he died, aged 34, he became the lover of Anne, a community member.

For a long time, Ricardo had been moaning at us to buy his farm, which included a huge area of virgin forest. We simply had no money, our environmental campaign had scarcely begun and large sums of money (like $5,000) were not our forte.

But Ricardo knew how strongly we felt about trees and made a clever move. One day, when I was resting with the children on our 'afternoon log', we were jolted out of our reverie by the hideous sound of chain-saw teeth snarling and gnawing nearby. Then the inevitable sickening thud. Then another. And another.

Ricardo was felling the forest that stood between his farm and ours. The children and I held on to one another in tears. Louise, 15 at the time, quietly and savagely muttered: 'I hope a tree falls on him.'

Ricardo's smart move did wonders for our Green Campaign: in pain at the tree felling, I wrote an impassioned plea for help to the green movements of Europe. The miracle happened: an English couple I will probably never meet sent the money and we saved the rest of Ricardo's forest, leaving him the already opened land.

Surprisingly, our friendship with him deepened, though it never cured his grumpiness. He brought me flowering shrubs and tree cuttings to plant. He asked to come along and support us when we had a big meeting with the southern-region guerrilla commander to get permission for some young Irish people to make a video of the area. And, most amazingly, he showed interest in giving up his disco and turning it into an environmental center.

I started giving him beautiful maps and posters of Amazonia, which he stuck up on his walls next to pictures of naked women on motorbikes, photos of Rambo and paintings of a self-pitying blond, blue-eyed Jesus.

One day I left for a rare trip to Bogotá. Soon after, Anne phoned me. She was choked with tears. 'Ricardo is dead,' she sobbed.

In Colombia, it is so unusual for a man to die young from anything other than violence that they specify 'Murió de muerte natural' – he died from natural causes. Ricardo had been fainting a lot. Anne insisted he saw a doctor, who found nothing wrong. A few days later, Ricardo dropped dead from a massive brain hemorrhage while digging out a huge pit to make a fish farm next door to us.

Some months later, I was discussing the dangers of tree-felling with a neighbor after one of our lads had an accident.

'Yes,' said the neighbor, 'that's what happened to Ricardo – his fainting fits began after a branch fell on him when he was cutting the forest next to you.'

Going home
Why the quiet stream near home is quiet no longer.

There will definitely be no buses running today. We don't need to trek the three hours down the steep muddy mountain path to the road to find this out. All we do is listen to the rain. And view the landslide outside our shack which removed two cesspits and a lot of beautiful greenery in the night. There is a crack forming in the bank near our open-air natural shower-place. From the usually placid little waterway five minutes from our house we can hear a thundering noise.

At least there is still forest all around us: below the house, there is none, just ugly yellow fields of rough pasture and scrub. Down there, conditions will be much worse.

When you travel the unsurfaced mud roads in the valley below, you don't have to be an engineer or a clairvoyant to see what will happen next: on one side of you a deep ravine where the river Oso runs; on the other, the next landslides waiting to happen. These are not miniature ones like those round our precariously perched home, but great mountains of sodden clay that slip by the dozen onto the road. They will take the bulldozers (if and when the council in far-away Neiva sends them) days or weeks to clear. And then they slip again as soon as the next rain comes.

Practically everyone in the area is now aware that these landfalls are caused by deforestation; you really don't need to be a geographical genius to pass your eye along the scar of the road running through these once-forested mountains to see this. 'Yes, but that man has lots of children and he needed to plant maize – he has no other land,' comes the excuse.

The landscape changes continually in the rainforest. Sometimes this is due to natural causes, more often it is caused by humans.

It is not the first time our little stream has changed into a torrent. A year ago, on a sunny afternoon, my friend Anne and I were chatting in my cabin when a terrible roaring began. 'Listen! What's that?' I said, running outside.

'It's the stream,' suggested Anne.

'No, it never sounds like that, even in the heaviest rains,' I said, horrified at the volume of the noise. My two youngest daughters ran off to look at the stream.

I stared at the forest below us and suddenly pointed, incoherent with shock. Anne tried to see what I was seeing; white waves at tree height. Then she saw – but the waves were green now as hundreds of trees tumbled over one another, bowled along by water where no water ought to be, accompanied by the crackling of a million rifle shots.

'My god, what is happening?' Then I remembered the children. 'Ned!' I yelled to one of our men. 'Get the kids!'

We didn't need to; they came panting back up the path, white with shock. They had been down to our normally babbling brook, in time to see a huge wall of rocks, trees and orange water coming down towards them. They had been able to scamper back up the steep path just in time.

The roaring and cracking continued for about three-quarters of an hour. Then all was silent. Gingerly, we made our way down to our stream, the one you can jump across in one leap. In front of us was a chasm, up to six meters deep and ten meters wide, full of huge rocks that had not been there before. Thousands of trees had been ripped from the banks and the ones left standing were scarred and battered to a level high above our heads.

Later we discovered that four streams nearby had suffered the same 'flash flood'. No-one knew where the phenomenon began nor how far down the valley it extended.

'Could it be deforestation higher up?' I asked my neighbor. They nodded glumly. It wasn't even raining.

'What if this happened right above our house?' asked one of my daughters.

'We'd have to run,' I said grimly, and we all agreed on the most practical escape route. 'And do not stop to save the guinea-pigs,' I warned the children.

Killing connections

Mourning the death of another friend and pondering the paradoxes of Colombian 'justice'.

Luis Arenas was a retired police official and a supporter of the Colombian Conservative Party. He read of our ecological community in the Conservative daily newspaper *El Tiempo* (The Times) and wrote to us of his own environmental efforts down in the flat, hot country of Caquetá – Port Milán on the River Orteguaza.

I made the journey to meet him at the beginning of 1995. Luis was 62 and the sort of person who made you mind ever so much whether he approved of you; his wife Dolly was plump, warm-hearted and soon became my friend. I had long, deep conversations with Luis about the social and environmental situation and local political opposition to his work. I was moved by the depth of his caring; saddened and depressed so see how alone he was in his efforts and determined to work with him in any way that I could.

Several months, river journeys and letters later, I received a note to collect a registered letter from Neiva post office, a day's journey away.

I collapsed on the post-office floor: 'Luis has been assassinated,' wrote Dolly. 'A hired killer slaughtered him with 19 machine-gun bullets. Please come and see me. I am living in Florencia: it is not safe to go to Milán.'

I got out of the taxi and fell into Dolly's arms. 'Who was it? The narcos?' Luis had been fighting for the substitution of the coca crop, ubiquitous in this region.

'No, no.'

'The guerrillas?'

'No, of course not.'

'Who then?'

'The Alcalde (Mayor) of Milán.'

Luis's political rival: Luis's popularity had been rising rapidly because of his efficient, honest, communal and environmental work; he would undoubtedly have become Mayor in the next elections. Does Colombia know no other way of arguing?

I knew privately that I would go to the guerrillas once I got home. They are the only people who do anything about anything and they take their time about it. But Luis' family were hugely bourgeois – university lecturers, lawyers, highly placed social workers – I couldn't talk about that side of Colombian reality with them. Yet when I suggested going to the Security Police, they had a fit. They definitely wanted me to do something, and kept looking at me intently as if I should know what they meant. I didn't.

I don't know how my mono-linear European brain finally caught on. When I at last came out with it, they all heaved a huge sigh of relief and became immensely enthusiastic: they wanted me to go to the guerrillas. I felt like a five-year-old, struggling to learn to read.

I had never met the Mayor, though one day in Milán Luis had taken me to see him, only to find that he was out. So, just in case all my informants were wrong and he was innocent, I did my own test. I sent him two poems, one 'To Luis Arenas' promising to carry on his green work; the other 'To Luis' Assassins' ending with the line 'Luis is at rest now. And you, little people, are you sleeping peacefully?'

I heard some time later that the Mayor was telling everyone he was 'receiving death threats from Neiva'.

Months passed. Fear paralyzed Luis' family from taking further action. One day, 'chance' took me into Neiva, the nearest town. Passing a newspaper stand, I saw the headline: 'Mayor of Milán accused of murder of Governor.'

He's done it again, murdered someone else. I ran to the newspaper headquarters, breathlessly told my story in all its details. They dialed the number of Luis' family.

'Will you give me permission to speak now?' I asked them.

'Yes,' came the reply.

The newspaper director drove me to the Public Prosecutor where I recorded everything I knew on tape.

'This will help to keep him in jail,' they told me.

I left the office, quietly saying my last goodbye to Luis.

Today, one memory nags me. I remember telling Luis the story of a young American traveler who had been machine-gunned to death in the nearby coca town of Getuchá.

'But he was a *vicioso* [an addict],' Luis had said. 'You must understand that this is the people's way of cleansing society.'

Of poppies, plantations and parents

Jenny looks out over opium-poppy fields just five minutes from her cabin.

The poppies in Colombia aren't red, like those that grew in the cornfields of Kent when I was a child. They are every delicate pastel shade from pink to mauve to purple.

When they drop their petals and form large seed-cups, young children and muscled men who could be doing much heavier work bend over the vast fields, making fine razor-cuts in the pods. Then, day by day, the sticky ooze that emanates from the cut is collected. Final destination: heroin on the city streets of the Northern Hemisphere.

Poppies grow best on recently deforested cool mountain slopes; for at least a year the floor of the slaughtered forest will be fertile.

The nearest opium crop to us is about five minutes from our central cabin. The occupant of the versatile sprayer-plane that swooped down right over our heads as we weeded our vegetable garden would naturally have thought the crop was ours; in fact, its owner lives one hour down the mountainside. So far, we have avoided being sprayed by aerial herbicides; not so our nearest neighbor Chucho, just ten minutes along the muddy track, nor Don Carlos, just beyond that. Don Carlos is an Evangelist and preached to me how he would 'never hurt other nations' by growing poppies. Now he has several hectares of them. There is no other form of agriculture in this area, now that a ban on logging has finally been imposed.

The FARC (Revolutionary Armed Forces of Colombia) guerrilla force have been known to kill drug users, after the customary three cautions – or at least to drive them from the area. But they support the peasants and oppose aerial spraying. So do I.

Martyn, aged 15, was standing with some neighbors outside their shack watching the aerial antics. He had a small radio with him and caught the aircraft's frequency.

'Look at those sons-of-bitches watching us. Perhaps they'd like another dose,' said one of crew of the Colombian armed helicopter crew, directing and protecting the US pilot of the spray-plane.

Martyn, being Irish, could understand both the languages spoken in the air above him.

It's handy for the Colombian Government that the Americans have decided it is easier to attack Third World peasants rather than deal with problems back home; the Colombian Government likes attacking peasants too, especially in guerrilla-controlled areas.

Meanwhile, we heard that my daughter Louise, also 15, was working on a poppy farm. She had told us that she and her teenage boyfriend, Alvaro, were tasting life in the nearest town.

Martyn's mother, Mary, hit the roof, and eyed me for my reaction. I shrugged. I was caught somewhere between not wanting to play the authoritarian parent and feeling indignant that Louise would risk sullying our anti-drug reputation, thus weakening our environmental arguments. Mary flew off.

She returned many hours later, rosy and pleased with herself, with a pale Louise in tow. Mary and the neighbor's poppy workers had enjoyed the brawl. Alvaro had not. He was trained that it was not nice to hit ladies, even when attacked, and ended up being chased round the opium plantation by the robust and not-very-inhibited Mary. The plantation owner was also not pleased: Mary gave him an Irish-Colombian earful and he has not spoken to us since.

Louise was relieved to be rescued; she had hated every minute of her escapade. I couldn't help a little private amusement as I mentally perused the generations: my own mother, born in 1910, had shocked her Victorian mother by leaving home at 22, becoming a professional artist and joining the Communist Party. I'd horrified her by beginning my sexual life at 14; what could Louise do in her turn? Well, she could go and work on an opium-poppy plantation.

Our children's blood

Jenny tells of the death of her grandson.

My grandson Tristan and my 'son-in-law' Javier, both 18, were murdered in Hoya Grande, Icononzo, about half an hour from where we used to live.

Tristan was about to go to Ireland and wanted to say goodbye to his half-brother, who lives with a peasant family in Icononzo. Javier, native to the area, went to say goodbye to his parents as he had decided to join our community forever and come south with us.

Anne first noticed something was wrong when the boys didn't turn up for a theater engagement a week later. Tristan had always been one of our best actors, a very moving, natural mime artist; a conjurer, comic, dancer and acrobat, unicycle and juggling expert.

Javier joined us during our forcible removal from Incononzo by the guerrillas a year ago by helping Anne get our old bus unstuck from a mud patch. A beautiful, tall, dark-skinned boy, it didn't require a psychic to predict that he would fall for my rather gorgeous blonde daughters and they for him.

When I first got the news in Puracé that the boys had been kidnapped, I entered an unreal world. My heart and breathing stopped; when I thought of writing to Tris to tell him how much we all loved and cared about him, I knew I would not be writing to anyone; and I began to prepare myself for news of his death.

Anne's meeting with the leader of the assassins in Icononzo and his absurd and brutish lying left her in no doubt. She was probably very near the boys' bodies as she watched him wriggle and concoct and contradict himself. And threaten her.

For days, weeks, we cried, agonized, philosophized, went to hell, came back fighting, phoning, always phoning: the Red Cross, the FARC (Revolutionary Armed Forces of Colombia) headquarters, the press, the United Nations, talking on TV, on radio, to newspapers, to the public prosecutor, to the leaders of the Communist Party. People on the street and on buses recognized us from TV news programs. A man who sells newspapers on the corner of Anne's street refused payment when she went to buy a paper with our report in it – and has refused payment ever since. Neighbors and friends rallied round with love and assistance. People we barely knew asked what they could do to help.

I would wake at some unearthly hour to the disbelief and torture of a new day. I gave myself the task of convincing the children and Javier's parents to give up hope, that hope only prolonged the inevitable agony of knowing that Tris and Javier were gone forever. It was my way of trying to believe it myself.

We were powerless to help our boys, but we could help all the other people bound in terror and silence in that region of Tolima; peasants used to being cowed by both sides in the war. Don Pedro, our beloved friend, was murdered by the same gang, so was the local nurse and her husband, killed after Tris and Javier. Gonzalo, the brutish commander who forced us out of the area – so people say, to steal our farm – and his cohort, a peasant neighbor called Anita de Jesus Caro and her two delinquent sons, together with a large band of *milicianos* (militia) using the FARC name and weapons, were running the region as a private enterprise, murdering anyone who stood in their way. We have every reason to believe Anita was implicated in instigating the murder of our boys. War always gives a moment of terrible power to embittered souls.

Now, about to leave Tabio forever, I am endeavoring to bring on the future, something I thought I could never find the strength to do. I have gone through Tristan's clothes, found his books in Spanish on marine engineering, astral navigation and sea diving. I have noted the immaculate way he kept his things, I have seen his queer spelling (academic subjects did not come easily to him), I have given away his possessions, I have slept under his duvet and called his name aloud in helpless desperation. I have agonized a hundred times over the terror the boys must have felt when they realized they were trapped by murderous lunatics; I have tortured myself over the morality of having the kids here in the first place and I have wept over Katie's nascent song about him. She can get no further than the line, 'I will never forgive the years they stole from you.'

When all the sharp and crippling pain of a new and violent death has dulled just a little, the mind's clouds begin to clear. Tristan wanted to live, to find a girlfriend, to go to Ireland to seek his roots; he cared not one whit for politics, he hated the FARC; and he frequently disagreed with his granny's choices. He was careful, conservative and materialistic. We were absolutely respectful of his differences and were doing our all to facilitate his return to Ireland. Several people, including Javier's parents, the adoptive parents of Tris's half-brother, and our friend Gilberto – the last people to see the boys alive and happy – begged them not to go out that fatal night, begged them to wait at least till light of day. Even Javier said they shouldn't go. But Tris was a Taurus, strong and stubborn.

The boys walked into sudden, mind-numbing, senseless death. We have all died with them, over and over again. But now we must live.

Soon the youngest kids will go to Ireland; the rest of us are opting to stay in Colombia through the war ahead and to go to where we are most needed. To the area the Americans in their infinite arrogance and stupidity are about to attack – the *zona de despeje*, where they are using the excuse of their fictitious 'war on drugs' to rearm the corrupt Colombian Army, backed by ruthless paramilitaries, so as to seek and destroy the FARC. And of course an indiscriminate number of peasants who happen to be in the way.

The irony of our situation will invite disbelief: we have lost two farms and forest reserves and now two cherished young men to maverick FARC commanders. And yet we are thinking of accepting their request to help them with drug-crop substitution and organic and ecological agriculture. The FARC are bending over backwards to see justice done. They know that had we chosen to, we could have handed the British and American governments an immediate excuse to get even more aggressive in their intervention. We have respect for the serious nature of their leaders which is in stark contrast to the brainless gunmen we have had the misfortune to cross at local level. The paradox of the Colombian situation is that, for all its hideous mistakes, the FARC is the only force in Colombia we know of that is seriously capable of bringing about a vital, radical change.

On television, we were asked time after time: will you all be leaving Colombia now? We answered: 'No, our children's blood on this land ties us to this country more than ever before.'

Tris, forgive us. We were not there to save you, to stand in front of your self-appointed executioners and say, 'You'll have to kill us first'. We let you go off on your young man's adventure, and like many a young mountaineer, motorcyclist or soldier, you were cut down before you began to live. And now your outrageous grandmother, and your talented aunts, and your carers and helpers amongst the grown-ups are going to work with those whom the media would love to label the devils in this story.

But the truth of this country is subtle, sophisticated, ever surprising, deep and hopeful amidst all the death and destruction. And so we are choosing to walk into the eye of the hurricane to honor you, your sacrifice, and our chosen path.

Letters from Tsengel (Mongolia), 1998-1999

Louisa Waugh

Louisa was born in Berlin, grew up in Liverpool, and spent several years living and working in Mongolia in the mid-1990s. After two years in the Mongolian capital, Ulaanbaatar, she moved to a village called Tsengel in the remote Altai mountains of western Mongolia in 1998. During her year in Tsengel (which translates as 'Delight') she wrote her monthly letters for the *New Internationalist*.

Louisa's letters are intimate and candid accounts of her time in this small, remote community, where people survive without electricity or running water, and where death is very much part of life.

When she finally returned to Britain, Louisa wrote a book about the people of Tsengel. *Hearing Birds Fly: a nomadic year in Mongolia* won the inaugural Ondaatje Literary prize in 2004 for 'the book which best evokes the spirit of a particular place' and was also shortlisted for the Thomas Cook Travel Book of the Year Prize.

Louisa's second book *Selling Olga: stories of human trafficking and resistance* was published in 2007 and was a groundbreaking investigation into human trafficking across Europe, including Britain.

Louisa has discussed human trafficking with numerous British and international audiences, and has written extensively about international human rights. She is now researching human rights violations in the Gaza Strip, and also taking notes for her third book, which will be a personal account of living under siege in Gaza. In her spare time she studies Arabic, and is a kick-boxer.

Changes in Mongolia

Famous for its vast steppe and nomads, Mongolia is also one of the most sparsely populated nations on earth, with less than 2.5 million people living in an area larger than western Europe.

Approximately half the Mongolian population is still nomadic; herders migrate to fresh pasture five or six times a year, though many families use the same routes year after year.

Mongolians form one of the main ethnic groups of northern and eastern Asia, and, under the brutal tutelage of fifth-century Attila and his Hun or Siung-nu forces, they conquered, and terrorized, much of historic Europe. Some 800 years later, at the beginning of the 13th century, Temujin, better known as Chingis (or Genghis) Khan, and his hordes swept across Central Asia and Eastern Europe.

The Mongols established the largest empire the world has ever known. But, like all empires, theirs too eventually imploded and crumbled, and Mongolia was itself occupied, first by the Manchurians, then by the Soviet Union.

The Soviet forces took over Mongolia in the early 1920s. In 1924 Mongolia declared formal independence – but nonetheless the Soviets stayed in power for almost another 60 years. The Stalinist Government collectivized the economy, and terrorized the revered Buddhist lamas (monks). Monasteries were razed and monks slaughtered en masse. Soviet troops finally withdrew from Mongolia in 1992. But, despite 65 years of Soviet-style regime, even in the capital, Ulaanbaatar, half the population lived in traditional *gers* (domed tents), with rudimentary electric and water supplies.

In the mid-1990s democratic reforms swept Mongolia's US-funded United Democratic Coalition into power. They were determined to employ 'shock therapy' to liberalize and privatize the economy. Despite subsequent changes in government, the economic Westernization and privatization of Mongolia's economy has continued ever since. In 1998 a new law required the use of surnames, which was unprecedented in traditional Mongolian culture, and US President George W Bush visited the country in 2005, to thank the Government for supporting the invasion of Iraq and sending 100 soldiers.

The tensions between traditional rural life and the economic forces of modernization and globalization were already being played out while Louisa Waugh was living in Mongolia. However, the bitter winter she survived in 1998 was followed by even more brutal winters in both 2000 and 2001. These were the harshest Mongolian winters for half a century – resulting in the death of more than six million livestock, and crippling the hundreds of thousands of nomads still herding out in the vast empty steppe.

Mother Rock
Visiting a sacred shrine in the steppes.

The rumor started many years ago. Amidst boulders littered across the steppe 70 kilometers southwest of Ulaanbaatar, the Mother was healing and answering prayers in return for gifts and worship.

Mongolians flock to this bulbous, three-meter-tall rock, carved by the elements into the crude outline of a woman. They come weighed down with bottles of vodka and milk, food and the brilliant blue-silk *hadags* (scarves) they use to adorn temples, cairns and all things sacred and powerful. This worship of the land, trees, mountains and the startling blue Central Asian sky is older than Mongolia itself and existed eons before Buddhism was introduced here in the 13th century.

I visited the rock with my Mongolian friends at the end of my second winter here. We'd just spent a weekend horse-riding and camping with some local nomads. One of my friends, Tsetsge, suggested we detour to the Mother on our way home to Ulaanbaatar, as she wanted to pray for her 68-year-old father who'd become seriously ill.

'Worshipping at Mother Rock and other shrines and Buddhist temples was outlawed for nearly 70 years after the 1921 socialist revolution,' she told me during the grinding, roadless journey.

'It was only when we got democracy at the beginning of the 1990s that we were allowed to return and practise our rituals. The irony is that Shamanism and Buddhism are becoming more important now, as though people need to make up for all that lost time.'

I was excited about this visit. Ever since I first briefly glimpsed Mongolia while on the way to China in 1993, I'd vowed to return to the steppe, to learn about the traditions of this still-thriving nomadic culture. I had been living in the capital, Ulaanbaatar, since 1996, writing, editing and teaching a bit of English.

And now we were heading through the heart of the mysterious steppe. As we sat crushed in the back of a dilapidated Russian jeep with three other Mongolian friends, we laughed at a herd of Bactrian camels meandering across the trail. The whole herd was shedding its winter coat. Sheets of matted brown fuzz trailed from them as they swayed in front of us. We mocked their scruffiness as they regarded us with haughty camel contempt.

Suddenly we dipped into a valley, and there she was – Mother Rock.

The stench hit me as soon as we scrambled out of our jeep. Littered with rotting food, fermenting milk and shattered vodka bottles, the shrine at first resembles a sacred rubbish tip. But I was enthralled – the Mother, swathed in hadags, was being encircled by a coil of Mongolians, including many young people. Everyone was carrying bottles and packages which they placed in front of the rock as others bowed their heads and murmured prayers. The shrine was enclosed by a crumbling wall made entirely of black tea: dried, compressed into bricks and stacked a meter high.

Tsetsge and I entered, pushing through hundreds of hadags tied to a makeshift wooden archway. Smoke rose from a small fire choking with incense as we picked our way through food debris towards the rock. An elderly woman, bent almost double by a life of herding and foraging, leaned her forehead against the rock, wringing her hands as she prayed.

Tsetsge took a turquoise hadag from her sheepskin jacket pocket and delicately wrapped it around the neck of the rock. She whispered prayers for her father and gently laid a wedge of cheese and a small bottle of yoghurt on the heap of offerings.

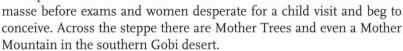

We were surrounded by the devout and the hopeful. Students arrive at the rock en masse before exams and women desperate for a child visit and beg to conceive. Across the steppe there are Mother Trees and even a Mother Mountain in the southern Gobi desert.

Older people stubbornly held on to the beliefs of their ancestors through the Soviet period and are now enjoying the freedom to worship, and they encourage their children to do the same. My landlord, Batbold, who's a 32-year-old cancer specialist, has told me in all seriousness that visiting Mother Rock annually for three years ensures health and well being.

'But only,' he reiterated, 'if you revere the Rock and present her with hadags, food and milk.' Mother Rock demands – and gets – respect.

Tsetsge's father, by the way, is doing fine.

Tuya's tale

Discovering a different world at an orphanage in Ulaanbaatar.

Erdentuya lives in Yarmag *ger* district. Like just over half of Ulaanbaatar's 600,000 residents she has electricity, but no running water, and an outside toilet in a fenced yard. The view from her house looks out over the meandering Tuul river, which divides Ulaanbaatar, and monstrous power station Number Four, which belches out fumes day and night. Erdentuya lives with 41 other homeless children in a shelter run by an Australian woman and a team of Mongolians. She's 10 years old.

I met Tuya, as she's known, in the spring, when I visited the shelter to talk about starting an English class for the older girls. This short, plump child with cropped hair and a habit of staring at the ground to disguise her shyness, could have been a boy or a girl. But her passion for red nail-polish and her gentle manner charmed me and she almost immediately became my blatant favorite.

She was picked up by Ulaanbaatar's children's police two years ago, living on the streets at the age of eight. After being held by a state-run orphanage for several weeks, she was handed over to the shelter along with five others.

It took some time before she would tell her story. Her family of 10, who live together in one room just streets away in this unpaved, decaying district, survive on less than seven dollars a month. Tuya's father worried about money, drank cheap, toxic vodka to forget, and died young, leaving his wife to fend for the kids any way she could. The family house was rented out to pay for food and clothing and, living literally on top of each other, tempers frayed. Tuya says she ran away because her mother beat her, and now has no contact with her immediate family. When Dee Dee, who runs the shelter, asked her gently what she'll do when she gets older, Tuya murmured that she's going to gather and sell fallen coal from the wagons that rumble in and out of Ulaanbaatar's only train station. This, after all, is how her mother fed the nine children.

Yarmag is the only future Tuya has. Without the shelter she'd be on the streets, forced to beg or scrounge for food and clothing. She could even be reduced to living under the streets, in the sewers, an airless network of hot water and raw waste pipes, which are home to several hundred street children. As it is, years of chronic malnutrition have led to her being physically stunted and developing learning difficulties. She reads and writes a little, but struggles even with basic numeracy and science. Tuya's unlikely to marry and so will always need some kind of support. She is bullied here and does catch the occasional dose of

scabies from one of the new arrivals. But she is safe, well fed – and cared about.

During one of my recent classes – which she attends, though saying little – she fell asleep leaning against my shoulder. She snoozed for half an hour before an older girl poked her and ordered her to fetch water. Blinking sleepily, Tuya tottered to her feet and searched for her boots.

This water-carrying is eternal labor. As I walk through Yarmag every Friday afternoon on my way to the shelter I see children, adults and pensioners hauling enormous metal cauldrons, and lines of people waiting patiently to fill their bottles. Cows lumber through the area, grazing on garbage and weeds, and on every corner there's a small kiosk selling a mixture of cigarettes, noodles, washing powder and sweets. This doesn't feel like central Ulaanbaatar, where I live with my running water and nearby supermarket – it doesn't even feel like the same city. It's just seven kilometers, but a world away from Ulaanbaatar's new neon lights, Western-style bars, foreign cars and fast-food cafés.

After my teaching, habitual cup of tea and gossip with the workers, one or two of the children walk me back to the bus stop. Tuya has never come – the older girls who dominate my time and energy, desperate for attention and affection, elect themselves as escorts. But Dee Dee, who knows of my love for this beautiful, shy child, tells me Tuya is standing up for herself a little more these days. 'The attention,' she says, smiling quietly, 'is obviously doing her good.'

Journey to the end of the earth

Setting off for Tsengel, a village in the far west of Mongolia.

My friend, Sodnem, whose postbox I share, was on the phone.

'There's a letter for you from someone called Abbai who lives in Tsengel village in Bayan-Olgii. It says they do want an English teacher. What's it all about?'

I stiffened. 'Oh God,' I thought. 'Now I have to go!'

For the previous eight months I had talked almost incessantly to friends and colleagues about going to live in the Mongolian countryside. I'd made and changed plans, switched my choice of landscape (Mongolia has desert, mountains and steppe) and my earnest ramblings had gradually become a standing joke.

The problem was that Tsengel village was about as hidden and rural as you can get. Bayan-Olgii, Mongolia's westernmost province, is popularly known as the Tibet of Mongolia. Its stark, fierce mountains and treeless valleys are home to Mongolian minorities – Kazakh herders and Tuvans from the nearby Central Asian republic (part of the Russian Federation). Tsengel, population 3,500, and more than 2,000 kilometers from Ulaanbaatar, is Mongolia's westernmost village.

After a sleepless night sitting up persuading myself how wonderful it all would be, my friend Chimgee and I rang Abbai to verify my arrival a month later. The crackling connection took 45 minutes to secure, only confirming my view that I had booked myself into a place at the end of the world.

Abbai, Tsengel's governor, said the local school director was already drawing up the schedule for my visit. The panic started. I began to shop for a siege – buying coffee, canned fish, pasta and tomato paste in bulk – trying to wind up my journalism and eating as much good food as I could in preparation for several months of noodles and boiled meat.

And then, just two weeks before my scheduled take-off, I fell in love. I didn't move to Mongolia to meet an Englishman, but Gulliver, a shy gentle musician, captivated me. While I nervously tore around saying goodbye to my friends and panicking over what I hadn't done, we spent every spare moment wrapped around each other ignoring my imminent departure. I looked around at Ulaanbaatar's rubble-strewn streets and tiny candlelit kiosks and felt sick with nerves. I knew this city with its dodgy heating system and power cuts. Tsengel had four hours of electricity a day (usually), one shop and no running water. This was going to be tough.

The evening before I left, my friends came round, helped me finish packing and left me laden with books and chocolates. Gulliver and I fell asleep halfway through the night, exhausted by my emotional turmoil. I awoke with a jerk and with a feeling of panic rising in my chest, looked at my clock and swore. It was 6.15am – in 15 minutes I had to be at the airport 25 kilometers away or risk losing my seat.

The driver of the first car we hailed tore along the almost empty streets towards the airport and I finally checked in at 7.35. At 8.10, still waiting for the boarding sign, I wandered over to luggage security to have my hand baggage (which included a bucket full of toilet rolls) checked. The officer took my flight bag, frowned and said casually: 'You're very late –

the plane has gone.' A terse conversation was barked between officers and we were suddenly herded through several corridors to the departure hall. Another officer glanced at my ticket and shook her head, 'The flight has gone!'

I was shaking my head and weeping. Gulliver speaks no Mongolian and just looked confused. But a well-dressed Mongolian tapped me on the shoulder, saying: 'The plane is going, but if you run fast you can catch it.' I momentarily threw my arms around Gulliver's neck, and then I ran out onto the tarmac. A woman was gesturing frantically to me and pointing to the plane being towed toward the runway. 'Run, run!'

After 100 meters I abandoned my bags and ran blindly towards the plane waving my arms. A figure appeared brandishing a walkie-talkie.

We scurried towards each other and I gibbered, 'Bayan-Olgii.'

He retrieved my bags while speaking into his radio. Three minutes later I shakily boarded the plane. An immaculately dressed stewardess smiled at me and said, 'I'll take your bags. You go and sit down.'

I was on my way to Tsengel.

The death of Kalim

Why it's hard to be young, male, unemployed and a Kazakh in Tsengel village.

My friend Ayush and I were wringing out our washing when we saw the procession snaking up the hill towards the ancient cemetery that stands above Tsengel village. Silent men and women picked their way through the intricate clay and wooden tombs until they came to a freshly dug grave.

'It's the funeral,' said Ayush calmly. 'His father hasn't even arrived from Kazakhstan. But the Kazakhs always bury their dead the next day.' She bent her head and continued rinsing her sheets. I stared at the small crowd across the rocky hillside and thought again about the rage and despair that killed Kalim.

'I went to school with him,' she told me later that afternoon as we sat in her small wooden house drinking bowls of tea. 'He really was one of the brightest in the whole year. Maybe that was his problem. There wasn't anything to occupy him here.' I nodded, drumming my fingers slowly on the table.

'What happened after he left school – what did he do then?'

Ayush shrugged. 'He went to the old Kazakh capital, Alma Ata, to study. Lots of the Kazakhs do. He came back here to Tsengel, got married, I don't know. He didn't work.'

She lowered her voice, though there was no-one else in the room and it was her house. 'That's when he started drinking and they began,' she gestured, 'you know, fighting. His wife Kulgan left him once a couple of years ago, after the first child. But they got back together again and he promised to change.'

Ayush is Mongolian, but our small village and the surrounding mountains and deserts of Bayan-Olgii province are home to most of Mongolia's 90,000 Kazakhs. Traditionally nomads, they herded here in the far west of Mongolia before anyone thought of international borders, tending their camels, goats and sheep in these barren mountains, always living on the edge of Mongolian society. Many of them don't even speak Mongolian. They don't want to belong to Mongolia – the strength of their own identity leaves room for no other.

Many, but not all, Mongolians despise the Kazakhs and don't want to work or socialize with them. So most of the Mongolian Kazakhs have kept to these remote western mountains, as far from the capital Ulaanbaatar as possible. In the early 1990s, lured by the promise of a new, more prosperous life, thousands trekked back to newly independent Kazakhstan. But they didn't feel welcome back 'home'. In Kazakhstan they were ironically identified as Mongolians and treated with subtle, unnerving contempt. Life was hard. So many returned to Mongolia and continued to play their beautiful, haunting music and worship Allah in exile. Kalim was amongst them.

I'd only met him a few times. We'd been introduced when I'd just arrived in Tsengel village. Kulgan told me her husband was a driver. But Kalim wasn't working – because like most people here, he didn't have a car. Ayush and I saw him again a couple of weeks later. He was coming out of a narrow shop doorway as we were entering. He reeked of vodka and had a swollen black eye.

At the beginning of the summer he and Kulgan fought again bitterly, shouting through the night. Kalim was drinking heavily, cheap local vodka. He didn't stop when Kulgan left the house early that morning for her teaching job. He could have slept it off, nursed a hangover – they could have made it up once more. But Kalim took down a wire clothes line and hung himself from the wooden rafters of their house. Their neighbor was walking across the yard to the communal toilet when he heard Kalim choking to death. He was just too late.

Kalim's suicide disturbed me because I realized what a terrible place Tsengel could be. The men have hardly any work here; the small clinic and the school are mostly run by the women, who are also constantly busy raising their children, cooking and cleaning. The men spend their time hunting and then hanging round the village square, trading wool or skins. There's little else to do.

For Kalim, aged 27, bored, clever, drunk, without money, unable to work and unwelcome anywhere else, Tsengel was all he had – and it just wasn't enough.

Tea and delight

Two birthday celebrations.

Kultii was hacking at a huge slab of fresh, moist beef. 'Louisa, it's my birthday on Sunday,' she said, wiping her damp forehead with the back of her bloodstained hand. 'Come over in the afternoon and drink some *chai* [tea] with Delgermaa and Javhlan.'

'That would be good,' I nodded, blowing on my own bowl of steaming black salty chai. 'What time shall we visit?'

I was perched in the spartan but vigorously scrubbed school kitchen, which has been ruled by Kultii, Delgermaa and Javhlan for the last 19 years. They bake and boil meals for 85 pupils each day without electricity or running water and have 20 kids of their own to look after between them. The school food is very basic – even potatoes are scarce here. People in these remote western mountains live on rice, flour, meat and milk. But there's always a bowl of tea and usually some hot food for anyone who drops into the kitchen. People in Tsengel village know how to give.

I arranged to meet Delgermaa and Javhlan and left them kneading a mountain of dough for the thick crusty bread they bake on the blackened wood stove. I strolled to one of the cramped wooden cabins that sell flour, rice, soap – and a lurid assortment of boiled sweets. I rarely buy this stuff – I don't need to, for every time I browse I am given a handful of sweets or biscuits. The traders spoil me. But now I bought half a kilo of sweets for Kultii.

A couple of sunny, windswept days later I head over to her house with Delgermaa, Javhlan and a posse of local women. We crowd into Kultii's two-room log cabin, gather round the table and pass each other bowls of milky tea. Kultii's table is laden with everything she can afford to buy or bake for her friends – fresh bread, fried dough sticks, sugar, biscuits and dried milk curds.

'Have some more food,' she urges me, 'and give me your cup, Louisa. You need some more tea.'

Mongolians are dedicated tea drinkers. We crouch on narrow stools drinking, nibbling and gossiping. Delgermaa and Javhlan prompt the ritual singing, more women arrive with young, shy children and we get noisier and gulp even more tea.

Kultii, sweating next to her wooden stove and breastfeeding her eighth child, suddenly claps her hands. 'Louisa, did you bring your camera? We need pictures!'

Fourteen mothers rush for the mirror, straightening headscarves, passing a single lipstick back and forth (it's me who is camera-shy here). The table is pushed back against the wall and my friends line up like soldiers. I start laughing, 'No! Act natural!' and snap photos of the beaming group. We toast the birthday girl (who is 41) and wander outside into the autumn sunshine, lingering with the yaks and goats.

Four days later it is my own birthday. By midday my arm is aching from shaking hands with half of Tsengel. People dismount from their horses and camels to greet me. Men, women and children shyly push bouquets of plastic flowers into my arms, give me chocolates, miniature bottles of perfume and bags of those glistening sweets.

Kultii, Delgermaa, Javhlan and my other friends arrange a disco in Tsengel's ancient, generator-powered theater (there's no electricity here). Two hundred people turn up and we dance all evening. Then, under duress, I clamber up onto the narrow stage, thank everyone in Mongolian – and sing a Beatles song.

By midnight a small group has settled in my felt *ger*, pushed the desk back and presented me with a midnight feast. Kultii's bread, home-made cheese, meat fried in precious onions and, best of all, four fresh apples Delgermaa charmed off someone who'd just been to Ulaanbaatar. Here, where there is so little, I am utterly indulged. We get out the guitar, sway to lilting folk songs and stay up with the stars. I fall into bed at dawn,

still slightly drunk.

The next morning I wake up late with a hangover. As my head slowly clears I smile, recalling Javhlan trying to explain to me what the name 'Tsengel' means. I sluggishly reach for my dictionary, and there it is in black and white. Delight.

A frozen world

The extraordinary experience of Mongolia's midwinter.

I wake up and my world has frozen. Everything, and I mean everything – my water, tomato paste, soap – is encased in thick, milky ice. I light a candle, stand up in my sleeping bag and pull on another layer of clothing. Shivering, I take a knife to the water bucket and hack at the ice until bubbles rise to the surface. Lighting my small stove is tough because the wood, which was damp, is now frozen. By the time my smoky fire is finally crackling and heating the water and ice in the kettle, the outside temperature has risen to -25 degrees Centigrade. I've never been so cold in my life. I know the mountains surrounding my village will be drenched in fresh snow but I can't see anything because my window is coated in thick ice.

On this dark, freezing winter morning, venturing to the communal outside toilet is quite an endurance test. But, after two cups of steaming black coffee I am bundled up and off to work, just as the sky is gradually brightening.

My school is a ten-minute walk alongside the Hovd river which flows through the village. The river is now so solid that horses are being ridden and cars driven over it. Everything but my eyes is concealed from the freezing air – my gloved fingers pushed down into my pockets.

'Louisa – off to work?' calls my neighbor Sansar-Huu. 'Don't worry,' he teases me, 'it's quite warm today – just wait till it gets really cold!'

Our school has no electricity or running water, but each small classroom is heated by a wood-burning stove. This morning we all wear our coats during lessons. Wind-burned children from herders' settlements outside the village board at the school 12 to a dormitory. Their parents pay the fees in meat and wood.

At break we jostle to be near the staff-room stove and my colleagues pull their fur hats back on. 'You sit by the fire, Louisa – you must be freezing,' offers Sansar-Huu's wife Gansukh, my fellow English teacher. I am.

After our classes Gansukh and I cross the street to the post office, which is crowded, as the weekly post has just arrived. Beaming and clutching two letters, I walk home with Gansukh and a couple of our students, passing herders trading camel, sheep, goat and wolf skins. We stop en route for bowls of tea at a friend's house.

At home, I need more water. Armed with a bucket, I lift the creaking lid of the well opposite our yard. But the water is so frozen I can hear the rocks I fling down the shaft ricochet off the ice. Taking the ax, I set out for the nearby river to forge my own well.

That afternoon it snows heavily as Sansar-Huu and I saw logs in the yard. 'How long will it be this cold?' I ask him as I stand panting, my face flushed and numb. 'Oh, it gets as low as -48 here,' he tells me, grinning. 'But we need this snowy winter. Even by October it's really too cold to live in a felt ger here – so the herders in the mountains move up into their winter log cabins. Their livestock live on hay and the herders melt snow for all their water. They slaughter sheep and cows for food at the start of winter, when the animals are still fat, and the ice stores the meat till the end of spring.'

'So, if the snow comes late, like it did this year, what then?' I query, resting on a white log.

'That's when the steppe gets overgrazed, which means spring will be very tough. Remember those trucks loaded up with ice driving way into the mountains?' I nod.

'The ice was for herders who didn't have enough snow and weren't near the rivers.' Sansar-Huu pauses to wave and call greetings to a local who trots past, his horse crusted in frozen sweat. I look around me at the snowscape – silent mountains on all four sides, pack camels weighed down with flour and hay, children skating on the river – and the deep, untrodden snow.

I pick up the ax and raise it to my shoulder just as Sansar-Huu turns back to me. 'You know,' he says, 'the herders are fine now – the snow is here for the winter. Oh, we'll be waiting for spring and warmer weather to arrive – but hopefully not too soon.'

In the eye of the beholder

People's names are not always what they seem.

At the end of a romantic evening in Ulaanbaatar, Bilguun tenderly called me his 'ugly Louisa'. I was a bit taken aback as he was my lover and had his arms around me at the time. But when I complained to a couple of Mongolian friends at work the next morning, they simultaneously burst out laughing.

'Oh! He only said that because he loves you!'

The Mongolian word for ugly (*muhai*) also, in the right context, means 'darling'.

Since I moved west to the mountains my Mongolian has improved considerably. So when I found out that one of my neighbors here in Tsengel is called Mene ('many') and his wife's name is Cow, I couldn't resist giving my friends a Mongolian translation. Here, if you have many cows (or yaks or camels), you are rich, which Mene incidentally is.

But it is the literal meaning of Mongolian names and the reason they are given in the first place which is really tantalizing. My teaching counterpart is Gansukh (Steel Ax). Her husband is Sansar-Huu, which translates as 'Son of the Cosmos'. One of Gansukh's students is Zerleg, which means 'savage' or 'barbarian'. And I have a student called Chudruck, or Fist. Then there is poor Neer-Gui, whose name is 'No-name'. Neer-Gui sits next to Butta-kuz, or Camel-eyes. Sazug meanwhile sits at the back of the class, which may be the best place for him, as his name means 'smelly'.

I quizzed Steel Ax one day about these bewildering names.

'Why would anyone call their child "Camel Eyes"?'

'Have you ever looked at a camel's eyes?' she replied. 'They're beautiful'.

It's true – Tsengel is full of long-lashed, coy-eyed camels. So Butta-kuz is really quite a compliment. As for Smelly, that took a bit more unraveling.

'It's affectionate,' said Steel Ax. 'No-one thinks it is offensive. As a name, in Mongolia, it actually implies that he smells quite nice.' (I thought of Bilguun, and my being ugly and beloved.)

This is good news for another student, ten-year-old Zolbin (Stray) who, Steel Ax assured me, is a very loved child.

Zerleg was given his savage name to bring him strength. It's a way of asking the gods to protect him, as is the name Fist. But Steel Ax became very somber when we got around to discussing Neer-Gui.

'She had four or five brothers who all died young. Her family begged the lama for a name that wouldn't anger or insult our Buddhist deities. He advised them to call her No-name. It's a humble name and she's a healthy child!'

Steel Ax has four brothers and sisters who all have names with a similar meaning to hers, symbolizing strength and might. Her own son is called Yalvita (Victory) while her daughter is named after a medicinal plant. Many girls have the word Tsetseg (Flower) in their names, while the male-only name Buga (Bull) speaks for itself.

Parents hoping for a son often give their new daughter a male name – and vice versa. It's another way of petitioning the gods, in this case for the gender of their next child.

Until very recently large families were the norm in Mongolia, especially in rural areas where children are the only security parents have in their old age. Mothers used to be awarded medals for having five children or more, so naming all your kids could turn into quite a challenge.

Mongolian names range from the poetic – Altan Duul (Golden Flame) is my favorite – to the ferocious. Malmas is a placid, happily married man in his forties, who works in Tsengel as an accountant. He's named after the legendary Almas – a towering, ferocious, coarse-haired beast, who apparently still lives in the remote Altai mountains and carries off the occasional nubile young man or woman to satisfy his rapacious appetites.

No-one has quite been able to explain that one to me.

A sheep for the Shaman

Meeing people who communicate with the spirits in the remote land of Tuva.

Tuvan is the most beautiful language I've ever heard. Words and phrases linger in my mind like bars of music and I repeat them just for the pleasure of the sound they produce.

Here in the far western mountains there are more Tuvans than anywhere else in Mongolia. Tuva, Mongolia's northwestern neighbor (and one of Russia's many republics), is an obscure land, best known for its quirkily named capital, Khyzl (pronounced Kizul), where an obelisk marks the absolute center of Asia. The Tuvans first crossed the Altai range to Mongolia because this seemingly barren landscape in fact offers good grazing for their livestock. Today they herd their animals alongside Mongolian nomads.

But there is a difference between them. While the Mongolians worship Buddha and the local Kazakh community pray to Allah, the Tuvans have no God. They are Shamans. Shamanism is not a religion, but a practice, with the Shaman being the link between the animal and land spirits and those who revere and pray to these spirits. Only the Shaman can communicate between these two worlds.

My colleague and friend Gansukh was giving me a Tuvan lesson when her brother Dorj arrived with a host of relatives from these nearby mountains. No-one schedules visits here; hospitality is endemic. Crumpled grandparents, florid husbands and wives and wiry children poured into Gansukh's wooden home, greeting and gossiping as they crowded round the wood-burning stove, the older people crouching on the few narrow stools, the youngsters kneeling on the floor.

Gansukh brewed a vat of salty milk tea, as Sansar-Huu took his dagger outside to slaughter a sheep. A resigned-looking ewe had her throat cut and was instantly skinned, as the guests blew on their scalding tea and warmed their stubby hands.

I helped Gansukh clean the warm internal organs, the stomach and the intestines, which would all be eaten. Everything is used. The head and hooves are boiled and the flesh scraped off and chewed. Every ounce of fat is saved and the skin sewn into the lining of winter clothes. For an ex-vegetarian, I've come to appreciate sheep.

The organs were simmered on the stove for several hours, while the guests settled down. Sansar-Huu splashed potent local vodka into a shallow wooden bowl, dipping his left ring finger into the clear liquid three times and spraying the drops around us, to toast in turn the spirits, the mountains and the land. I frowned, bemused, as he passed the bowl to a young woman: the men are always served first here.

'Why is she so important?' I whispered to Gansukh.

'Because she's the Shaman,' she hissed. My eyes bulged. I'd heard much about Enktuya, whose spiritual inheritance descends from nine generations of female Tuvan Shamans. I'd been told she was just 23, but her age was impossible to determine: her face was youthful, but she had the gait of an older, more tired woman. Enktuya would spend just one night in the village – a Shaman, Gansukh whispered, can rarely leave the mountains. Now I understood why the ewe had been slain. It was in honour of Enktuya's visit.

When the sheep was finally tender Gansukh took a knife and silently tossed a small section of bone, meat, dried blood and a slither of the heart into the stove flames. Tuvans believe there's a spirit in all fires and this was an offering. They never burn soiled or blood-stained papers or rags, which are instead buried outside.

We feasted, washing down the chunks of dripping meat with more tea. The grandparents relaxed, inhaling snuff from tiny stone bottles and smoking pungent shredded tobacco wrapped in strips of old newspaper. By evening the guests were drifting off to visit other homes and relatives.

Gansukh and I finally finished my Tuvan lesson and began her English revision (I am training her to take over as the teacher in the school when I leave in a month's time).

'So many visitors!' she sighed. 'Some of them will come back here and stay, so we'll be up late and I'll be tired at school tomorrow.'

'Don't you want them to return?'

She smiled in the candlelight. 'Of course I do, Louisa. I couldn't ever live in a place where people don't visit and wouldn't be welcome to stay as long as they wanted. This isn't just our home; it's also theirs.'

A month in the country

Visiting nomadic friends – and their animals – in Mongolia's remotest mountains.

'That goat, the black one over there,' called Hulan. 'That's the one we need.' She gestured vaguely towards a cluster of black goats who all eyed me suspiciously. It was eight in the morning and we were in the throes of milking 50 goats who all had to be tethered first. I was already exhausted. Goats are faster than you think – and they all looked the same to me.

Hulan, one of my teaching colleagues in Tsengel, had invited me to spend a summer month horse-riding and herding with her nomadic family. I was delighted. I pictured myself lolling next to a cool river, collecting stories for my book, swimming, horse-riding and learning to milk the odd goat or yak. I couldn't have been more wrong.

Mongolian herders are busiest in summer – milking their goats, sheep, cows and yaks, shearing the sheep (with scissors) herding on steep mountain slopes, collecting dry dung for fuel, and water for cooking and washing. The work is endless.

Hulan's mother Dere-Huu, a statuesque 56-year-old with cheeks burned to the color of oak, always rose at 5.00am. The rest of us got up at 6.30 every morning. When I could finally bear to open my eyes, the early-morning light was gorgeous. We were camped 90 kilometers west of Mongolia's westernmost village. The mountains were snow-capped, the hills coated in dense pine-forest concealing ripening berries, and the rivers clear as glass. But I've never worked so hard in my life.

Goats aren't difficult animals to milk, but it takes a bit of practice. That first morning Dere-Huu was on her eighth goat while I still grimly tugged at my second. To add insult to its reluctant dribble of milk, the third goat kicked my pail over. I was mortified.

We lived on goat- and yak-milk – boiling and separating it to make thick crusted cream, curdling it into soft cheese and yoghurt, fermenting gallons to produce Mongolia's famous *airag* drink and even distilling the airag for *shimin arkhi*, the purest vodka you'll find anywhere.

While the menfolk went off hunting, Hulan and Dere-Huu patiently taught me to wash sheep wool, stretch and dry it on the rocky riverside, beat the wool with sticks until it was fluffy and finally roll it into layers of new felt for the walls of the *ger*. I learned to churn butter, to dry cheese into rock-hard but edible curds (*arrul*) and to cook marmot, a large steppe rodent Mongolians are partial to.

But we did relax – at dusk every evening we sat around the cracked tin stove drinking hot, frothing yak's milk. The wooden door of the *ger* was open, animals silhouetted in the long shadows. Friends and relatives visited on horseback almost daily. We were invited en masse to a nearby wedding party, where we toasted the bride and groom with shimin arkhi, ate platters of fresh mutton and horse meat with our fingers, and the Mongolians sang their hearts out. Toddlers laughed and cried while older people, their faces creased from lives in the sun, recited poetry. I just sat and beamed.

The day after the wedding, I swam at lunchtime. But by early evening the mountains directly behind us were dusted with fresh snow. Now the cold rain battered our *ger* every two or three days. The roof leaked twice and we had to bail out, crouched by the stove, drenched and shivering.

'How do you survive here in winter?' I asked Dere-Huu, who had spent her life in these mountains.

'Oh Louisa,' she replied, grinning broadly, 'the snow can come up to here'. She slapped one of her broad thighs. 'But the men gather hay for the livestock in autumn and we move to our wooden cabin 60 kilometers from here.'

Dere-Huu and her family move five times a year. The people go on horseback. Their large *ger* and all their possessions – the ancient chests and wall-hangings, the stove and the two narrow beds, are all carried by their three camels.

Our final morning with Dere-Huu and her family dawned sunny and cool. A truck was heading back to Tsengel and so, unfortunately, were Hulan and I. Laden with arrul and cheese, I hugged Dere-Huu. We clambered up on to the open truck and waved as it clumsily wove its way eastwards.

Going home

Louisa ponders on what she will miss about Mongolia.

I knew I was leaving Tsengel village when the weekly mail arrived. Wedged in the bundle of letters handed over to Nina in the post office were three airmail envelopes addressed to me. They were all letters from my family and all said the same thing: 'When are you coming home, Louisa?'

I re-read the thin sheets of paper sitting in my yard with a cup of coffee. Afterwards I looked around me and pursed my dry lips. This small herding community had been my life for the last year. I knew all the local gossip, the simmering feuds and illicit affairs; the celebrations, traditions and drudgery that made up this secluded mountain village. But, after almost three years away from my own country, I suddenly reeled with homesickness, and knew with a somber certainty that my days in Tsengel were numbered.

I thought I was ready to leave. I couldn't face another raw, freezing winter in the mountains. I was sick of fetching slopping buckets of water from the river and washing myself in a tin bath. My skin was dry and my feet were cracked. I told myself there was a lot I wouldn't miss about the countryside.

Over the weeks before I left Tsengel, friends and neighbors crowded into my wooden cabin and constantly invited me for dinner. My stomach bulged after numerous mounds of horse meat and mutton noodles. Mongolians lavish food on guests who are embarking on a long journey – I ate and drank my way around the village, took endless photos and promised to return. In between the feeding frenzy and the farewell disco, I wandered along the river bank alone, absorbing every detail of the wild, silent landscape around me.

Landing in the capital Ulaanbaatar at dusk was a revelation.

The taxi driver, who looked as though he was about 15, accelerated through the streets as high-pitched pop music screamed out of the tinted car windows. I laughed out loud as the illuminated city center zoomed past. In the year I'd spent in Tsengel, there'd been electricity for exactly three weeks – and that was for four hours a day. Most people in Tsengel have never been to Ulaanbaatar and I suddenly felt like a flustered tourist, although I'd lived in the capital for two years prior to moving to the mountains.

I stayed with my friend Javhlan, who was amused by my waiting for the kettle to boil for ten minutes before realizing I hadn't flicked the 'on' switch.

'You spent too long in the countryside,' she commented wryly, as I eventually poured the coffee. 'Just wait till you get back to England!'

But I knew it wasn't returning to London that would floor me – the contrast between life in Tsengel and Ulaanbaatar was far sharper than the differences between two capital cities.

I stood in front of a department store counter for 15 minutes one morning, trying to decide which brand of shampoo to buy. I'd ended up washing my hair with laundry soap in Tsengel (and it didn't look any the worse). Now labels dazzled me. Javhlan howled with laughter when I came home one evening with three different kinds of beer, because I couldn't remember which type I liked best any more.

All these choices were making my life difficult.

The day I booked my ticket to London, I sat in Javhlan's centrally heated lounge and mentally rewound the previous year. I had a host of memories from Tsengel impressed on my mind: my decadent birthday party, the chaotic school classes, seeing wolves for the first time, meeting the formidable Shaman.

Now I was heading back to constant hot water, bookshops, English cinema and good pizza: all the things I thought I'd longed for. But what, I pondered, would I miss from Tsengel most of all?

It was the people, the immense indigo sky – and the post office. I'd always raced to the tiny, cold post office at 11 o'clock on Wednesday morning. Every week I'd felt nervous and excited when the decrepit delivery van rolled up. If I had mail, it made my whole day: I'd read and re-read letters, friends would visit my home to see photos or magazines I'd received; a parcel would send me into raptures. Getting a letter would never be quite so precious again.

Letters from Beirut (Lebanon), 1999-2006

Reem Haddad

At the age of four, Reem's life drastically changed when Lebanon's civil war erupted in 1975. For the next 11 years she, like other Lebanese, learned to dodge bullets and seek shelter from bombs. In 1986, the family finally fled the country to the US. Five years later, the civil war abruptly ended. By then a university graduate, Reem wanted to see her country at peace and made the decision to return. Over the next 13 years, she saw the rebuilding of the country and witnessed people daring again to hope and dream.

Reem married a British journalist, Nicholas Blanford, with whom she had two children: Yasmine and Alexander. Today, the family still lives in Beirut. On one hand, life in Lebanon is wonderful. The streets are busy and cafés are full. On the other hand, it's deeply unsettling given the extreme political instability. While many families have chosen to leave the country, Reem and her husband have made the decision to stay. It was a difficult decision, taken in the knowledge that things may suddenly 'blow up' if tensions continue to rise. But the family believes that the Lebanese love their country and do not want to see another civil war.

Reem is now working for the International College in Beirut and writes their tri-yearly newsletter. She also freelances for several international and local publications.

Changes in Lebanon

Lebanon has had such a tortured modern history that its image in the world's eye is of a blasted landscape scarred by war and bitter conflict. The Lebanese people endured 15 years of civil war from 1975 to 1990 that cost around 150,000 lives and left the capital, Beirut, in ruins. The war was usually characterized as a Christian-Muslim conflict. But it was much more complicated and at various stages also involved Christians against Christians, Palestinians against Lebanese, Shi'a against Shi'a, Islamists against Communists. It was also a war in which regional powers backed rival militias. The Israelis at one point supported Maronite militias while a host of Arab countries supported other secular, Islamist, Lebanese and Palestinian militias. The war broke out after years of tension building between Lebanese Christians and the Palestinians, whose influence and growing military might many Christians feared would lead to a reshuffling of Lebanon's sectarian political system.

By 1999, however, when Reem Haddad started writing her series of Letters, Lebanon was shaking off its past woes. Beirut was being reconstructed and regaining its former title as the financial hub for the region and gaining a new one as a major holiday destination, particularly for cash-rich Arabs from the Gulf. Reem continued her correspondence for six years – longer than any other contributor to the series – and her vignettes embraced gentrification of old districts and the growth of Arabic media as well as portraits of street children and environmental campaigners. In 2005 she lamented the assassination of Rafik Hariri, the entrepreneurial prime minister largely responsible for the country's revival, and reported on the 'Cedar Revolution', as massive nonviolent demonstrations resulted in the withdrawal of Syrian troops.

But the civil war and its echoes were never far beneath the surface – and returned to haunt the Lebanese in 2006, when Israel invaded and bombarded the country in a vain attempt to obliterate the armed Shi'a group Hizbullah. Over 1,000 Lebanese civilians were killed – a third of them children under the age of 13. The war lasted 34 days and ended as suddenly as it had begun. A strengthened UN peacekeeping force was deployed along the border. Reem contributed a one-off letter to the *New Internationalist* (included here) about how the renewed conflict had affected the lives of her and her children.

The political situation in Lebanon remains complex and chaotic. In 2006 leading Christian cabinet minister Pierre Gemayel was shot dead and further assassinations followed in 2007 and 2008 – usually by car bomb. The country remained politically split down the middle and its parliament proved unable for many months to agree on a new president. In these circumstances, the chances of normal life being resumed seem remote – yet the yearning for peace comes through again and again in this series of letters.

Candles, courtesy of Israel
Life in Beirut after another Israeli bombing.

I suppose one could look at the romantic side of being bombarded by Israel and anticipate candlelit dinners each evening. That is, if one could ignore the hassle of cooking by the feeble light of candles and battery-operated lanterns, bathing in freezing water and shivering with cold in front of a redundant electric heater.

The worst part is that people were just beginning to recover from the previous Israeli onslaught only eight months after the warplanes of our friendly neighbor bombed two power stations in Lebanon, plunging much of Beirut into darkness.

Thanks to donations, power plants had been coming back to life and homes were enjoying almost full-time electricity.

And then, on 8 February, Israel struck again. This time the excuse was that the Hizbullah fighters, who are trying to oust Israeli occupation forces from south Lebanon, killed five Israeli soldiers in the previous two weeks.

I suppose a twisted logic could justify that the Israelis injured 17 civilians, deprived around 3.5 million people of heat in the middle of winter, inflicted at least $40 million worth of damage in a country still struggling to recover from a civil war – just to teach the Lebanese not to resist an occupation force in their own country.

The day after the shelling of Lebanon, the international media plastered pictures of 'poor' Israeli civilians huddled in bomb shelters. I couldn't help but notice that they had televisions, lights and heaters. And I couldn't help wishing I had a bomb shelter to hide from Israel's bombs.

But there was one thing the Israelis did not count on. After 16 years of civil war, the Lebanese have become an amazingly resilient people.

The day after the shelling, the reaction was

subdued. With a collective sigh, people just pulled out their generators – still placed on their balconies since the war days – refueled them and continued with their business.

Those who didn't have generators went to their local neighborhood electricity supplier. There, a huge generator operated by an entrepreneur who had the far-sighted vision to invest in these motors rented electricity lines to neighbors.

Abu Hussein, for example, in the picturesque community of Gemaizeh, provides ten amperes to nearby households for $80 a month and five amperes for $40 a month. It's enough to power the refrigerator, heater, television and lights in an average-sized apartment.

Others, who couldn't afford the services, shrugged their shoulders and also went about their businesses.

'I just close down my shop as soon as it gets dark,' said an owner of a clothing store. 'I won't subscribe to a generator now or ever because I simply can't afford it.'

'Let them bomb us all they want. We don't care,' said another store owner. 'Of course, the power cuts are making life difficult but we refuse to show the Zionists that we are weakened by their terrorism.'

I am ashamed to admit that as much as I want to be stoic, I long to watch TV, take a warm bath, cuddle by the heater and see what I'm cooking. At the moment there is strict rationing of electricity, but as luck would have it my neighborhood is getting much of its ration after midnight.

So I head towards Abu Hussein and request a power line from his generator.

'I have no more lines to rent,' he said. 'In fact, I have exceeded my limit.' I plead.

'I just can't,' he says. 'May God help you find another way to power your home.'

So far, God still hasn't found a way for me. So I console myself by placing scented and colored candles around the house.

I have learned the secret of surviving – God forbid – future missile attacks on power plants. Abu Hussein has confided in me that as soon as the Government repairs the electricity, some of his members will stop buying electricity from him.

'And then all you have to do is hook up a cable to my generator and pay me ten dollars a month on top of what you pay for government electricity,' he said. 'So when Israel bombs again, you have nothing to worry about. I'll immediately provide you with power.'

I think I'll do just that.

Across the fence

Families reunited after 52 years of separation.

It was the last thing I expected and for a few seconds I stood there dumbfounded. I was climbing a small hill in the village of Dhayra in south Lebanon. Somebody had told me that I might be able to find some members of the South Lebanon Army, Israel's proxy militia until their withdrawal in May this year (2000) after 22 years of occupation. As a journalist, I thought this would make a great interview.

Instead, I came across dozens of people standing in front of a fence. They were tearfully calling out people's names. On the other side, others were doing the same. In between the two groups was a barbed-wire fence – all that now separates Lebanon from Israel.

And then it dawned on me: these people were Palestinian families torn apart 52 years ago when the state of Israel was created. And today they were seeing each other for the first time.

Palestinians on the Israeli side had made their way to the fence and asked Lebanese villagers to send a message to certain Palestinian families living in refugee camps in Lebanon. Somehow the message had spread and a busload of Palestinian refugees had made their way south.

On both sides, men, women and children arched their necks trying to recognize each other.

'I am Itaf, the daughter of Rihan,' an elderly woman yelled from the Israeli side. 'Who are you? Do you know me?'

Immediately, screams rang out from the Lebanese side as cousins extended their hands in the air as if to reach her. Itaf and other Palestinians stepped over knee-high barbed wire and walked to the fence. Her hand reached through it to grasp the hands of her relatives on the Lebanese side. She had not seen them since 1948.

'How did this happen to us?' she cried out. 'Oh, how did this happen?'

Itaf was born in the Acre region in what was then known as Palestine. Her family fled to Lebanon in 1948 and contact with relatives ceased.

All around, sobs filled the air as relatives either recognized each other or met for the first time. Most were children when they fled. Only childhood memories remained of their friends and relatives. They persisted, calling out the names and trying to identify who was standing in front of them.

'We were neighbors, don't you remember?' one woman shouted from Lebanon. 'Tell me, what happened to your uncle and your aunt?'

Suddenly I noticed an elderly woman next to me silently shedding tears. She turned to me and grasped my hand. Her name, she said, was Myriam Moussa.

'I was only 13 when the Israelis made me go to Lebanon to join my Lebanese fiancé,' she said. 'I didn't want to go. I went alone and never saw my parents, brothers or sisters again.'

I gathered she was around 65 but she looked more like 80. The last time she saw her siblings, they were just small children, some even toddlers.

'Look over there,' she said still holding on to my hand. 'These are my sisters, and that man over there is my brother, Ahmad.'

From across the fence, an elderly man with white hair stared back. He seemed in a daze. He must have been around ten when his sister was forced to leave.

Nearby, their children held hands through the prickly barbed-wire fence. 'You're my first cousin,' said Yusra, holding on to a man's hand on the Israeli side. Both started crying. Neither one seemed to be able to let go.

Meanwhile, dozens of voices exclaimed joyfully when identities were established. Youngsters kissed the hands of the elderly extended through the fence.

Not knowing what to give her relative on the Lebanese side, one woman handed over a Pepsi can with Hebrew lettering. Another man threw over a *keffieh*, the traditional male headcovering, requesting that it be given to his brother. One family exchanged photographs.

The day ended all too soon. As I helped Myriam Moussa down the hill, her tears flowed again. 'What if they don't let me see my brother and sisters again?' she said.

I could only hope that perhaps, just perhaps, two warring nations might see beyond their hatred to allow wrinkled and youthful hands to touch through a prickly barbed wire.

It was not to be: a week later Israeli Prime Minister Ehud Barak prohibited Palestinians on the Israeli side from approaching the fence. Those on the Lebanese side came and waited for hours.

I wondered if Myriam Moussa was among those who finally turned away and walked slowly back down the hill.

Neighborly love

Reem realizes why she likes living in Lebanon.

It took the death of an elderly neighbor to remind me why I am still living in this chaotic country.

That day, I woke up to the wailing of several women. I looked out the window to see a coffin being brought into an apartment just opposite mine. Our buildings are so close that I could easily see the proceedings. Three women were staring in shock at the coffin, holding each other and crying out for the return of their loved one. On the balcony, several men paced nervously and fumbled with their cigarette packs.

Disturbed by the tragic scene, I began to turn away when I noticed almost all the neighbors in the four buildings which make up this small community standing on their balconies, heads bowed. Some were praying, others were wiping away silent tears. Young and old stood in silence.

I vaguely remembered the elderly man and his wife standing on their balcony staring at me and my husband only a few months ago. We were newlyweds and moving into our first home. I found their stare disconcerting and commented to my husband on their perceived rude behavior. Much in the impatient spirit of a young career couple, we pointedly turned our backs to them.

In the days to come, however, I found many of the neighbors' attitudes annoying. I thought that living in a community with buildings so closely facing each other would be rather exciting. Before moving here, I lived in a high-rise apartment and had a lovely bird's-eye view of some parts of Beirut. In this community, however, the view was people staring at us from their balconies.

But as I watched the neighbors standing in silence that day, shaking their heads and weeping over the man's death, they suddenly took the shape of caring neighbors rather than nosy ones. It dawned on me that they stared at us for a purpose. In this closely knit community, women wanted to know if new tenants posed any threat to their offspring running round the neighborhood and men needed to study the strangers who might intrude in their families' lives.

I also began to notice other details. Men, for example, came out on their balconies when pedlars arrived.

By now, neighbors had figured out that my husband has late working hours and I am often alone in the evenings. Visitors are dutifully noted.

When a visiting girlfriend inadvertently blocked the entrance of a nearby building with her car and came up to my apartment, neighborhood boys knew exactly where to locate her – and kindly helped her find another parking space.

It was then that it occurred to me that it's the people who tie me to Lebanon. There's the cobbler down the street, for example. When my car was giving me trouble he promptly shut his shop, climbed into the passenger seat and took me to his mechanic nephew. Then there's the grocer. Knowing that I'm still learning how to cook, he picks out the best produce and gives me a new recipe each time – adding a few items without charge 'just to give your stew some more taste', he assures me. There's also the shop owner who runs to take some heavy bags from me and carries them the whole block to my building.

And, just the other day, I was in a hurry to leave for a weekend holiday. I was carrying a big bag filled with blankets and, of all things, my mobile phone. It was only hours later as I opened the trunk of my car that I realized that I had left the bag on the sidewalk and made off without it. Two days later I returned to the scene. I didn't have much hope of finding it. And then I spotted the bag – my bag – on the top of a car.

Next to it an elderly tailor was sewing a pair of trousers.

'Some young people found it on the sidewalk and brought it to me,' he said. 'I thought I'd keep it until its owner turned up.'

I could have hugged him.

When Beirut's heavy traffic, potholed roads, nightmare of bureaucratic government offices (it's too much work even to report a theft), and the inconsistent electricity irk me, I remind myself of the cobbler, grocer, shop owner and the elderly tailor.

As for my neighbors, my husband and I are no longer items of curiosity. The staring from balconies has drastically decreased. We are now officially accepted in the community. However, there are some new tenants who have moved into a flat in the opposite building.

I think I can get a better view of them if I stand on the balcony.

A visitor in the mountains

Searching for her grandparents' grave, Reem relives the pain of a region's past.

I had envisaged laying down flowers on their graves, saying a small prayer or even introducing myself. But nothing had prepared me for this scene. Instead of the gravestones with loving inscriptions of my grandparents' names, I stared at skulls and bones strewn around the small cemetery. The marble tombs had been smashed open and the bones and skulls lay scattered carelessly around the overgrown graveyard.

I wasn't sure which skulls belonged to my grandparents and which to other relatives. It was an ugly scene and one which told the story of the hatred which engulfed these mountain villages during the Lebanese civil war.

I was still a child but I remember well my parents talking about the War of the Mountains. I remember hearing the deafening booms of rockets and artillery shells going over our heads from one village to another whenever we approached the mountains. They were times no child could ever forget. I remember hearing of relatives who were killed in the War of the Mountains. And I distinctly remember my father's warnings to the family that we should stay away from the mountain villages for the time being.

As Christians, we were no longer welcome. Neighbors and friends had turned against each other. For centuries, Christians and Druze (an offshoot of Islam) had coexisted in the mountains. True, there had been massacres two centuries ago when Lebanon was a hotbed of European political interests, but life had since settled peacefully around the two communities.

In 1982 Israel invaded Lebanon and led the way for its Christian ally militia, the Phalangists, to enter the mountains. One former militia member later told me: 'We went to help the Christians in the mountains, but they were not grateful and treated us badly.'

Small wonder. It was this 'help' that led to fierce battles in the mountains. Surrounded by Israeli troops, villagers found themselves fighting off the Phalangists. Many atrocities were committed by the Christian militia on Druze villagers. In turn, the Druze fought back and vented their anger on Christian villagers. Suddenly neighbor turned against neighbor. Some Christian villagers joined the Phalangists. To make a long story short, the Phalangists lost and Christian villagers were forced to flee from most of the mountain villages.

That's how it seems to be in a war. If a Muslim militia attacks you,

you begin to hate all Muslims. If a Christian attacks you, then you hate all Christians. Cool heads don't prevail. Revenge and anger are all one sees.

And it's obviously all that could be seen by the people who desecrated my grandparents' grave. Since the war ended in 1991, formal reconciliation – overseen by the country's president – has taken place in some of the villages and Christians have been allowed to move back.

But this is not the case in my village. The hatred still runs too deep.

My grandparents loved their village. I never met them but I have always heard a lot about them. Countless stories have been told by my older cousins about the pre-war visits to my grandparents' house in the mountains. My grandmother, Rose, was a good cook and delicious food was always available. My grandfather, Salim, ran a hotel in Jerusalem, Palestine, but returned to his village after Israel was created. They were hard-working village people. Both died before I was born. And according to my cousins, I missed out on meeting two wonderful people.

'We will never forgive what the Christians did to us, never,' said one angry shopkeeper as I stopped to buy some refreshment. 'We don't want them back.'

Later I met some distant relatives of mine. When prompted to relate the past, their answer was immediate. 'The Druze attacked us too,' said one. 'Let me tell you how.'

But I didn't want to hear any more. It didn't really matter. As far as I could see, both groups had committed atrocities. It was time to start anew.

A few weeks later, I met a young Druze man who is from my village of Abey. We have since become good friends. The past didn't matter to us. He promised that the day will come when I will build a home in Abey and we will become neighbors. Once our elders are gone, he said. I think about my family's cemetery sometimes. I know I should attempt to collect the skeletons and rebury them with new gravestones. But at the moment the task is too daunting for me.

I haven't told my father about his parents' desecrated graves. But somehow I think he knows.

Heart's desire

Pregnant with her first child, Reem seethes at her well-wishers.

I stood there waiting for the pronouncement which would inevitably come. I put on what I thought was an expressionless face. I was tired of arguing. And, as usual, it came: 'If God is willing, it will be a groom' – the Lebanese way of wishing upon me a boy. I murmured an incomprehensible appropriate reply and walked away.

I was pregnant with my first child and my husband and I had decided not to find out the sex of the baby. We really didn't care, much to the disbelief of many people. 'It can't be,' said one man. 'You must wish for a boy. Every family wants a boy.'

Strangers on the street would stop me to tell me that I was, for certain, carrying a boy (apparently if the belly bulges upwards, it guarantees a boy). 'He will no doubt make your husband happy.' I was seething. I imagined the baby growing inside me, if it were a girl, seething as well. I found myself reassuring my protruding belly that a girl would be greatly loved.

'What if the baby can hear all this and she's a girl?' I complained to my patient husband. 'She won't feel special and won't want to come out.' I admit that pregnancy makes one lose some of one's logic.

The more people wished a boy upon me, the more I fervently hoped that the baby was a girl. 'Let's hope it is a boy,' said a woman at the gym as we walked on the treadmill. 'But just in case it's not, here, look at her.' She jumped off her machine and ushered in a little girl. 'This is my daughter. She's nine years old. Isn't she beautiful? Twahameh. Twahameh.'

This is an Arabic expression reserved for pregnant woman. It means if I stare long enough at the child, my baby will look like her. The mother planted the bored-looking child in front of my treadmill, ordered her to remain there and went off. I managed to finish my treadmill session very quickly.

I dared to scratch my face in the supermarket some time during my eighth month. A hefty-looking woman descended upon me. 'Are you carrying a girl?' she demanded. 'For if you are, she is going to have a birthmark on her face in the same spot that you've just scratched. And she will have trouble finding a husband later on.'

There was no escaping. I had some workers install a closet in the nursery. 'You must put in more than one closet,' said the carpenter. 'That way if it's a girl, you will immediately try to have a boy and the closets for each would be ready.'

I was beginning to acquire an attitude. 'I want a girl. A girl,' I would say to anyone who greeted me. 'I hope it's a girl. I definitely want a girl.'

My mother sought to comfort me. 'You must be carrying a girl,' she said. 'You are looking radiant. Only a girl could do that. If it was a boy, you wouldn't look pretty at all.' I'm not sure that was much comfort.

So many others wanted to make me 'feel good'. 'This will be your first born,' said my neighbor.

'So it wouldn't matter if it was a girl.' I purposely bought a few little dresses and hung them out on the balcony for the neighbors to see. It was my declaration to the world: I want a girl.

On 28 June at 12.35pm my wish came true: I gave birth to a beautiful baby girl, Yasmine Alice. We were thrilled. I couldn't wait to take her out for a stroll. I proudly wanted to show her off to the world. As I expected, people stopped me in the streets and peered in the pram. My beautiful little darling cooed at them. After uttering the necessary compliments and blessings, they smiled at me.

But as I smiled back, I suddenly froze. 'If God is willing,' they said without missing a beat, 'the next one will be a boy.'

The perfect wife

A disturbing recent trend among well-heeled Lebanese bachelors.

It sounded rather preposterous to me but my new friend, Toufic, was nodding his head vigorously in excitement.

'I think I have found my bride,' he said. 'She's everything I've ever wanted. I can't wait to marry her.'

'When is the big day?' I inquired, amused at his excitement.

'I don't know,' he said. 'I suppose some time after I meet her.'

I must have looked shocked, for Toufic burst out laughing. 'It's true,' he said. 'She's a mail-order bride from Russia.' I must have looked even more shocked. 'Everyone is doing it,' he rushed to explain.

Well, maybe not everyone but certainly many men, I later found out. Much to the disgust of young hopeful Lebanese women, some men have turned to the internet to find brides.

'All the Lebanese girls I dated just want too much from me,' he said. 'They want to have a house in the most expensive area in town, cars and maids.'

But the internet sites which provide Russian brides promise something different. 'Russian women,' one site claimed, 'are unspoiled. They tend to be devoted, adoring wives.'

They are also beautiful, slender and willing to relocate. Pictures of the women, their profiles, hobbies and the qualities that they are looking for in men, are on display. Men have to pay a certain amount for each email address.

At first, Toufic decided on 21-year-old Olga. But Olga informed him that her monthly internet connection cost $50 and she therefore couldn't communicate with him. Toufic obligingly offered to pay.

When it became apparent that Olga's English was very weak, Toufic found himself paying for English lessons. Olga also received a mobile phone with a bill which conveniently made its way back to Toufic. She also demanded clothes, jewelry and a weekly allowance. Toufic obliged.

After two months of 'dating', it was time for Olga to come to Beirut and meet her future husband. And so Olga and her mother arrived in Lebanon where a fully paid hotel suite awaited them.

After a two-week all-expenses-paid stay, the women agreed to the marriage if Toufic provided them with a brand new Alfa Romeo car, a luxurious apartment registered in Olga's name and a generous monthly allowance. Olga and her mother were soon sent back to Russia.

Toufic had since been 'dating' Julia. 'And I think she may be the one,' he said. 'I have already sent her air ticket and booked a hotel suite for her. I can't wait to finally meet her.'

Suddenly I see a lot of Russian women in Beirut. Some have children in tow. 'I miss Russia,' one woman told me. 'But I like it here too.' Her name is Anna. She met her husband over the internet. He sent for her and after a few weeks together, they decided to get married. 'My family is very poor,' she explained. 'A Russian husband cannot give me what my husband here does. I have a nice home and good life now.'

But not all the women have met their husbands over the internet. Some met their Lebanese husbands when they were students in Russia or Europe. Others were among the hundreds of Russian cabaret dancers who have been arriving in the country for the past several years.

'I make $40 a month in Russia as a dancer,' one woman told me. 'As a cabaret dancer here, I make about $500. My family doesn't know I am a cabaret dancer. I send them some money and they think I am dancing in a ballet abroad.'

The dancing itself is innocuous: there's no stripping involved and performances are in a troupe. But the audience is entirely male and dancers are encouraged after their performances to mingle with their admirers and get them to spend as much cash as possible on drink. Several such meetings have ended in marriage.

But Toufic had no intention of setting foot in a cabaret venue to meet the 'right bride'. 'Not my style,' he said disapprovingly.

The last I saw of him, he was busy preparing for the arrival of Julia. Spending money, jewelry and clothes had already been sent. His experience with Olga had, however, scared him. Just in case Julia wasn't the 'one', Nathalie would be arriving from the Ukraine a few months later.

That was over a year ago. I haven't seen Toufic since and often wonder if he ever found 'the perfect wife'.

Judging by the amount of email I receive advertising mail-order brides mostly to Western men, I can only hope that some Russian brides are living happily ever after.

Taking the veil

Why Lebanese women are covering up.

I remember a time, not so long ago, when wearing a veil was seen as unacceptable – at least in certain social circles. Educated women, it was thought, did not wear veils. Only five years ago, when a friend decided to don one, it was the main item of gossip in town. In hushed and shocked tones, friends spread the word that Samia *tahajabit* (put on a veil). Many felt awkward around her and Samia sought new friends.

Two years ago, another friend who lives in the US suddenly decided to turn religious and donned the veil. In a fury, her mother flew across and talked her out of it. 'No daughter of mine puts on a veil,' she told me sternly.

But since 11 September 2001 things have begun to change. It has become more acceptable for middle- and upper-class women to wear veils. As one put it: 'With all this anti-Islam in the world, I began to take more of an interest in my religion. And one of the duties of Islam is to wear the veil.'

Yasmine Dabbous, who is 26, couldn't agree more. There was a time when she wore shorts, tanktops and swimsuits. Exploring her religion, she made a point of wearing long skirts. Then she began covering her arms. Finally she donned the veil. (In Lebanon, veiling is restricted to covering the head and hair – the face is usually left uncovered).

'This is a personal decision,' she said. 'No-one has forced me.' Her father was livid. 'He thought my veil would tarnish the family's image. He saw the veil as primitive and barbaric.' So she held off until she got married. Her sister soon followed suit.

'It's beginning to be acceptable now,' said Yasmine. 'I don't think the events of 11 September are the main reason for the change in people's attitudes. But it's certainly part of it.'

Her husband, who was studying in the US at the time, grew a beard as if to challenge the anti-Islamic feeling that swept the country. He immediately shaved it off upon returning to Lebanon.

The new shift in attitude is completely unnoticed by Nabil, a taxi driver, who frequently chauffeurs me around the city. To him, all Muslim women should be veiled. 'It's their duty,' he told me. 'My wife is veiled.'

He had been asking his teenage daughter to don the veil for several years, meeting each time with refusal. 'God is certainly frowning on me for letting my daughter leave the house with her head uncovered,' he said. 'I don't know what to do.'

One day, Nabil picked me up, his eyes shining. 'My daughter has agreed to wear the veil,' he said in excitement. 'Her only condition is to wait until after she is married. I have agreed.' A few months later, the 17-year-old girl was wed. A month later, she donned the veil. 'I am so relieved,' said Nabil. 'I have succeeded as a father. God will reward me.'

I never really understood the pride that accompanies wearing a veil until I met 13-year-old Nawal Youssef. Her poverty-stricken family lived in a Palestinian camp crowded into two small rooms. They only had one bed and this was given to Nawal. The child had brain cancer and was paralyzed after a faulty operation. She could barely mouth a few words. A few weeks before she died, Nawal asked to be veiled.

At her funeral, her father couldn't stop talking about it and seemed to draw comfort from it.

'No-one expected it,' he said. 'She was a very sick little girl. But she insisted. So we got her a veil. She even fasted during Ramadan. We begged her not to but she was a believer. I know that God has welcomed her into heaven. I'm so proud that my daughter wore the veil.'

It hadn't occurred to me to ask my unveiled Muslim friends why their heads were uncovered. When I did, Rula stared at me blankly.

'Well,' she hesitated, 'I don't know. It's not something I ever considered or thought about.'

She called her mother over. Afaf, in her late fifties, is a practising Muslim who prays and fasts but is not veiled.

'I would be miserable if my daughters wore the veil,' she said. 'There is absolutely no mention of the veil in the Qur'an. This is all about men containing women. The men were in charge of making the laws. It's all about power, nothing more.'

As the veil becomes more popular, new businesses have crept up: stylish clothes tailored to the veiled woman, scarves decorated with new twists and even a sea resort where men and women are segregated for swimming then reunited for dining and family activities.

But a word of warning from Yasmine. 'Wearing the veil doesn't mean fundamentalism,' she says. 'I am against it. Islam preaches moderation, not extremism. We are still the same people. We're just veiled. That's all.'

Worlds of words

The beautiful bewilderment of Lebanese proverbs.

Much of the time I don't know what people are saying to me. I respond with a smile, a murmur, an unintelligible answer, and hope that I appear all-knowing. The Lebanese are fond of using proverbs to express their feelings – according to a Lebanese researcher, we have over 4,000 proverbs. Most of them rhyme and are quite pleasing to the ear. I confess, however, that it takes me some time to decipher them.

'If you are afraid, don't speak. But if you speak, don't be afraid,' I was told when I entered the field of journalism.

During interviews, I would often find myself on the threshold of a small house in a poverty-stricken area wondering whether my photographer and I would find a place to sit in the family home. But the welcome was always the same: 'If our houses are too small to receive you, our hearts will do so.'

My father has absolutely no luck in business ventures. When he bought some real estate, the Lebanese civil war erupted and the land became worthless. When he invested some money in stock, the market crashed. 'If he should go to sea,' my mother is fond of saying, 'the sea would dry up.'

My mother seems to understand the world of proverbs. 'He who gossips with you will gossip about you,' she would say sternly to me when a friend came over with an exciting piece of news.

She strongly believed in family unity. My two sisters and I grew up listening to her favorite proverb. 'You and your sister against your cousin,' she would repeat when refereeing fights between us and friends. 'And you and your cousin against the stranger.'

At times when I stubbornly refused to comply with her wishes, she would patiently say: 'He who doesn't agree with you, try to agree with him.'

And when I suspected a neighbor of swiping one of my toys, my mother was quick to advise: 'Shut your door rather than accuse your neighbor.'

At times I resorted to proverbs myself. A favorite proverb that I used frequently as a child to lord it over the neighbor's younger kids goes: 'She who is one day older than you, has one year more experience than you do.' And with that I was deemed worthy of making up the rules of our games.

During my wedding reception, a guest studied my husband. 'He seems a good man,' she whispered to me. 'Put your hands in cold water.' In other words, rest assured.

As my parents bade me goodbye at the end of the reception, I must have looked rather forlorn, for the same guest approached me again. 'Remember,' she said, 'the home which reared me doesn't forget me.'

In many ways, Lebanon remains a traditional country, especially with regard to women. Virginity is prized. In fact, men prefer to marry a woman whom 'no-one has kissed on her mouth but her mother'. Many parents are eager to marry off their daughters as 'a girl's marriage is her protection'.

And so it goes.

A man is 'well fed from his mother's milk' if he is strong and healthy.

A person who takes 'one step forward and two steps back' is hesitant.

And a person 'above the wind' is rich and prosperous.

Young people are told: 'Lying will get you lunch but not supper' – meaning a liar is soon discovered.

Up-and-coming career persons are warned that 'there is not a tree which the wind cannot shake'.

The wealthy are reminded that 'money from earth remains on earth' – in other words, you can't take it with you once you're dead.

When someone suddenly reappears after a long absence, it is said that 'it has been a long, long time since this moon made its appearance'.

A proper Lebanese person would have a ready response, ideally another proverb. Unfortunately, words fail me in such situations. If my mother is nearby, she rises to the occasion as I stand there helplessly nodding. But my father – who, like me, gets lost in the world of proverbs – taught me a trick.

'Just say "May God bless you" to everything,' he said. 'It gets you off the hook.'

I've tried it. And except for a few strange looks, it works most of the time.

I've also managed to memorize two or three proverbs. I am still waiting for an occasion to use them.

Fundamental flaws

Why many Arabs are growing tired of the blame game.

It was unnerving for all the residents in the building when the couple and their four children moved into a recently vacated flat. All of us, Muslim and Christian alike, talked in shocked tones.

'I can't believe we are going to be living with such people,' said a neighbor.

A devout Muslim herself, she could not tolerate the fact that the couple that had moved in belonged to an extreme Islamic fundamentalist group. The man sported a long beard and the wife was completely shrouded in black. I have yet to see her face. Several times per month, they held meetings for men and women separately – we guessed for religious studies. Christmas decorations in our building lobby were frowned upon and we heard of their displeasure.

In time we got used to their presence. We later found out that the man's own parents had been highly disapproving when he became a fundamentalist. Father and son were not on speaking terms. But it is becoming a common story in Lebanon – some children of modern Muslims are turning to fundamentalism. In hushed tones a good friend of mine confided to me that his younger brother had become a fundamentalist. The family was aghast. The father threatened to cut off all inheritance if his son didn't leave the group he had joined. The son refused and left the family home.

The trend has not gone unnoticed.

'I'm worried,' said Othman, a devout Muslim and father of three grown children. 'Fundamentalism is increasing. I worry for the future of the country. I worry about my children and grandchildren.'

Fundamentalists will quickly point to the 'evils of America and Israel' when asked to identify the big Satan. US policy, which tends to side with Israel against the Arabs, has left many feeling that the only way to fight the two allies is through force. And if fundamentalism blesses this force, so much the better for them.

'They think that the only way to change things is through extremism,' said Othman, some of whose friends' children have turned to fundamentalism. Othman himself stared at his daughter in shock when her first reaction to a forthcoming US trade exhibition in Beirut was 'Let's blow up the place!'

'I know she was joking and she would never do it,' said Othman. 'But this is a frightening reaction. This hatred against the Americans is spreading more and more and it's very scary.'

The bombing of the UN headquarters in Iraq in August has sent shudders throughout the Arab world. The targets are no longer just the US and Israel. The international community and Arabs themselves – as the bombing of the Jordanian embassy early that same month proves – are targets too.

Lone voices in the Arab world are beginning to cry out.

'It's time we examined our own societies,' said one analyst in Saudi Arabia. 'How are we producing such sons who are killing in the name of religion?'

The Saudi Arabian security authorities are reportedly worried that 3,000 young men have disappeared from the kingdom and are believed to have infiltrated Iraq to conduct attacks against Western – and maybe Arab – targets.

'We cannot keep blaming the US and Israel for the increase in fundamentalism,' said Othman. 'There is nothing we can do about Zionism and the US Congress. But there is a lot we can do to improve our own societies.'

Voices like Othman's are calling for a change in Arab societies. Many Arab governments – including Lebanon's – are riddled with corruption. Laws exist seemingly only to protect the powerful. Those without political backing are basically on their own.

This, sociologists argue, is creating a high level of frustration. Fundamentalism begins to look more and more attractive. It certainly looked rather inviting to a friend of mine. A few years ago while at university she began secretly to attend religious meetings – the first step towards joining the group. Hoping to convert me, she dragged me to one of the meetings.

The experience was enlightening to say the least but after a heated argument between myself and the teacher I was no longer welcome. A few weeks later, her father found out and banned her from attending the meetings.

While Lebanon is a long way away from producing a generation of fundamentalists (fortunately we love our night life and are slaves to the latest fashions), some parents have begun to keep a watchful eye on their grown-up children's activities. No-one can forget the story of a young, attractive, cleanshaven Lebanese Muslim man who was educated at a Christian school, enjoyed parties, drinks and having a good time. His name was Ziad Jarrah and he was one of the 11 September hijackers. His parents never knew he had become a fundamentalist.

Life lessons

A voice from the past brings back a life touched by brilliance – and suffering.

I kept staring at the tall, lanky young man sitting across from me. 'I don't want money or food,' he said, lowering his eyes. 'But there is one thing I want more than anything. I have one dream and you're the only person who can help me.'

At 24, Shadi was living alone in a rat-infested room with no electricity, running water or even a toilet nearby. Like his father, he was a squatter in a privately owned building. He searched the city dumpsters every night to find recyclable cartons or plastics to sell. He hadn't eaten in days but refused to let me buy him lunch.

'More than anything I want to learn English,' he said. I continued to stare, stupefied.

'Reem, you started me on this, remember?' he said. 'I loved school and hated my father for what he did. It's too late for me to go back to school but not too late to keep learning. Please help me again.'

It was 13 years ago that I had first met him and his sister, begging on the streets of Beirut. Something in the little girl's face caught my eye. Her eyes were partly hidden by long, jet-black hair and she peeked at me from behind her brother. Refusing to give them money, I offered to buy them lunch instead and we sat together, slowly getting to know each other. Our lunches became a daily rendezvous. The girl, Hala, was 9 and the boy, Shadi, 11. Neither had been to school. Their mother was dead and their father made them work the streets – just two of the many street children who appeared right after the 1975-90 war. They were squatting in a room that had once been a university dormitory. The father's bloodshot eyes said much about his pastime. I was still in university and thought – as the young tend to – that I could save the world, beginning with these children.

So I spent all my free time with them.

I found a barrel of water in the rat-infested building in order to bathe them. I begged friends for clothes and talked a nearby theology school into providing lunch for them. Their father continued to send them to the streets. Worried, I would search for them in the middle of the night and find them huddled together. Turning to the law was useless. Except in cases of severe physical or sexual abuse, parents had the ultimate right when it came to their children. After many months, the father relented and allowed his daughter to attend a few hours of classes set up for illiterate children, so long as she begged on the streets afterwards. To my surprise, he allowed the boy to attend a boarding school. But never having been taught right from wrong, Shadi stole from school friends and bullied students. In desperation, I would travel the two hours to the school and beg him to stop. He didn't. Almost two years later, the principal called me in.

'This boy,' he said as I braced myself for more complaints, 'is highly intelligent.' Shadi had managed not only to read and write but had caught up with his peers in just two years.

'His conduct is beginning to change,' continued the principal. 'He's calming down. He needs more time but he'll get there and I think if he continues his education he'll make something of himself.'

I was thrilled. But two weeks later, I got another call. Shadi's father had taken him out of school. I looked all over Beirut for the children but they were gone. Disappointed, I chided myself for getting involved in the first place.

Years passed. I graduated, worked and got married. Every New Year's Eve, exactly at midnight, I would get a call.

'Happy New Year,' a youthful voice would say. Before I could respond, the caller would hang up. Over time, the child's voice changed into a teenage croak, then a young man's tenor. Finally, a few months ago, the voice lingered.

'Will you meet me somewhere?' it asked hesitantly.

And now here I was, meeting Shadi again. Needless to say, he enrolled in English classes and came up with the highest scores. This time around, I didn't feel thrilled at his success. Only extreme sadness at a wasted life. With his exceptional intelligence, Shadi could have amounted to something. I passed him a few times at night rummaging through the garbage or selling flowers to passers-by.

Now that I have a child of my own, I think miserably of a father who denied his children the few opportunities they could have had. The children's picture – in their newly washed hair and clothes – still hangs in my home. Many times I find myself thinking of Hala, who has since become a prostitute and of Shadi, whose dream, amid the squalor he inhabits, is to learn English.

Written in the stars

Railing against the fatalism of the Lebanese.

I listened with shock to my carpenter relating the events of his weekend. His young brother-in-law and wife were killed in a car accident, leaving their three-year-old-child an orphan. The bewildered boy kept calling for his mother.

'That's terrible,' I said, on the verge of tears.

My carpenter nodded his head. 'Terrible or not, it was meant to happen,' he said. 'Don't waste your tears. It was written that they should only live so many years. Nothing could have changed that. We must accept it.'

And there it was again: fate. Most Lebanese are great believers in it. Your life, they believe, is written for you before you were born. *Que será será*. Fate dictates everything that happens to you: your birth, marriage and death.

'It's sad, but don't dwell on it,' said my carpenter as he continued his job.

I've seen it many times before: strength in the face of death. Some years ago, I covered the aftermath of the April 1996 massacre at Qana where over 100 Lebanese civilians were killed in an Israeli artillery bombardment as they took shelter in a United Nations base. The 17-day-old baby of Fatmeh Balhas was decapitated by a lump of shrapnel as she held him in her arms. Fatmeh's husband, 16-year-old brother and her two other children had also been killed in the shelling.

I personally don't think I could have gone on with life, but Fatmeh did. She eventually remarried and had another baby.

'It was my baby's fate,' she told me sadly. 'It was meant to be.'

A few years later, I was covering an Israeli air strike against a Lebanese

electricity plant. Flames were billowing from the wrecked machinery and a group of journalists was begging the army to let us in to look at the damage. As the army refused, fire engines arrived. We stood aside and looked at the firefighters rather enviously. The younger firefighters had heard our pleas and smiled sympathetically at us. I remember their faces well. No sooner had they entered the burning electricity plant than we heard the sound of returning Israeli jets. I saw a lightning flash followed by a huge explosion. We ran screaming in all directions and took shelter behind some fuel tanks in a gas station. The stupidity of hiding from missiles in a gas station sent us running away again. When the sound of the planes disappeared, we approached the electricity plant trembling. In silence we stared at it. None of us dared to ask. Then we knew. Most of the firefighters had been killed. Ambulances rushed in.

'It was their fate,' I heard someone murmur behind me. 'It was their fate and not ours. Not ours.'

The next day I was assigned to cover the funeral of one of the firefighters. He was 19. Unfortunately I showed up at his house as his mother was being told that her son was dead. Apparently, no-one could bring themselves to do it during the night. Her screams echoed through the neighborhood. Family and neighbors did the only thing they could. They held her and kept repeating that it was fate, hoping that that would bring her comfort.

For weeks afterwards, many journalists who had been begging to go inside the plant were asking themselves why fate had spared them.

Fate, or *nassib* as it is better known here, also dictates your choice of spouse. I have seen many women suffer in marriages with abusive husbands. 'It was our nassib,' they would say. 'What can you do?'

'A lot,' I would respond passionately. But they would only look at me with pity. 'Accept your fate,' they would reply.

When a woman does not marry – still considered strange in this society – the parents' excuse is invariably: 'There was no nassib.' In other words, her fate in life did not include marriage to a suitable man. This immediately lifts any embarrassment at having an unwed daughter.

My marriage to a British man five years ago displeased many acquaintances. 'Aren't Lebanese men good enough for you?' I was asked. Or: 'How could you marry someone with different values?' The questions were endless.

At first, I would patiently explain that I fell in love and that my husband has become quite familiar with Arab culture and I with the English one. But to no avail. The frowns and questions would continue.

Finally, I realized that there was only one word that would stop them in their tracks: nassib. That's all I needed to say. Nothing else. In reply, they just nod their heads in understanding and walk away.

Motherland

Reem is shocked to be denied Lebanese nationality because she married a foreigner.

I stared at the woman in frustration. 'But I am Lebanese,' I said. 'I was born in Lebanon and raised in Lebanon. My daughter was born in Lebanon and is being raised in Lebanon. I don't understand.'

The woman nodded sympathetically. The walls of her drab office were bare except for a mandatory picture of a smiling Emile Lahoud, the Lebanese President.

My daughter, Yasmine, had only been born a few months earlier and I had come to apply for her Lebanese nationality. Yasmine was rejected.

'You, my dear,' continued the Government official, 'are a woman. And when a Lebanese woman marries a foreigner she cannot give her husband or her children Lebanese nationality. It's just how things are.'

I married a British national five years ago and although I am entitled to UK citizenship through him, I cannot offer my husband Lebanese nationality. The most I am allowed to do by law is grant him an annual residence visa to live in Lebanon.

I consulted a lawyer but there was nothing he could do. Anyone born of a Lebanese father – whether the child was born in Lebanon or abroad – has the right to Lebanese nationality. The mother, however, doesn't enjoy the same privilege.

And yet women have made great strides in the country. An estimated half of college graduates are women and working women make up 30 per cent of the total labor force. Three seats have been taken up by women in the 128-seat parliament. There is speculation that one of the women MPs could one day even run for the presidency.

But that same woman could not have given Lebanese nationality to her children had she married a foreigner.

My irritation subsided somewhat when I met Hanan – after all, her situation was even worse. As a Lebanese married to a Palestinian, her children have been denied citizenship. While she has access to government healthcare and services, her three youngsters can neither attend government schools nor benefit from any services. And since Palestinians are barred from working in over 60 different kinds of skilled jobs and from owning property, their future seems bleak.

'I can't believe I can't give my own children the same privileges that I have,' she said. 'What is to become of them?'

I recall when my friend Saria had a big row with her family. She had fallen in love with a Palestinian and wanted to get married. But Saria's family took a firm stand against him.

'Your children will have nothing,' yelled Saria's father. 'Nothing. Do you hear? They will be Palestinian.'

The father prevailed and the couple separated.

Women's rights movements have been lobbying vigorously to have the antiquated law overturned. But like everything in Lebanon, the decision is a political one – and it takes time. The fear, as a high-ranking politician explained to me, is that Palestinians will take advantage of the relaxation of the law to marry a Lebanese and remain in the country. The Lebanese have long been concerned at the prospect of the Palestinian refugees – today estimated at 350,000 – settling permanently in Lebanon and becoming assimilated into Lebanese society.

Since the end of the war, in 1990, the Palestinians have remained confined to their camps surrounded by Lebanese soldiers. The result of this uncompromising policy has condemned many Palestinians to a fate of grinding poverty and despair.

My son, Alexander, was born last October and like his sister will grow and love a country which will never accept him as one of its own.

I admit my worries are selfish ones. My children will always have the right to live in Britain – a privilege desired by many Lebanese. But I am a typical Lebanese mother who wants her children around her for as long as possible. I want them to attend university here. I want to see them marry and settle down near me. I want to live near my grandchildren.

But as non-Lebanese they might not be able to do that. As 'foreigners' they will require expensive residency and work permits. They will be barred from unions and many jobs. Their future is almost certainly abroad.

The loss of my and other such children – well educated and trained – will surely be Lebanon's.

Speaking in tongues

The language her daughter speaks causes Reem some soul-searching.

I'm not sure how but I have managed to produce a daughter whose sentences can only be understood by the Lebanese. For only they can understand the bizarre mix of Arabic, French and English.

'Ana going aa' ecole,' (translation: I am going to school) declares three-year-old Yasmine in the mornings.

My British husband often seeks me out to translate his child's sentences. 'I think I know what she's saying but I'm not sure,' he says, looking a little ashamed. And so Yasmine repeats her mixed-up sentences and I dutifully translate.

At first, I worry. 'By age three,' a magazine article declares, 'your child should make clear sentences and use proper words.' I begin to panic. Yasmine's sentences are far from clear. I blame myself. I decide to read her books only in one language. I put away the French and Arabic ones. Yasmine has a fit. I bring them back.

Then I decide to speak to her solely in Arabic. Not an easy task. I am a typical Lebanese who floats from one language to another. I don't know the Arabic words for many things. I usually just use the English or French word. So I buy a dictionary and spend time looking up the proper Arabic words.

But the headteacher of her school frowns. 'How do you expect her to compete with other children if she doesn't speak French?' he practically bellows. 'Speak to her only in French.'

And so I switch to French. Yasmine continues to speak Arabic but incorporates some French words here and there. And since her father only speaks English, the child's sentences become trilingual.

'We're back where we started,' I complain to my husband.

Lebanon, a French mandate between the two World Wars, is well known for its multilingual talents. Nearly a quarter of a century of French rule has strongly influenced aspects of life. French was first taught in Lebanese schools in 1834. But when American missionaries arrived in the region in the middle of the 19th century, they founded several English-speaking schools and universities. While French continued to flourish in the Christian areas, English grew increasingly popular in the Muslim regions.

During the 16-year civil war, thousands of Lebanese fled the country. Many settled in Anglo- and Francophone countries. When the war ended in 1990, many returned bringing with them French- and English-speaking children. There's also a strong US influence – with the introduction of cable television, viewers here are bombarded with non-stop American films.

As a result, English and French words continue to enter the Arabic language mainstream.

Today, when registering their children at elementary schools, parents have to choose whether to put their

children in an English or French section. While some class material is taught in Arabic, most is taught in the language chosen by the parents. At a certain point in school, all three languages are taught simultaneously.

Children end up imitating their parents, whose business and social conversations often contain mixed sentences. This is particularly annoying to visitors from Arab nations where Arabic is considered the main language in schools.

'Why can't you just stick to one language?' asks a friend visiting from Jordan. 'Do you think we can stick to Arabic?'

I try. But it's hard. Conversations just don't flow as easily. I revert to the dictionary. My friend sighs. 'Arabic should be your main mother tongue,' he reprimands. 'If you want to speak English, speak purely English. If you want to speak French, speak purely French. But stop mixing them. It's annoying and I can't understand you.' I'm relieved when he leaves.

When my son, Alexander, was born a year ago, I was determined to use only one language when speaking with him. I chose Arabic. I thought myself wise.

One day I was trying to coax Alexander (in Arabic of course) to follow me to the elevator. He refused to budge. Yasmine, watching us, looked at me disdainfully. Finally, she came and stood squarely in front of her brother.

'Alexander,' she said, 'taa go to ascenseur. Rahan walk bil jardin maa mommy.' (Alexander, come let's go to the elevator. We are going to take a walk in the garden with mommy.)

An excited smile appeared on my little boy's face as he jumped and crawled after his sister.

Running out of lies

Over a year of warfare in Lebanon means Reem has spent over a year lying to her children.

I'm desperately trying to find a way to tell my little girl that she will not be graduating from preschool. She has been practising her dances and songs for the past few months now. She can't wait to wear her little graduation robe. Or for her parents and grandparents to come and see her perform. I have told her so many lies since last summer that I don't have any more in store.

'That's just thunder,' I told her over and over again as Israeli planes dropped bombs on Beirut last July. Yasmine and her little brother, Alexander, would run to the window every time to look out for the rain. The rain that never came. Instead, we watched mesmerized as two missiles fell on the port of Beirut not far from our home.

'That's fireworks,' I exclaimed. Yasmine looked at me suspiciously. For a little person just turned four, she was amazingly perceptive.

'Didn't you know that some fireworks are so strong, they make houses shake and windows rattle?' I added. But the windows wouldn't stop rattling and we fled to the mountains. The windows rattled there, too. Sonic booms.

'Lots of wind up here,' I lied to the children. We were in the midst of a hot July summer. There wasn't any wind. I could see Yasmine puzzling over my statement.

By then, my journalist husband had disappeared to the south of Lebanon – which was bearing the brunt of the Israeli attacks – to cover the war. As thousands were massacred, I would sometimes hear from him and sometimes not. Roads to and from the south were shelled. There was no way for him to return home.

'Where's Daddy?' Yasmine asked.

'He's doing some interviews,' I lied.

The days and weeks began to blend and Daddy's 'interviews' didn't finish.

Beirut airport was bombed. My parents, who had gone to Spain for a two-week holiday, couldn't return. The children kept asking about them. 'They decided to travel to other countries,' I lied.

A few days into our refuge, our household help and friend decided to be evacuated with other foreign nationals. We begged her to stay but in vain.

The children were in tears. 'Why is she going, Mummy?' Yasmine cried. 'I want her to stay with us. I love her.'

'She wants to visit her mummy and daddy,' I replied.

'And then she'll come back?' asked Yasmine.

'And then she'll come back,' I lied.

We were now well and truly alone in our mountain refuge.

A third of the dead were children. Their pictures blazed over the television. Yasmine managed to glimpse some scenes before I quickly shut it off.

'Why are those children all sleeping?' she asked. 'It's still light out.'

'They're just so tired, Yasmine,' I lied. 'They want to lie down a little.'

'Then why are you crying, Mummy?' she said, looking at my puffy eyes.

The images of dead children, who looked so much like my own, were still in my head.

'I just have a cold, that's all,' I lied.

The war ended in mid-August. My husband came back to us after 33 days and we returned to Beirut to rebuild our lives. The damage to the country was tremendous. Thousands of people lost their lives and homes. For weeks, people walked around in a daze. It took a while for life to resume but it finally did.

Four months later, in early December, the Government became divided. The opposition group rallied its masses as thousands of demonstrators took over the downtown of Beirut that houses the government buildings. They set up their tents and started a long vigil. Downtown – a busy hub of shops and cafés – was effectively closed.

Sectarianism reared its ugly head. Deeply divided, the country seemed on the brink of a civil war. From our home, we could hear the angry mobs.

'I hear lots of noise outside,' declared Yasmine.

'Oh, it's a wedding,' I lied.

My instinct, my full instinct, was to keep the children ignorant of the country's instability. My earliest memories of my own childhood were of the Lebanese civil war, the pervasive fear, the sleepless nights.

Yasmine and Alexander must never experience this devastating fear.

And so I continued to lie.

Somehow, we got used to this new lifestyle. The tents were still there and the Government remained divided, but we managed to live our lives rather normally. Social events resumed and the children couldn't keep up with birthday parties. My sister arrived from the US in late May with her two young children for a two-month stay. The family was elated.

A few days later, Islamist militias with ties to al-Qaeda in the north of the country attacked the Lebanese army. Intense fighting between the two continued for weeks.

And then it began.

I jumped from my bed as the sound of the explosion resonated in our flat. A bomb had been detonated in front of a busy shopping mall just before midnight.

Over the next few days, four bombs exploded during the night and one during the day, killing a pro-Government politician. And they continue.

Fear, panic, but mostly depression has spread in Beirut. The streets are almost deserted. Parents rush their children home from school and we all basically stay indoors. A frantic husband back in the US insisted that my sister leave the country immediately. She did.

And, of course, I lie to the children as I rush them past parked cars. They all look like potential bombs to me.

Several unrigged bombs were found around the country, triggering many schools to end the year suddenly. Other schools canceled their planned events. Among them was Yasmine's preschool.

And now, I face the biggest lie of all. I know only too well how it feels to practise for a school dance or recital which never happened because of 'the situation'. I distinctly remember the bitter disappointment of not having my family watch me perform because it was too dangerous. And now, I have to watch my own child weep in disappointment.

I haven't yet decided what to say to her. It has to be a good lie. A convincing lie.

It's the only way I know how to protect my children.

Letters from Bambous (Mauritius), 2006-2007

Lindsey Collen

Born in Mqanduli, South Africa, Lindsey has lived in many parts of South Africa, in London, upstate New York, in the Seychelles, and, since 1974, with her husband Ram Seegobin in Mauritius. From when she was a child she had two passions: political action, and writing stories. At school in East London she organized a hunger strike and a ceremony of peer-group 13-year-olds to set alight the apartheid South Africa flag. She also kept a diary every day for four years at high school. At the University of Witwatersrand, she was on the Students' Representative Council and was also editor of *Critique*.

In Mauritius she participated in the nationwide general strike movement in 1979, and is a political activist and commentator. Her novels include *There is a Tide*, *The Rape of Sita*, *Getting Rid of It*, *Mutiny* and *Boy*. Her *Misyon Garson* is the first ever full-length novel in Mauritian Kreol, while *The Rape of Sita* was banned in Mauritius for being 'blasphemous'. Two of her novels have received the Best Book in the Commonwealth Writers' Prize for the African region, *The Rape of Sita* and *Boy*. The BBC commissioned the story 'Breaking Point', which she read at the Manchester Literary Festival.

Her novels have been translated into French, Turkish, German, Dutch and Danish.

Changes in Mauritius

Mauritius is peculiar in having two 'official' languages, neither of which is the first language of more than five per cent of the population – less than one per cent speak English as their native tongue and less than four per cent French. The peculiarity emerges from the island's tangled history – named after a Dutch prince (Maurice), it was colonized by the French in the 18th century but administered by the British after the defeat of Napoleon. In the 19th century most of the population were slaves but by the 20th century two-thirds were workers imported from India to replace slave labor on the sugar plantations. The Kreol, or Morisyen, language spoken by 80 per cent of the island's people was born suddenly, rising out of the ashes of the social destruction of slavery, and is today used everywhere: in the judiciary, in advertising, on radio, but it is only now being introduced in schools. The country's diverse ethnic and religious make-up is even more complex than its linguistic one.

Britain reluctantly agreed to grant Mauritius its independence in 1968 and the country finally became a republic, divesting itself of the British Queen, in 1992. One significant legacy of British rule remains very much a live issue, however – one reflected in Lindsey's letters. In 1965 Britain removed the Chagos Islands from Mauritian jurisdiction and leased Diego Garcia to the US for 50 years in exchange for a discount on its purchase of nuclear arms. To make space for new US bases, the people who had been living and working there for generations were forcibly removed to Mauritius, where they remain, despite having won the right to return in British courts.

The country's politics have been fiercely contested ever since independence by a rich array of parties and alliances. In the late 1970s and 1980s, hit by high oil and low sugar prices, the country was forced to seek loans from the IMF, which insisted on the usual deeply unpopular austerity measures in return – and, as Lindsey's first letter shows, the impact of globalized economic policies is keenly and often painfully felt in this Indian Ocean island of 1.25 million people. The fallout from 9/11 and the 'War on Terror' was also felt even here: in 2002 two successive presidents, under popular pressure, resigned rather than approve new anti-terrorism legislation allowing suspects to be detained for longer periods and reducing their right to legal representation (the legislation was eventually signed into being anyway by the Chief Justice).

The letters give a fascinating insight into the cultural and political life of a small nation far from the global centers of power – with a particular focus on women's myriad struggles – while also giving a sense of the rhythms of daily life on a tropical island that many would consider a paradise.

A yellow flag in the sunset

Setting out to repair her boat, Lindsey reflects on the ripples of change lapping at Mauritius's shores.

The fishing pirogue Ram and I bought old in 1983 started taking in a bit of water recently, and right now is when we need it. It's the season when the sea is beautiful way out beyond the reef, for fishing, playing with dolphins or watching whales.

'I'll get her out on my trailer for you,' offered Patrice last week. He moors his pirogue in the same cove as us in Flic-en-Flac, which isn't far from the village we live in. This way Ram could quickly redo some of the plank joints with new wick and sealant and get the boat back in the water. For a living, Patrice dives down and hand-nets exquisite teeny-weeny deep-sea fish, which he has to carry from the dark depths up, in delicate stages, to different pressure levels over about 24 hours, until they're ready to hand over to an intermediary for export.

As well as being a diver, Patrice is one of the 5,000 'fisherfolk' who are skippers of boats now defined by the Government as 'pleasure crafts', so he's got exams coming up. He's got to get a license now, in order to make him WTO-compatible. Mauritius has offered up 'tourism services' to the World Trade Organization, for companies worldwide to be able to 'invest' in without hindrance. But for that to come about, and to ensure there's no 'unfair competition' from local people who happen to live there, there are rules, rules, rules.

But rules or no rules, pirogue fisherfolk haven't got much choice. Catches have decreased so dramatically that the only income they can come by these days is from taking tourists out trailing, diving or on a picnic to a little island somewhere. Now they find there are exams to pass just to stay in the new niche they've found.

But anyway... When we went to take the pirogue out, we saw this amazing sight.

Two young men were standing calf-deep in the middle of the turquoise lagoon near where the boats were moored and, in their arms, were holding a reddish-maroon, three-seater, fully upholstered, beautiful couch. A settee. They stood there, looking ashore, waiting. Then they proceeded, after a lot of instructions yelled at them from the beach, to place it carefully in the water. Meanwhile someone had tied a different-colored flag on to the top of the mast of each pirogue in the cove. Ours got a yellow one. And a huge four-foot-high stage had popped up on the beach, between the pirogues and where Patrice and Ram intended to pull ours up. A lone dancing girl was standing up there on it in scanty attire while a film crew from Bollywood, busy as a Bruegel painting and surrounded by gawkers, prepared a song-and-dance sequence. That's another niche – the Government encourages filmmakers to come and film scenes in Mauritius, hoping this creates a few jobs here and there.

The wooden pirogue, old as it is, looks beautiful out of the water as well as in. Hand-crafted by lone master marine carpenters, Mauritian pirogues are unusual in that they've got a mast that isn't upright. It slopes quite markedly towards the back of the boat. The front sail works from the top of the mast to the bowsprit, and then there's a second mast – the vergue – which is a very long bamboo on to which you tie your mainsail before hoisting it up through pulleys and lashing it to the top third of the mast.

The members are cut from mature jackfruit trees – dug up root and all – from the angle incorporating the trunk and the root; this way they are strong because the curve runs against the grain of the wood throughout. But jackfruit trees are becoming rare now. And anyway there's quite a sizeable industry producing fiberglass boats that replace the old pirogues. When we bought ours from a retired fisher in Le Morne Village in 1983, everyone predicted that it was already too old. But it's back afloat after its repairs now.

So, watch out for the one with the yellow flag, if you come across a Bollywood film with a song-and-dance sequence that has pirogues in the background. And take care not to miss the upholstered-settee-in-the-sea scene.

The slide of sugar

How globalization ruined Kawlowtee's life.

A friend of mine from the women's movement, Kawlowtee, announced in 2001: 'I'm fed up! I'm taking my VRS!' She was referring to the Voluntary Retirement Scheme.

She's a big strong woman, who for 14 years had worked as a laborer on a sugar estate in the south. This meant she'd led an orderly life. Generations of cane-workers had struggled for it. The work is hard, so the hours had got short. The sun is hot, so you start work early. You have time: for family, the women's movement, St John's Ambulance, to play in a band, whatever. You get new work gloves every three weeks. And extra money for cutting cane on a slope. The pay's OK too, totaling around $120 a month.

Kawlowtee and her husband bought their house when the Government was selling them off cheap. Then they had taken a bank loan to add three rooms for the children. Their daughter, a cashier in a transnational retail firm, and an older manual-worker son could both help with repayments – as well as with their younger brother's schooling.

Then Kawlowtee's life got hit by globalization: the price of sugar is to be fixed by the free market now.

During decolonization, when countries like Mauritius were faced with the riddle of how to be 'independent' with a monocrop economy invented to foster dependence, the Lomé Agreement between Europe and its ex-colonies solved it, fixing quotas at guaranteed prices. The agreement arguably also served to tie the economy even further into subservience and lined the pockets of the sugar oligarchs, but it did provide some security for workers like Kawlowtee.

Until liberalism came back. Now, the World Trade Organization's Dispute Settlement Tribunal finds Europe to be 'illegally subsidizing' sugar. Its judgment in favor of Australian, Thai and Brazilian sugar producers who cry unfair competition is binding. Sugar prices will fall around 40 per cent in the next few years.

The estate owners and the Government see only one way out: cut costs by destroying jobs in their tens of thousands.

Kawlowtee doesn't agree. 'I don't want to retire!' she said. 'Who would at 42?'

But after the first batch of older women nearing retirement age accept the VRS package, work gets tough for the rest. Workloads increase, unemployment rises, casual workers move in on lower wages. The bosses put the screws on younger laborers to take their VRS too. Kawlowtee, a union organizer, realizes they'll find a pretext to kick her out anyway. So she takes her VRS. With the sum of $2,125, plus the promise of a tiny plot of land, she becomes unemployed.

At this point, her husband runs off with a younger woman. So Kawlowtee and her children continue the $75 repayments on the house. She lands a job with a cleaning company. She gives a false address because they won't take someone from the south because of the bus fares. So, part of her pay goes on transport. How much is her pay? $75 a month.

And work is chaotic. The hours are long and shifting. Every morning, the supervisor calls Kawlowtee on her mobile to tell her when and where to report for work. Go clean a supermarket here! Scrub a government building there!

'The boss can get at me,' she marvels in disbelief, 'even when I'm at home in pajamas! That's globalization for you.'

Kawlowtee chips away at the VRS money for loan repayments. She buys a computer for her son doing A-levels. 'May help him get a job next year,' she says. Then her daughter falls in love with an Italian colleague brought in to fix computers at work. More VRS money goes into the wedding and her daughter emigrates.

Her older son, having become unemployed, ends up, like thousands of youngsters, in jail – stole a mobile phone from a tourist.

Bank repayments become impossible. So the bank is foreclosing. Her house is the collateral. She, like her workmates, still hasn't got the promised bit of VRS land. And when she does get it, divorce being an archaically slow process, Kawlowtee will probably only get half. By law, half will belong to her 'husband'.

Kawlowtee's isn't a hard-luck story. She'll manage. But her story is typical. The lives of everyone in Mauritius are in similar disruption and disequilibrium. It's not unlike the wild descriptions of 19th-century liberal capitalism that Karl Marx and Frederick Engels gave in their Manifesto and, interestingly enough, a Mauritian Kreol version of that has just been launched in both book and audio CD format.

'I see a human being'

Why Mauritius ties itself up in knots over race and religion.

Imagine this. You are in Mauritius in 2000, and not, by some space-time warp, in apartheid South Africa. You distinctly hear a lawyer, Yousouf Mohamed QC, in the Supreme Court putting it to a defendant, as lawyers are wont to do: 'Mr Sardanand Lilldharry, you wrote on your nomination paper that you are a Sino-Mauritian?'

The candidate in the general election replies: 'Yes, I did, My Lord.'

'What do you see when you look at yourself in the mirror in the morning, Mr Lilldharry?'

A thoughtful silence. Then to the Judge Dhiraj Seetulsing, the candidate says: 'I see a human being, My Lord.'

The lawyer sighs, glances at the ceiling fan, changes tack: 'Are you a religious person, Mr Lilldharry?'

'This is a private matter, My Lord.'

The judge sighs this time. The next defendant is called.

'You wrote on your Nomination Paper, Mr Radha Kistnasamy, that you are a Muslim. What is your father's first name?'

'My father is dead, My Lord. People called him "Tamby".' Line of questioning a cul-de-sac.

'Are you married?'

'Yes, My Lord.'

'Who conducted the ceremony?'

'A civil status officer, My Lord.' Another dead end.

'Do you have children?'

'Yes, My Lord, a boy.'

'What's his name?'

'Ryan.'

Yet another line of questioning to find out Radha Kistnasamy's ethno-religious 'belonging' fails.

Witnesses are called. One is a Muslim religious leader. He testifies to the effect that by someone's name, he can know whether they are Muslim or not. Under cross-examination by Advocate Rex Stephen for the defendant, he concedes that Ahmadiya people do have Muslim names but they are not, according to him, Muslims. Witness falls.

The Supreme Court, after hearing this kind of evidence, has to decide, according to the Independence Constitution, on the 'community' or ethno-religious classification of some 25 candidates of three political parties – Lalit, Nouvo Lizour and Tamil Council – whose nomination papers are being challenged. Lalit and Nouvo Lizour candidates had filled in, as the Constitution requires, their 'community'. But they selected which of the four communities to inscribe by drawing lots.

Every general election since Independence produces an ever more bizarre court case. Judges have to sweat away to interpret anew a devilish little Schedule to the Constitution that bears the curious appellation of 'Best Loser System' – this was one of those divisive 'concessions' to ethno-religious lobbies made by the British as they left in 1968. The concessions were ostensibly designed to limit the racism-cum-religious politics we call 'communalism', but they end up forever after engendering it. The Schedule poisons the political process by infusing it with racial and religious classification. After voting for candidates as individuals and as party members, electors find their votes later allocated proportionately to candidates of different 'communities' so that eight 'best losers' can be named to 'restore' after the fact any imbalance in communal representation.

Judge Seetulsing in 2000 classified everyone before him as 'General Population', a holdall for anyone not in the other three, which are defined by religion and geographical roots of ancestors. In a future election this community could also be challenged by any elector.

In the 1982 elections, the Supreme Court had a different problem to solve. One of the parties won all the seats in Parliament. The best loser system, however, was drafted with the idea that there would always be an Opposition, so that four of the eight best losers can be used to re-establish the balance between parties after four are nominated on purely communal grounds. With no Opposition, this couldn't be done. The Constitution had to be amended piecemeal to allow for this turn of events.

In the run-up to the 2005 general elections, Judge Balancy held that candidates could stand even if they did not fill in their 'community'. They would form a kind of fifth community of conscientious objectors. This well-meaning though perhaps misguided judgment has since been overturned by the full bench.

Back to square one. But square one is a dodgy little square. In 1982, there was so much popular opposition to classification that the Government removed the question on community from the Population Census. The statistics on community in use today therefore date from the 1972 census.

In a country where class differences are vast and increased class-consciousness would be salutary, this kind of race-religious classification is pernicious and should be done away with. The overwhelming majority of Mauritians want that. But the powers-that-be seem to have a persistent interest in maintaining it.

The breadfruit tree
Cajoling the man with the buzzsaw.

The breadfruit tree out front has got too big. Glorious, but ridiculous. That's what happens if you miss one pruning season. Trees get out of hand. Now it's gone and grown too tall. Too wide, as well. And generally spreading. Everything's like that here. Grass invades the tar on the Government's motorways, weeds have to be fought back from people's verandahs and paths. An old abandoned sugar mill soon has a full-sized tree growing from its highest chimney, your house can get a pawpaw tree growing out of its gutter if you don't watch it, while mango trees push the wooden tiles out of the roofs of abandoned houses from the inside. Any neglected back garden turns into a wilderness of green.

So we ask Fareed Tronsonez, who makes a living in our village from his electric saw, to come around. Which he does, little grandchild on his hip, to discuss the matter of the breadfruit tree.

We know we've got a big job on hand. How to persuade Fareed, although it is his living, to cut back such a beautiful tree. Not cut it down. Just cut it back.

He stands with one hand affectionately feeling the smooth grey bark of the three-trunked breadfruit tree. He looks up adoringly at its huge leaves. Half a meter long, almost as broad. And thousands of them, layer upon layer. He smiles.

It will all depend on our arguments. Only the most delicate and the most rational will do. They will have to be developed at some length, and at a gentle pace. Fareed loves trees.

So we stand around, his grandchild playing about our legs. Ram begins. 'You'll notice, it's impinging a bit on the sun-space of the mulberry and the fig. They could end up stunted.' Subtle argument.

'A problem,' Fareed nods. Anyone can see he is unconvinced. The trees both looked spindly anyway.

Silence. Then I mention that we're having this bit of difficulty managing the pruning now that it's that tall. The ladder doesn't reach, and the branches are rather too thick up there to cut with an ordinary saw. This could perhaps make upkeep dangerous.

'True,' Fareed mumbles. Not too convinced. We look too fit for such arguments.

More silence. I try another tack. The profusion of fallen leaves, going dry, that we have to sweep up. Day in, day out. And if we can't keep up, how this will breed mosquitoes, what with each leaf being like a big bowl on the ground, catching rainwater; how mosquitoes will in turn spread Chikungunya (viral fever). Not to mention, I add when he seems unmoved, the hundreds of male fruit that fall male-shaped all over, that also have to be swept up. I make them sound positively rude.

'Exercise,' he says, now swinging his grandchild between his legs, 'is good for everyone.'

And another thing, I go on bravely, is that the bright green football-sized vegetables, with their tiny hexagons carved all over, so beautiful to see, to pick, to hold, are now growing too high up to get to. So we can't harvest them properly any more, nor share them with neighbors. We can't get to boil them and serve with butter, salt and a bit of chili. Nor to make mash, nor to use them as stuffing in faratas. Nor to parboil them, and cut them up for chips, nor to make a dry curry, nor to let them ripen, pull out the big stem, fill the hole up with brown sugar, rum and raisins, and bake them in their skins.

They get left up in the sky until, of their own accord, they plummet down in a big over-ripe plop. This is hard to clean up.

'Problem,' he nods, reverting to the second-last point, pointedly ignoring the last one as invalid, 'when you can't enjoy the fruit. When neighbors can't either.'

I'm pleased. At last an argument worthy of consideration.

Ram thinks it's time for our trump card. The most important

argument must be left for last. 'You know, there's a danger to such a big tree in the next cyclone. Isn't the season getting nearer? And now this side of the tree is right above the corrugated iron roof of Lindsey's writing den. Those huge branches break so easily.'

'Yes, maybe,' Fareed says, 'maybe she'll have to be cut back a bit.'

We've probably won. But he adds: 'I'll think it over, let you know tomorrow.'

Empire's exiles

The women of Diego Garcia who have kept the flame of longing for their homeland alive.

'Never heard of it,' well-informed people from all over the world used to say when I asked them if they knew about Diego Garcia. Some even asked, 'Who's he?' And when I embarked on telling them how the British and US governments in the late 1960s forcibly removed the 2,000 inhabitants of the islands of Diego Garcia in a genocidal mass kidnapping in order to install an exponentially expanding military base, then people just used to look at me as though, having thought up to that point that I was perfectly nice, it was now dawning on them that I was in fact stone mad.

If such things were true, they thought, how could they possibly not have known about them? Such was the success of the conspiracy to hide the operation. People worldwide didn't know.

How did they find out? Some may have heard that B-52s were taking off from there to bomb Afganistan or Iraq. But it didn't mean much to them.

Then a judgment of the High Court in London in 2000 hit the front pages of British newspapers. Once the 30-year censorship of the British Official Secrets Act expired and the official papers that prove the whole murky deal became available, the Mauritians from Diego Garcia and the rest of the Chagos Archipelago could put in a legal challenge about their forcible removal from their native islands. The judges exposed a hideous plot where 'the British authorities [were concerned] to present to the outside world a scenario in which there were no permanent inhabitants on the Archipelago' and followed a policy of what one memo at the time described as 'quiet disregard – in other words let's forget about this one until the United Nations challenges us on it'. And the people won the right to return.

But the Blair Government promptly issued two Queen's 'Orders in

Council' to override the
judiciary. Earlier this
year, judges threw out
the Queen's decrees
and the right to return
was won again.

The people of Diego
Garcia and Chagos
hadn't just been sitting
around waiting all
those years. They never
stopped struggling. To
get back to their islands. To reunite the country. To get the military
base that was the cause of all the problems closed down. And it was the
women especially who acted. 'Two of my children died of sadness when
we were left stranded here,' Marie-Magdalene told me, 'and my heart
has been left heavy because I couldn't tend my grandmother's grave on
Diego Garcia. From this suffering, I got my strength.'

The first time I met women from Diego Garcia (and became lifelong
friends with some of them) was when I went to an all-night candle-lit
vigil in 1978 alongside a hunger strike in a poor suburb of Port Louis.
Then, in 1981, we held big street demonstrations three days running to
highlight yet another women's hunger strike. Eight of us were arrested,
during a confrontation with riot police, and faced a long trial for
demonstrating without police authorization. The trial became a further
focus for protest.

From 1997 onwards we attempted to get hold of a boat so as actually
to go to Diego Garcia. At one point Greenpeace had one of its ships in
line, but it fell through. In 2004, at the World Social Forum in Mumbai,
yachters offered to join a 'Peace Flotilla' if we got hold of a main boat.
But in the meantime, the right to return has been won.

In the women's movement we received a gift from the women of
Diego Garcia who had lived in a matricentral society and worked for
equal pay on their home islands. They showed us how to face up to
patriarchy in one of its worst forms: the police. The women from Diego
Garcia felt no fear of them. I remember one police officer who made
a quietly spoken 'proposition/threat' to one of the women during a
protest stand-off, only to have her reply loud enough for everyone in the
crowd to hear: 'And what's so special about your dick, then!' The man
crumbled.

In a million ways they shared with us that there's nothing special to
fear about any men – or their State hierarchies. Somehow they know

that women hold the power. And this knowledge has in turn given them power. And with the recently won right to return, the womenfolk of one of the smallest communities in the world has succeeded in calling to task the biggest power of all, the empire of the US-UK military alliance. They know that empires are not eternal.

To a place of healing

Lindsey reflects on the change in attitude towards rape.

Twenty-five years ago, there was great consternation in the village I live in, Bambous, when a young woman neighbor, Santa, was abandoned by her fiancé after he had tricked her into accompanying him into an empty house and then raped her. The consternation was around how to pressure the man to make amends for the rape by forcing him to go ahead and marry her. This was done by a band of Santa's male relatives going over to his village and threatening to castrate him. The Criminal Code, as the band of men knew, specifies that castration is 'excusable' (meaning has lesser penalties) if carried out in direct response to an attack on a woman's 'chastity'.

Santa had acquiesced in the original marriage proposal. 'I'm already 25,' she had explained to me, 'and my mother is a poor widow. She's so pleased she's found a suitable boy for me, because he owns a plot of land.' But from the beginning Santa found the man repugnant. The rape obviously disgusted her further.

However, a shotgun marriage went ahead. Such was the attitude to rape, only 25 years ago.

I was among the women who had tried to give Santa the courage to refuse the marriage. But, after failing, and with the wedding preparations going ahead, I still had to face a serious moral dilemma when Santa asked, 'Will you help me? Will you type a few wedding invitations?'

Anyway, the marriage lasted no more than three months. 'I'm back!' Santa announced one day. She got a job in a factory, made lots of friends, and lived happily ever after with her mother.

In those days rape within a marriage was not only not illegal, but was generally deemed impossible, a contradiction in terms. Marriage entitled a man to his wife, so how could he rape her? In the District Court in Bambous, I heard a barrister for the defence in a rape case get away with openly deriding two women who had been raped by police officers inside a police station.

It was against this baseline view of rape that, when my novel *The*

Rape of Sita came out in 1994 and I came under death threats from some religious fundamentalists and under attack from the Government, a long debate ensued. It was something of a turning point in attitudes towards rape. Rape, once perceived as being 'the woman's crime' could not go on being so. Old women who couldn't read at all supported me for 'allowing women who'd been wronged to walk with their heads held high', as they put it.

I often wonder how it was that attitudes changed so much and so fast. Rape is now universally denounced. Woman speak out in public. Marital rape has been made an offense.

Perhaps the main underlying reality is that women's oppression in Mauritius has always, since slave times, through indenture and into the modern epoch, been countered by a surprisingly strong women's consciousness. Women never seem to have accepted the idea of being inferior. Oppression was imposed, resented and resisted. From the 1950s onwards a very organized, vocal women's movement grew up around the political issue of the right to vote. Today there are over 600 women's associations in Mauritius, and almost all of them have a dimension that is both emancipatory and political, as well as the jam-making and embroidery. There are two in Bambous.

Come 2001, when a Mauritian woman, Sandra O'Reilly, spoke out publicly about two double-rapes she suffered in one night, consciousness had reached such a height that the more advanced sections of the women's movement put forward and won support for the demand that rape victims be able to report directly to a hospital and not have to go to a police station.

And by the end of 2006, after some women's mobilization, the Women's Rights Ministry, together with five main hospitals, issued a 'protocol' on what everyone should do after a sexual assault. You, as victim, can now go direct to a hospital for all the care you need, and a woman police officer interviews you as a witness, far away from the patriarchal structure of a police station. Police medical officers now examine you in a place of healing.

So women in Mauritius avoided making the demand for 'Women police officers in each police station!' or for 'More punishment for rapists!' Demands which, if won, probably would only strengthen, instead of weakening, the very patriarchy that allows such a thing as rape to exist.

Tongue twisters

A child's questions cast light on the politics of language.

I'd popped in to see my friend, Anne-Marie, for a few minutes of chatter and laughter while she was doing housework. But her four-year-old was bent, it seemed, on interrupting any conversation between us. As soon as we started talking: 'Mom, when you went to the shop this morning, did you have to cross the road?'

Anne-Marie turned to her patiently, despite pulling a face suitable to a ridiculous question. 'No, I went to Madame Labutik's.'

Her daughter was satisfied. No sooner had we started up again than: 'Mom, when I go to school next year, will I have to take a bag?'

Anne-Marie, slightly less patiently: 'Of course, of course.'

I noticed her daughter was testing a new and difficult grammatical structure. She was generating questions about conditionality – 'When x does y, does x have to do z?' – and checking to see if the constructions registered accurately with her mother.

'And I was convinced she was just doing it to annoy me!' Anne-Marie put her head back and laughed at herself.

When her daughter goes to primary school next year, the teachers will completely ignore her already highly developed linguistic skills in Mauritian Kreol. They will systematically repress any spoken Kreol in the classroom, and never ever use a word of written Kreol. God forbid!

They will attempt to teach her everything from the very first year of primary school through the medium of two languages she doesn't know at all: English and French. Her cognitive development will be held back to the level of her painstaking formalistic learning of foreign language constructions. Pedagogues call this kind of language policy a 'violence', and say the damage done to children's learning when they are taught through unknown languages (usually colonial or élite ones) takes some seven years to repair. And of course the emotional and psychological damage is difficult to quantify.

Anne-Marie's daughter is not alone. The Government Census says 93.2 per cent of children usually speak Mauritian Kreol and/or Mauritian Bhojpuri at home. Both these mother tongues are stifled in schools and denied status as a medium. If anything, Bhojpuri is more repressed than Kreol.

So, as Anne-Marie and I watched her daughter, now speaking to herself as she drew pictures, we continued to marvel at the human language capacity. We like marveling when we meet for a chat. And then we thought maybe it's misleading to see language through the cliché that it's just a 'means of communication'. Anne-Marie's daughter obviously uses it as her means of thinking and of understanding. In fact, she wasn't communicating with her mother at all really, except to get on her nerves. With her two irritating questions, she was beginning to grapple with ideas of conditionality and causality, and to test them against the sophisticated concepts of past and future that she has already managed to embed quite naturally in her language.

'No wonder,' Anne-Marie said, hugging her daughter, 'no wonder 40 per cent of you will fail the primary school examination, if they destroy the learning process we've just witnessed in you!'

Our conversation meandered on. I'd had a visitor from abroad, a university professor of sociology, who had asked me the usual question: 'Is Kreol derived from French?' and, when I had hesitated, had added 'Or English?'

At least the question was up one notch from the previous generation of questions: 'Is Kreol broken French?' Globalized prejudice dies hard, we decided. Even here, where it's against oneself. We took a few moments to swear at the Minister of Education for perpetuating it.

Strange, we concluded, that for 40 years the linguistics departments of universities have known how the 80 to 100 Creole languages around the world were born, and how they, unlike the other thousands of languages in the world that evolve gradually, emerged suddenly from a break with other languages. They were generated collectively by a single generation growing up after a holocaust-like slavery, from out of the language-making capacity that we humans are born with inside our own heads. And yet even professors of other subjects, who would perhaps hesitate to hazard an opinion on quantum mechanics or phenomenology if it weren't their own subject, are oblivious to their own ignorance on human language studies.

'The walls at universities must be as thick as...' I began.

'Mom, when Pierrot goes swimming, does he have to...' And we all three laughed together as she completed her question.

Fetching grass

The wheel of change can crush convention. In Mauritius it flattens even the grass.

It's late afternoon and my neighbors, Prabha and Pulo, stop and, following convention, ask: 'Cooked your evening meal yet?' And while I reply, asking them the same question, the history hiding behind the conventional greeting suddenly strikes me: checking if we need to send a bowl of food across for a friend's children when mealtime comes.

Prabha says: 'About time you came with us again, when we go cut grass! You won't believe the change.'

'Tomorrow,' I reply, laughing.

So, next morning at dawn, after criss-crossing through the village and walking along a little path between some new but ramshackle factories of nondescript sorts, we begin to climb into the foothills of the nearby mountain, over rocks and around thorn and aloe trees. No sign of good grass anywhere. It's already been cut.

All five of us dressed in gumboots, long-discarded men's trousers under faded calf-length cotton skirts, long-sleeved shirts, long brightly colored cotton scarves over shoulder and across to hip with a plastic water bottle tied in. Each with a sickle over a shoulder. Prabha's scruffy brown dog tags along.

After an hour's walk, chatting about the whole world and everything else, we reach a place where there are still grasses, creepers and other weeds that cows and goats love.

Prabha only keeps two goats now, in the stable next to her house. Finding grass for the three cows she used to keep isn't possible any more. Most cow-keepers have given up. Pulo keeps one calf at a time now, for the same reason. These women in their forties and fifties have been fetching grass every day since they were 12. This work has been their insurance against the hardship of unemployment whenever it has struck.

There were always problems in daily grass fetching. Getting up the day after childbirth to fetch grass. Setting out in a cyclone to fetch grass. Periodic drought. Sugar estate bosses laying charges against you for stealing grass from their land.

Now, the very grass has been disappearing fast. Cane planted in every spare corner. Villages spreading out as the population increases.

Motorways and factories and stone-crushers taking up land. Golf courses being laid like carpets on grasslands. So Prabha and Pulo have to go further and further away, for less and less grass.

All five of us cut away with our sickles, climbing up on rocks for the high bits. Each one piles grass up for the bundle she'll carry home. I, the unskilled, contribute a bit to each bundle. When we're done, we lie back, laughing and talking as we drink our water to the last drop. I pour some into my hand for Prabha's dog.

'I'll help lift the others' bundles of grass, Lindsey,' Prabha says, 'then you help me get under mine.' Hers is famously the biggest. Two meters long, all wound up, weighing over 20 kilos. She places it at an angle to the ground to get under it. She reminds me how to lift the long end, to get it above the circle of cloth on her head, and then lower it, to avoid injuring her neck.

'God knows where we'll have to climb to next year!'

'My husband is being laid off by the sugar estate. Just when the shirt factory my daughter works at has closed down.' The dog runs ahead.

And somehow we all go quiet as we walk, homeward bound, four of them under huge bundles, me with just my sickle on my shoulder. Hard times are returning. Each family that once had four workers now has perhaps three, two of them in dodgy employment. The sugar estate owners announce they will get rid of all their workers, rely on seasonal labor. There is no massive agricultural diversification, the obvious way to create jobs, nor any land reform. The textile industry is crumbling under new WTO rules. Signs of the crisis being systemic are everywhere now.

My four neighbors know that masses of women won't be able to turn to this semi-peasantry ever again to escape poverty.

The phrase 'Cooked your evening meal yet?' comes back to me. We'll soon be asking this in earnest again. So we know whether to send across a bowl of food for the neighbor's children.

Where the streets have no shame

An age-old form of public expression is squeezed out.

On a dark and rather blustery night two of my friends were out in the capital, Port Louis, pasting up the usual big-format letter-press posters announcing a coming public political meeting to be held in the vicinity. Navy-blue ink on off-white newsprint. 'Grand Meeting', the posters announced (all meetings being 'grand').

While they were busy slapping on the home-made flour-glue, ready to stick up a poster on to the wooden-slatted wall of an ancient building on a side road, an old man's voice came from inside to break the silence: 'Are you folks pasting up posters out there?' After a short, guilty silence, one friend replied: 'Yes, yes we are.' He put his glue brush down in the dark, out of respect. 'For what party?' the voice asked. When they replied, he said: 'Go ahead!' Then the voice continued: 'When you've finished with that one, could you paste another one just here, a bit lower and further to your left?' He tapped on the inside of the wall next to his bed to indicate the place. 'Terrible draught coming in!'

In Mauritius, posters have always been an important medium for direct communication with people. They get pasted up in bus-stops, on electric pylons, on rubbish drums, on walls of nondescript buildings, on palings around building sites. You can judge the mood of the country at a glance. You are informed by them. You are invited by them. You are included by them. And the experts at pasting them up make an art of choosing strategic places, so that at the expense of only 50 posters, thousands of people can get the message from a club, association, union, political party, or a benevolent organization.

Most posters, just like the ones my friends were pasting up, are printed on the same few very old letterpresses still in action. They announce petanque tournaments in housing estates or five-a-side football fixtures in villages; a film in a big cinema house or blood donations needed at such-and-such a place on Sunday; religious celebrations of all denominations; fasts, processions, public forums on key topics of the day, fancy-fairs, hip-hop concerts, and of course the next important political meetings at a particular street corner. Other posters are hand-painted slogans – everything from 'We want price controls back!' to 'The right to strike at once!' In the past two decades, there have been multi-colored offset posters, too, when just the color alone tells you which party is holding an event.

And then a campaign started in the country. In schools, in the media. Posters, the campaign went, are dirty. They are an eyesore. What will tourists say? Posters spoil the environment. It's the fault of political parties. The country must modernize. Suddenly, the police began laying charges on people pasting them up, accusing them of not paying tax to the District Council. (No-one had ever taken notice of this regulation before, of course.) Or laying charges on the grounds that some factory owner had complained about posters on their perimeter wall. Do-gooders would get funded by business and, with the permission of a municipality, would scrub the walls of bus-stops 'clean' and then paint some childish fresco on it, showing tourists the cute naiveté of us, the local population.

Gradually this democratic space began to shrink. It's been almost closed down by vilification and by repression. It still exists, but it is humbled. In its place there is a new mass medium supported by very strong economic interests – and strong steel frames, too.

Bus-stop walls are now fixed up with square spaces for glossy advertisements for transnational fizzy drinks, cosmetics, disposable diapers/nappies, trendy jeans and mobile phones. Meaningless messages cover almost all the space the eye can see. Even dustbins now have 'sides' with frames for firms to rent or buy, covered with glossy ads for banks, insurance firms, shopping arcades, deep-sea diving. Giant billboards stand ostentatiously everywhere vaunting empty faces, dwarfing peoples' daily lives. Entire buses are disguised as a brand-name chocolate bar. Public space invaded and polluted by advertisements, a democratic space taken over by capital.

Capital already controls the press and most radio. Now even a place to paste up a poster is sold to the highest bidder. Leaving senseless messages pasted everywhere, unrelated to living, breathing society.

Of robbers and planners

Mauritius' economic crunch leads to desperate remedies.

The sun was already high in the sky, beating down hot that weekday. Four young men on bicycles arrived, one by one, outside a small hardware store in a sleepy residential area in Quatre Bornes. No-one noticed them as a team at the time. The events were only reconstructed in retrospect, and put together by all the people in the area going over what had happened.

'Look at that suspicious man with a towel wrapped around his head! Look – standing across the road, leaning on his bicycle,' the old lady in charge of the hardware store exclaimed to her only assistant, who happens to be a friend of mine. 'Probably got toothache,' Dojo replied, as he turned his back to dust the different-colored oil paint tins, shining on the shelf in the store's dimly lit interior. In a matter of seconds, a young man tore into the shop, grabbed Dojo by the shoulders and, at close range, sprayed some gas from a canister into his face, while another immobilized his elderly boss and gave her the same treatment. A fourth man then had just enough time to put his hand into the till, and grab a fistful of notes, then all four were off on their bicycles before the arrival of neighbors in response to the shouting.

Dojo laughs as he tells the story. This kind of thing has become so common in Mauritius as unemployment increases, that it has given rise to a brand new series of audacious robber jokes. Most often the robberies involve little or no serious injury. The serious injuries and murders, one cannot avoid mentioning, are left mainly to the realm of the family, which is imploding in senseless violence as the economic crisis puts increasing pressure on an institution with no access to land or income.

The taxi driver who drove Dojo and his employer to the hospital ended up needing treatment too. So strong was the gas still emanating from his passengers' clothing and hair that his eyes were burning too much for him to contemplate driving them home. Dojo recounts this, shaking his head philosophically.

At the exact same time that all this was happening, when the sun was up high in the sky, I was in a social center at a local women's association meeting on the outskirts of Port Louis. The association had invited our women's organization that day. So 3 of us joined 25 or so of their members and we all sat in four neatly prepared rows of chairs as their elected president formally opened their monthly meeting. Ironically, at the same time as the four young men on bicycles were addressing the economic crisis in their way, the ambitious theme of the meeting was the effects on women of the self-same economic crisis, and the political need for addressing the issues in a collective way.

After a short interactive DVD focusing on how the sugar industry's collapse is being handled, Marie-Antoinette explained, pushing back strands of hair, how she and her daughter both lost their jobs when a textile mill was closed. Her daughter then got a new job in a factory further away. 'Maybe I'll set up a small enterprise,' she announced, her voice tinged with sarcasm.

'Like me,' another woman laughed. 'I took one of those loans. Now I have to change what I make every few months. First, children's clothes, but I could only sell the initial few batches, so I turned to sewing flowers. That only worked for a while. Now I cover cushions.' An older woman in a sari solemnly predicted, from a lifetime of experience, 'Things will get worse'. Everyone smiled.

But perhaps most evocative was what Manta said: 'I finally got a permit to sell food inside a textile factory yard. So I took a loan and got a tricycle made, equipped with a big see-through box, handsome green parasol over it and all. My business was a success – until the factory closed.' She has loan repayments and nowhere to work.

'So you don't even have to work at the factory to lose your job there,' she smiled across to Marie-Antoinette.

Letters from Cairo (Egypt), 2007-2008

Maria Golia

Maria is a US expat, long-time resident of Egypt and author of *Cairo: City of Sand* (Reaktion Books, London 2004). Contributor to a variety of international publications, she also writes speeches for Egyptian politicians and tycoons. She is currently working on a cultural history of photography in Egypt, to be published in 2009.

She is a fellow of the Institute of Ecotechnics (London), the non-profit organization behind the building of Biosphere 2, a miniature Earth under glass, the world's largest laboratory for global ecology. She worked from 1985 to 1992 on an urban environment project where the Institute also served as consultant. The Caravan of Dreams Performing Arts Center in Fort Worth, Texas, was an attempt to revitalize the city's segregated and culturally sterile downtown. She was general manager of this nightclub, theater, dance and exhibition space, widely recognized as reintroducing the *avant garde* to the Texas arts scene.

Maria's work for the *New Internationalist* and other publications is largely social, political and environmental commentary based on two decades' experience in the Middle East. In her writing, Golia seeks to revisit cultural preconceptions, including the seemingly opposing notions of traditional versus modern, and to emphasize the value of inter-cultural communication as the basis for a more meaningful and constructive – as opposed to a purely economics-driven – model of globalization.

Changes in Egypt

Egypt has a long and rich civilization stretching back to the Pharaohs and beyond. In the modern era it is at the very heart of the Arab world – despite a period of ostracism following President Anwar Sadat's groundbreaking rapprochement with Israel in 1979. The US rewarded Egypt's peace deal with massive amounts of economic aid that are only now beginning to dwindle, and with military aid that is ongoing.

Egypt is of value to the US not only because it is prepared to take a relatively moderate line on Israel/Palestine but because it holds the line against the growing power of fundamentalism. Egypt's regime was concerned with acting as a bulwark against Islamist movements long before 9/11 placed it at the top of Washington's agenda. Sadat was assassinated in October 1981 by elements of the military opposed to repression of fundamentalist groups and his successor as President, Hosni Mubarak, has wrestled ever since with rebel groups seeking a theocratic state.

He has been aided in this by sweeping powers afforded by the State of Emergency that has been in place ever since he took office – and are routinely renewed every three years. This has allowed the Government to stifle opposition, censor the press and ban public assembly all in the name of national security. It has meant a clampdown not only upon the biggest rebel group, al-Gamaa al-Islamiya, but also upon the largest opposition group, the Muslim Brotherhood, which disavows violence.

Elections are rigged as a matter of course to ensure a majority for the ruling National Democratic Party. Almost every aspect of public life, from religion to trade unions, is heavily controlled. As a result, a culture of political apathy predominates. As Maria Golia puts it: 'Egyptians have never believed in their power, only in their wit.'

The politics may be problematic but Egyptian society remains vibrant, particularly as seen from its capital, which may be 1,400 years old but is a fantastically dense, sprawling megacity, over half of which has only been built in the last 20 years. Its predominantly young population is wrestling daily with the impact of Western-style globalization and industrialization on its livelihood, culture and religion, and it is the everyday intermingling of the traditional and the contemporary that Maria Golia brings to vivid life in her monthly letters from Cairo.

'We can take it'

The changes in people at a time of fasting.

When I arrived in Cairo in 1981, it was summer and I'd never known such heat: glaring white and suffocating, the kind that makes your calves sweat. I blamed the weather for people's daytime irritability, and it seemed reasonable that they spent the cooler nights eating, smoking and drinking tea until dawn. There was more to it than that, I soon learned – it was Ramadan, the Islamic month of fasting.

My Egyptian education has proceeded apace, but at that time, as I recall, not everyone fasted, and friends concur that many who did tailored their abstinence in ways they found appropriately challenging. People gave up smoking, drinking, or eating but not water so as to remain functional at work despite the heat. Plenty went all the way, but the great uniformity of today's Ramadan, with its sullen rigor, was absent, and no-one cared that much if you fasted or not.

I'd lived in Paris and Rome, but despite their sophistication found mid-1980s Cairo more deeply cosmopolitan and tolerant, its supra-human inhabitants able to leap tall contradictions, differences in wealth, temperament, background and spirituality, in a single gracious bound. Cairo was a city of grasshoppers in a world of nasty ants. Friendships could be forged in an instant; no-one saved for winter, or ever held back what they had.

When things went wrong, Cairenes said 'god makes it easy', a mantra that seemed to mitigate the pain of every loss. But the biggest loss was in the making. Egypt was enjoying its last moments of relative innocence and isolation from the culture of time and money – my culture, America's.

In 1985, circumstances sent me back to the States. When I returned, in 1992, Cairo had changed. In the wake of the first Gulf War, people had retained their humor, but the Government had opened Egypt as never before to Western-style consumerism and development. The backlash came in the form of terrorist attacks against tourism, a pillar of the (secular) state's economy, catering to foreigners and perceivably benefiting primarily Egypt's élite.

By the turn of the millennium, between tourism, satellite TV, and reports from relatives working abroad, average Egyptians had glimpsed lives full of the comforts, order and options that political greed and maneuvering had persistently denied them. Women started covering their heads, as if in mourning. Public expressions of religiosity grew alongside disillusionment with state corruption and injustice, and post-9/11 dismay at the unraveling chances for regional peace. Although ostensibly devout, people grew less considerate; men started harassing women in the streets. The punchlines to jokes became cruder, bitterer.

Today, Cairenes seem to match their surroundings: neglected, frayed. Tempers flare frequently, especially during Ramadan. The high-decibel vituperative of the imams' Friday sermons is like a volley of ringing, ear-reddening slaps. On the metro, in banks and doctors' waiting rooms, people chant the Qur'an aloud. At prayer times, building hallways and stairwell landings become mini-mosques, full of supplicants bowing to an elevator shaft, seeing past it, one supposes, to god and reward.

Many, like my friend Bassim, a lawyer and civil servant, lament the new religiosity, how everyone wants to make everyone else toe the line. No-one used to pray in Bassim's office but now everyone does – including him, he confesses, conspicuously, on the floor beside his desk. Prayer and observance was once a pact made with god, not your officemates. Now people do extra fasts throughout the year, to show off, Bassim says, but also because they're scared.

Indeed, despite their entreaties, god has made things harder, and I suspect he's been secretly reproached. People need forgiveness now, aside from help. Sick people fast, even though they're allowed to skip the days they're ill. Old people fast, though it can kill them, especially working all day without water. Kids fast, insisting they're old enough. Fasting says, 'we can take it'.

Egyptians never used to feel obliged to make such statements. Several millennia of group continuity buttressed their confidence in a unique identity, and in the higher powers that had helped them, despite invasions and other calamites, sustain it. Cairo's religious conformity, however often described as a reaffirmation of cultural identity, suggests to me its loss.

An artist friend tried to reassure me that the religious trend won't last, that Egypt would recover its idiosyncratic nonchalance. 'We Egyptians don't believe in anything,' he said, 'not in government, or hope, or in the future. We have enough history to entertain us for a lifetime. Who needs a future?'

How about the half of Egypt's population still largely in its teens, I inquired. My friend blinked. 'Only god can save them now', he said.

A marriage of convenience
The wheeling and dealing behind a Cairo wedding.

My neighbour Selwa is a jovial young woman, hefty and assertive, but when she visited the other day she was upset. She and her family live on the roof. Her father used to be the building's guardian, but he died recently, and Selwa assumed the role of her mother's right hand. She told me the family was in crisis, because of her brother Ahmed's prospective marriage. Ahmed, the eldest of six siblings, is 33. He left school at 10 and has since helped support his family. He too became a building guardian, earning around $50 per month.

Recently, Ahmed's mother arranged his engagement to Karima, a second cousin from their hometown in Upper Egypt. Since Karima's father is also dead, her brother negotiated the marriage contract, as is customary, on her behalf. Ahmed would supply the apartment, and certain furnishings. Karima's family would provide other household items, in addition to supplying Karima.

Selwa and her sisters were thrilled to have found Ahmed an affordable apartment ($35 per month) in a shantytown on the outskirts of Imbaba, a relatively central quarter. They secured the required furnishings with cash deposits, and organized the wedding celebration, paying in advance for a band and an outdoor space to hold the party not far from the couple's future home.

Then, just a week before the wedding, Karima's brother raised an issue. How could his sister live in a flat with no electricity? Unless a more suitable dwelling was found, the deal was off. Selwa's distress was equally distributed between her brother's thwarted chance for happiness and the cash they'd lose if the marriage fell through.

The family gathered, she told me, to examine their options – things like gas-operated generators, which were expensive. Kerosene lamps and candles were more typical solutions, but unsatisfactory to Karima's brother. They tried to explain that the Imbaba neighborhood would one day be embraced by the municipal grid and, if not, people would organize to pirate nearby electricity wires. Meanwhile, god had seen fit to position the flat in such a way as to profit from his light throughout the day. The brother remained obdurate and Selwa's mother, who suffers from diabetes and high-blood pressure, had, in the local parlance, 'blue genies dancing in front of her eyes'.

'What can we do?' Selwa asked. I suggested she tell Karima's brother once more exactly what she'd told me: that they'd done their best and it wasn't easy, and if he didn't like it, he could help pay to solve the problem himself. Otherwise they should drop the engagement. Better to lose money than for Ahmed to marry into a family of unreasonable ingrates. Selwa sighed. I wished her luck and gave her some money that she refused, as is expected, several times before accepting it.

I'd nearly forgotten about her visit when, two days later, I heard choruses of ululations coming from the roof. I figured they'd reached an agreement and Ahmed and Karima would marry after all. I was half right.

Selwa's mother came by to make sure I'd go to the wedding. I told her I was glad they'd settled things with Karima's brother.

'We didn't,' she said.

'What do you mean?'

'We found another one.'

'Another apartment?'

'No,' she laughed, 'another bride'. This was a third cousin by the name of Hind, who showed up moments later to introduce herself; a sturdy woman wearing jeans and a headscarf, who had known Ahmed for years and was apparently game.

I figured what the marriage lacked in romance it gained in practicality. Both parties were well past marriageable age, poor, uneducated and unlikely to find a better match, especially considering that their families' rapport was evidently longstanding and harmonious. Life is a difficult enterprise, requiring reliable partners. It was that simple.

The wedding party took place on an empty lot in a garbage-clogged maze of informal housing blocks. The band played beside a crude brick wall, with a swathe of printed fabric as backdrop. Several hundred people filled the surrounding benches, wooden planks that bobbed up and down as we sat or stood. Men were on one side of the stage, women on the other, with kids swarming back and forth in between. People danced, particularly Selwa, who moved with robust innuendo, as if her whole body was winking.

I slipped away after midnight, following a tight alley to something resembling a street, walking ankle-deep in the ghostly sun-dried shreds of plastic bags, like the skins of molting snakes. This is Cairo in pursuit of renewal: heroically defiant of the odds, hopelessly romantic after all.

The thinness of things

Living in Cairo means accepting much that isn't how one might want it – and that everyone looks good in pink.

I recently purchased a stepladder, only to discover it had one leg dangerously shorter than the others. When I returned it, the shopkeeper duly noted its wobble, then explained to me it was because the ladder was new. I asked if that meant the leg would grow as it got older. He shrugged, and offered me a cigarette.

It's a relief, especially during Christmas holidays, to live in a place where consumerism has not entirely caught on. Yes, Cairo has its mega-shopping malls and every fast-food joint imaginable, but many people can only visit them as you would a park or a museum, in order to look and not to buy. Egyptians are inconspicuous consumers who tend to buy what they really need. There are no coupon sections in the newspapers, no two-for-ones, few warranties. Until the ascendance of satellite TV, local commercials were generally boring, often featuring the same gaggle of girls singing jingles and jiggling their breasts. There's a joke that addresses the not-quite-fully conditioned response to commercial stimuli. It's about a farmer from Upper Egypt, who sees an ad for Marlboros, then goes out and buys a horse.

Nevertheless, the shopkeeper's nonchalance towards shoddiness was a typically Cairene attitude that has often troubled me. I may be a lapsed American, but I haven't lost the habit of expecting things to work. I realize most tradespeople have received little if any training, but it's hard not to get testy with the carpenter when he shows up without a hammer and asks to borrow mine. The hammer itself is an annoyance, a Chinese import whose head falls off each time you swing it back to strike a nail. The whole city resembles the Chinese goods that have invaded it; nothing is made well or to last. Momentary usefulness, or the mere appearance of utility, is often considered enough.

Sometimes even appearance is foregone in exchange for availability. Salespeople will offer whatever they happen to have on hand in place of the requested item, no matter how different the two may be. Ask the vegetable seller for cauliflower. 'Take the eggplant,' he'll tell you, because that's what he has, insisting moreover that eggplant is exactly the same thing – 'it's vegetable,' he says. Likewise the tailor who was meant to make a green shirt that somehow turned out pink. 'Pink looks nice on you,' he says. But it's not for me, I tell him. 'Never mind,' he counters, 'pink looks good on everyone.'

In time, I've come to savor these interactions and perhaps even grasp what lies beneath. It isn't facile salescraft, or apathy, or the desire to annoy me that makes people justify lacks or defects, but the belief that everything – and everyone – is multi-use and interchangeable. Why bother with foolish distinctions between thing and thing?

I've watched cab drivers mending engine gaskets with drops of plastic melted from their pocket-combs, seen garlic cloves chewed to a paste for use as glue, and Turkish coffee applied to wounds to staunch the flow of blood. I've been invited to two-room homes where several broken plastic chairs, inserted into one another, made a comfortable seat, and where the divan doubled as a marital bed under which was stowed a butane-gas burner that regularly produced a dinner for eight.

Most Cairenes live in makeshift houses, have makeshift jobs that hardly pay and go to schools where they're encouraged not to think. While governmental rhetoric hails Egypt's democratic progress, arrests of opposition types are common, and torture far from rare. 'Higher growth rates than ever!' the pundits exclaim, but the size of bread loaves has diminished from that of a dinner plate to that of a saucer and, for most Egyptians, a portion of meat is a sometime thing.

When the poet Paul Valéry wrote that 'god made everything out of nothing, but the nothingness shows through,' he might have been describing Cairo. People are so accustomed to the telltale nothingness, that the illusions of wholeness and solidity have been dispensed with altogether – everyone knows they're living in a castle built of sand. Nor do they harbor great hopes about what might eventually replace it, since in their experience, these distinctions too are largely artificial, boiling

down to a small, privileged 'them' and a great big 'us'. Yet Cairenes approach each day, by and large, with enviable equanimity. Nothing seems able to deter them – no objective or subjective obstacle – from pursuing the business of survival. Nothing, after all, is perfect.

A bag of lemons

An impulsive gift prompts some unexpected thoughts.

During holidays in Cairo, whether Muslim feasts or Christian ones, there's a phrase you're bound to hear repeatedly, which roughly translates as 'may your every year be good'. However genuine the sentiment, the saying often carries a well-known subtext – 'tis the season to tip more heavily than usual.

Holidays are cause for consternation as well as celebration. Average Egyptians, whose belts are already unconscionably tight, need extra food for families and guests as well as new clothes for the kids. Generosity at these times is especially appreciated, so you try and really let go, to empty your pockets whenever possible in an attempt to share the prevailing and specious hope that god will see fit to refill them.

Just after the recent feast, I went vegetable shopping, and having purchased several mud-laden bunches of spinach, some dented tomatoes and dusty potatoes – typical fare –stopped by the lemon lady. I call her the lemon lady because that's what she sells, in the sun all day, sitting on a cinder-block in the street at exhaust-pipe level. In summer, she props a broken umbrella between her feet and her wares; sometimes she just balances a half-full sack of lemons on her head. I've seen her breastfeed her child, there in the street, mother's milk laced with carbon monoxide. Although I've had ample occasion to admire her carved features, and how her country-style dress billows around her straight-backed squat, I've somehow never asked her name.

It is well known in Cairo that vendors rarely have change, especially in the morning. I had a single, tired and disintegrated one-pound note, but at the last minute decided to give her a ten, which isn't much, but it was crisp and about ten times what is called for. She looked up at me, shaking her head. When I said I didn't need change, and expressed the wish that her every year be good, she insisted I take several more handfuls of fat green lemons.

'I don't need them,' I told her.

'Make juice,' she said.

I felt embarrassed by her generosity, which so exceeded mine. Walking away with a bulging bag, I berated myself for having only given her ten pounds and for even considering giving her one.

Having lived so long in a place where the average monthly income is less than a sum I can earn in several hours, virtually every cash transaction is fraught with this sort of self-doubt. Do I really need another contour sheet, or to take multiple vitamins, when there are homeless children sleeping on my doorstep? This awareness of inequity can be paralyzing, but it is also instructive. As an American I must remind myself that being better-off doesn't necessarily mean knowing any better, indeed, being right is not among the inalienable ones. But it's an arbitrary universe, I'm convinced of it, and this absolves me temporarily.

My ruminations came to a halt a little later at the pharmacy when, fumbling among the lemons for my money, I realized I couldn't find the 100-pound note I was sure I took when I left the house. Then it dawned on me: the 100-pound notes resemble the 10-pound ones, so I must have given it to the lemon lady.

I was instantly pleased and more at ease recalling how enthusiastically she'd forced me to take so many extra lemons. One hundred pounds, after all, buys a lot of them. But yes, I was happy that I'd given her something to be excited about, and reminded myself of it so many times while walking home that I grew embarrassed at the pleasure it gave me, this unintentional gift for which I deserved no credit. Yet I was secretly proud to have surrendered the money, no trifling amount, without regret.

At home, unpacking my bag, at the very bottom amidst the lemons, I found the hundred-pound note – and felt like a maundering ass. I was struck anew with the woman's gladness in receiving the boon of ten measly pounds, and her compulsion to share it immediately and give back. My humility was restored (temporarily no doubt, and arbitrarily) alongside the knowledge that giving is a qualitative not quantitative matter, by a woman whose name, I've since learned, is Nadia.

A world apart

A dinner invitation offers a glimpse of the power, glitz and tact of Cairo's high society.

Back in the 1980s, Cairo's upper class fêted lavishly, as often in their flats and villas as on feluccas, the sailboats that ply the Nile, or moonlit desert caravans culminating in dinners beside the ruins of lesser-known pyramids. Nowadays outdoor parties are problematic, the flaunting of booze and wealth being increasingly unwise. People mostly meet at the pretentious restaurants and clubs that have multiplied in the last decade. So when my friend Kamal, a superb host, invites me to his home, it's hard to refuse.

Despite his aristocratic background, Kamal nurtures a lively curiosity in lesser-born humans. He's gay, older now and generally philosophical.

When I chide him for being so enamored of beauty – his house is crammed with costly oriental *objets d'art* – he quotes Nietzsche, saying 'the Greeks were superficial out of profundity', except he adds a 'darling' at the end. His guest list invariably includes representatives from the worlds of power, glamor and art. I suppose I fall into the last category.

People tend to arrive late at Kamal's, embracing, exchanging extravagant compliments, and displaying an almost unhinged pleasure at seeing one other. By tacit agreement, they're always pleasant, or if moody, attractively so. They never share deep concerns, only witty anecdotes, never lean too hard on an argumentative point, and never, above all, demonstrate any sort of need. Aside from the local moguls and vamps, Kamal's foreign guests included a maharajah visiting with his polo team, and a Kuwaiti gentleman, wearing a diamond ring so large that even without my glasses I spotted its prismic gleam from across the room.

At around 1.00am, Kamal's liveried Nubian servant did a little dance to indicate that dinner was served. The party of around 30 trickled into the dining room. I sat on a huge damask-covered throne, a painting of a rosy nymph wearing flowers and a strip of leopardskin behind me, and Cairo's incoherent lights spread out in front, through a series of high windows. The table was strewn with gilded leaves and acorns, Lalique butterflies, and brass pomegranates filled with geode crystals, the whole lit by candelabra attached to the wall in brackets shaped like muscular forearms and hands.

I assisted a woman called Nazli into the throne to my right; at nearly 90 she's a fixture at these gatherings, the last of a long line of Ottoman princesses and a living compendium of Cairo's players and scenarios throughout its various belles époques. An Egyptian telecom tycoon took my left. The hot conversation topic was the son of the President, who had recently moved to Kamal's neighborhood, and the distinct possibility of his succession.

'He's not a bad-looking fellow, but too serious by half,' someone said.

'If only he had a sense of humor, people would like him more,' said Nazli.

'He lifts weights to ease the tension,' Kamal added.

'The people don't want him,' I said. 'They're fed up. Why bother having a revolution to end up with another king?'

'I don't know why they bothered either,' said Nazli, 'the monarchy was paradise compared to this.'

'I share your nostalgia dear, but don't forget you grew up in a harem and had to bribe the eunuch to buy your cigarettes,' noted Kamal.

'At least we dressed well, and entertained in style. These poor girls in their black tents...'

'I suppose nothing ever changes in Egypt, not really. Isn't that why we love it?' asked Kamal.

'But it is changing, always has been, you just can't see it from up here,' I couldn't resist remarking.

'Darling, I know what the countryside is like.'

'Sure, because you're landed gentry.'

'No, because I'm interested. When was the last time you got your hands dirty with the *fellahin* [peasants]?'

'I don't have to go to the country for that. I've got them living six to the room on my roof, not to mention all around me.'

'I don't see what the problem is,' said the telecom billionaire, 'the son is a smart guy and, besides, he's my friend. It's not his fault that his father is the President.'

I laughed at this convoluted gem of logic – alone – and Kamal gracefully changed the subject. Then Omar Sharif arrived, looking marvelous, with a pan-Arab mega-diva on one arm and a Hollywood star on the other, and all else, for the moment, was forgotten.

Turn, turn, turn

Springtime in Cairo brings some unwelcome changes.

So much has changed in the years of my residence in Cairo that the city I once knew is nearly gone. The older generation that lived through it all, from colonization to so-called democratization, is dying out, and with them, not only history but ways of being and speaking, entire professions and trades.

We still enjoy a few pre-Industrial Age luxuries, like having clothes tailored, ironed and mended by career experts in these arts. But tailors can't compete with ready-mades, and while the ironers' services are fairly inexpensive, people are more likely now to buy their own irons. As for the *stoppeurs*, or invisible menders, no-one seems to have anything worth fixing any more. So the sons who once inherited these professions have moved on, or tried to, and the fathers, now well past retirement age, are shutting their shops, last vestiges of a more graceful, handcrafted era.

Until this year, each spring I took my sweaters to the stoppeur, Abu Rashad, to mend the desk-worn cuffs. A feisty gent, he shared a tiny but well-situated workshop with Mohammed, a shirt maker, close to the old stock exchange building which, since the socialist 1950s and 1960s, had gone, like the rest of downtown Cairo, more or less to hell.

Then a while back, the state refurbished the Bourse and spruced up the neighborhood to give the impression that Egypt was back in business. The surrounding streets were closed to cars and planted with flowerbeds and palms. When I visited Abu Rashad last spring, I found him in front of the shop, suturing a wounded woolen elbow, talking to Mohammed, who sat beside him sewing buttons onto a shirt.

I gave Abu Rashad my sweaters then lingered to examine some fabrics while eavesdropping on the conversation I'd interrupted and that they'd immediately resumed. They were talking politics, a typically seditious diatribe of the kind iterated daily by septuagenarians city-wide.

'Revolution my foot. Socialism be damned. Holy Law – nonsense!' Abu Rashad began.

'Don't forget this open market stuff.'

'Open? The only thing they know how to open is their mouths.'

'Hypocrites all of them. It's enough to make you long for the monarchy.'

'Right! Or even the Brits. At least they didn't bother pretending to like us, whereas these sons of whores have been sodomizing us in the name of patriotism for decades.'

'And remember how everything worked when the English were here? Not to mention they liked sweaters. God forgive me, but it's a good thing my brother died. There's not enough business to keep us both alive.'

'God have pity on him.'

'And on us. Especially if you-know-who [the President] doesn't join my brother soon.'

'Don't hold your breath. He's not going anywhere.'

'Can you believe the balls on this creature? He's older than we are and he still runs for office!'

'I'll tell you what's unbelievable, is that you and I voted for him.'

'Who else was there?'

'I swear to god we were better off voting for the other guy.'

'You mean the one who's still in jail?'

They laughed.

'But you know what really surprises me?' asked Mohammed reflectively.

'Say.'

'We thought we were poor back then and had nothing to lose, but after 50 years the bastards are still stealing it.'

'By god, that's the truth.'

I left the two men chuckling good-naturedly at the demise of the nation, acute observers over whose eyes the wool could never be pulled. If only they'd realized that apart from being witnesses to history they had also helped make it. But Egyptians have never believed in their power, only in their wit.

A sidewalk café now occupies Abu Rashad and Mohammed's premises, and boxes of cantaloupe-flavored tobacco and gaudy water-pipes have replaced the bolts of fabric on the shelves. Arriving there the other day on my springtime errand, I paused confusedly, realized Abu Rashad was gone, and moved on, figuring it was probably time to buy new sweaters anyway.

Walking home, past downtown's grand but dilapidated buildings, I felt the last puffs of cool issue from their lofty foyers onto the street, where they were dispersed in the gathering heat, like sighs.

Beyond nature

How 'other worldly' powers can deflect some earthly problems.

My friend and lawyer Bassim is a knowledgeable man, whose repertoire includes the salient points of Egypt's history and legislation, every joke, proverb, conspiracy theory and *fait divers* worth repeating, not to mention the Qur'an that he committed to memory as a boy. Jovial, sanguine, short and round, Bassim's wisdom is surpassed only by his generosity in distributing it. Like many Cairenes, he believes in god and the devil, as well as the power of invisible demons, or *jinn*. Also like many Cairenes, Bassim is obliged to hold down three jobs to survive, working for private clients in the morning, a state-owned bank in the afternoon, and playing the drums at night at parties.

Until recently, his spare moments were spent with his wife Afet, who suffered from diabetes, in addition, as Bassim often told me, to 'nerves'. The opposite of her extravert husband, she was terribly jealous, which weakened her health and strained their marriage. Bassim married Afet while recovering from a broken engagement with a woman who had proved unfaithful. Afet was the antithesis of a jezebel: plain, plump and devoted. She wore a headscarf and was painfully modest. Their lovemaking sessions, from what I gathered, caused her to faint away in a swoon.

Shortly after marrying, Bassim related an incident that shed light on his relationship. He took Afet on honeymoon to Sinai. Back in Cairo, he began dreaming of women, with whom he would 'make love completely' and then awaken, 'very tired in the body'. One afternoon, drowsing at his desk while a colleague read the Qur'an aloud (a common pastime amongst civil servants) Bassim felt someone violently grab his tongue, and speak in an incomprehensible language. The colleague confirmed Bassim's suspicions of being possessed, and recommended a sheikh specializing in exorcism.

In Egypt, jinn have a place in religious belief (they're discussed in the Qur'an) while coloring the popular understanding of emotional states ranging from rage to infatuation. Everyone has a personal jinn that influences them, often in negative ways, aside from the envious freelance jinn who can trespass another's territory. Either way, jinn, like weaknesses of temperament, can and should be mastered; they're here to test us, to see how we act when the chips are down.

Bassim duly went about the business of conquering his demons, and visited the sheikh. When the holy man called forth the jinn, she declared her love for Bassim, saying she would never leave him so long as he lived. The sheikh began smacking Bassim about the head, neck and torso, while addressing pious admonishments to the smitten and obdurate jinn. With a fusillade of blows, the holy man managed to corral the jinn into Bassim's little finger, which he pierced with a sewing needle to let her out.

It took, however, several more punishing sessions and a copper talisman to do the trick. The sheikh instructed Bassim to have sex with Afet while wearing the charm, and to throw it in the Nile afterwards. Bassim obeyed and was finally free. I asked if he still had those dreams, and he said no, but that he wasn't sleeping with Afet much either. 'She is tired', he told me ruefully, 'and now she snores – very loud. I think she scared the jinn away, not the sheikh.' So much for Bassim's first year of marriage.

Time passed and Bassim began praying more frequently, ostensibly for Afet's health, but also to get out of the house. Afet, for her part, had put on a lot of weight, which distressed Bassim, even though he was quite chunky himself. Moreover, Afet had failed to conceive a child, which reflected poorly in society's eyes on them both.

'Sometimes when I look at her,' Bassim said, chuckling uneasily, 'I see a bad thing... like a devil' (mispronounced to rhyme with 'evil'). Rather than admit his growing disillusionment with his wife, or acknowledge her commensurate discomfiture, Bassim was willing to attribute supernatural causes to their estrangement. Nor would pride allow him to seek a divorce and publicly expose the failure of his marriage.

Things seemed to have reached an impasse, when he called to say Afet had taken the initiative and requested a divorce. I thought he'd be relieved, but he was upset, and convinced against all odds she'd been cheating. Nevertheless, his sunny temperament soon returned, along with a wish to remarry. 'Maybe a Ukrainian, or a Japanese,' he mused, 'something different this time. Egyptian women are so complicated.'